# Old
# Snow
# Just
# Melting

# Old Snow Just Melting

## Essays and Interviews

MARVIN BELL

Ann Arbor    The University of Michigan Press

Copyright © by The University of Michigan 1983
All rights reserved
Published in the United States of America by
The University of Michigan Press and simultaneously
in Rexdale, Canada, by John Wiley & Sons Canada, Limited
Manufactured in the United States of America

1986   1985   1984   1983        4   3   2   1

**Library of Congress Cataloging in Publication Data**

Bell, Marvin.
   Old snow just melting.

   (Poets on poetry)
   1. Bell, Marvin—Interviews.   2. American poetry—
20th century—History and criticism—Collected works.
3. Poets, American—20th century—Biography.
I. Title.   II. Series.
PS3552.E5204   1983        811'.54        82-21972
ISBN 0-472-06342-1 (pbk.)

One of the ironies of the creative process is that it partly cripples itself in order to function. I mean that, usually, in order to turn out a piece of work the author has to exaggerate the emphasis of it, to oppose it in a forcefully competitive way to other versions of truth; and he gets carried away by his own exaggeration, as his distinctive image is built on it. But each honest thinker who is basically an empiricist has to have some truth in his position, no matter how extremely he has formulated it. The problem is to find the truth underneath the exaggeration, to cut away the excess elaboration or distortion and include that truth (elsewhere) where it fits.

Ernest Becker
*The Denial of Death*

It is a tremendous act of violence to begin anything. I am not able to *begin*. I simply skip what should be the beginning. Nothing is so powerful as silence. It would never have been broken, if we had not, each of us, been born into the midst of talk.

Rainer Maria Rilke
"The Young Workman's Letter"
trans. G. Craig Houston

# Acknowledgments

*Grateful acknowledgment is made to the following authors, publishers, and journals for permission to reprint previously published materials:*

*American Poetry Review* for "The University Is Something Else You Do," an interview by Nancy Bunge, *American Poetry Review* 11, no. 2; and for fourteen columns entitled "Homage to the Runner" which appeared successively in volume 4, numbers 1, 2, 3, 4, 5, and 6; volume 5, numbers 2, 4, and 6; volume 6, numbers 2 and 5; and volume 7, numbers 1, 4, and 6.

*Antaeus* for "The Hours Musicians Keep" published in *Antaeus*, Spring/Summer 1982.

*Associated Writing Programs Newsletter* for "Influences" published in *AWP Newsletter*, September 1981.

Confluence Press for "Richard Hugo: A Personal Foreword" which first appeared in *A Trout in the Milk: A Composite Portrait of Richard Hugo*, edited by Jack Myers. Copyright © 1982 Confluence Press.

*Field* for "How We Think Back," *Field* 15, Fall 1976; and "Noun/Object/Image," *Field* 24, Spring 1981.

*Iowa Review* for "Pain and Fear: Something about Them," *Iowa Review* 11, nos. 2–3; and "If a Poem Is Only Music, What

Chance Does It Have?," an interview by Lowell Edwin Folsom, David Groff, David Hamilton, Adalaide Morris, and Fredrick Woodard, *Iowa Review* 12, no. 1.

*Massachusetts Review* for "I Try to Feel What It Means," an interview by Joyce Renwick.

*North American Review* for "I Was a Boston (Marathon) Bandit on Assignment," reprinted with permission from the *North American Review*. Copyright © 1980 by The University of Northern Iowa.

*Poetry Miscellany* for " 'Self' Is a Very Iffy Word for Me," an interview by Richard Jackson which first appeared in *Poetry Miscellany* 10 (1980).

*Seattle Review* for "Auden Twice" which was originally published in the *Seattle Review* 4, no. 2, Fall 1981.

University of Michigan Press for "The Impure Every Time" from *Claims for Poetry,* edited by Donald Hall. Copyright © 1982.

*Unmuzzled Ox: The Poets' Encyclopedia* for "Entry for *The Poets' Encyclopedia:* Five-and-Ten," *Unmuzzled Ox* 4, no. 4.

*Every effort has been made to trace the ownership of all copyrighted material in this book and to obtain permission for its use.*

# Contents

# Preface

All of the essays in this book were written on assignment. My principles, if that is the word, have been: (1) to write prose only when asked to and, preferably, on an assigned subject; (2) to write informally and to follow my nose. These essays are, in part, improvisations.

There is some overlap here, which I have let stand in deference to the notion of context. There is some awkwardness, too, occasioned by visible thinking, which I have also let stand in honor of that person I was and the words by which he managed.

This book comes at the right time. After this, different.

I particularly wish to thank Arthur Vogelsang and Stephen Berg, who in 1974 convinced me to write for *The American Poetry Review*. This book is dedicated to them; to David Morris, who discussed ideas like these with me during long, slow runs into the countryside, sometimes uphill; and to Chester Osborne, trumpeter, historian, author and music teacher. The mistakes are my own.

Marvin Bell

# I

# The Hours
# Musicians Keep

ESSAYS

# Auden Twice

A friend wants to hear it again. It was some years ago, and I probably ought to remember how many, or find out, but I don't remember and I certainly don't want to find out.

Auden would be reading up the road at Cornell College in Mount Vernon, Iowa. I was a young poet, and I had read that essay in which Auden says that he likes the sort of reader who is on the lookout for odd metrical feet. I was on the lookout.

He read twice—afternoon and evening. I don't know why. I imagine that he was being paid handsomely—$2,000, say, at a time when poets would read for $150, and rarely. It didn't mean he would have to stay longer: two readings, one day, a couple of grand.

He appeared on stage in a sweatshirt bearing the name of Tolkien, or *Lord of the Rings,* or perhaps both. He had created a new format and he began by explaining it. He would read a certain number of minutes or poems and then he would step to the side for two minutes, during which time we would be free to converse or change cheeks. Then he would step back behind the lectern and we would listen. And so it went, through versions of Auden and Icelandic.

I was on the lookout and labored to discover odd, intricate meter in one of his translations of an Icelandic saga. I thought I noted, also, that when he would blow a line while reciting from memory, the mistake would usually consist of his having substituted for the correct word a word which appeared directly below that word on the page. This I took to be evidence of a photographic memory. I don't know whether or not he made such photographs and perhaps I should find out, but I don't know and I certainly don't want to find out.

At the end of his afternoon performance, he started to exit stage-right, almost throttling himself on the neck-mike he had forgotten to remove. Auden the yo-yo.

Afterwards, I walked with a friend to the student union. Auden was sitting in a booth, looking somewhat forlorn. It was decided that I should keep him company. I was reluctant but at least I had something to talk about. I let on that I had scanned the intricate meter in one of the Icelandic sagas. "Oh," he said, "that's just Common Meter."

That night, I attended his second reading and a small party afterwards. It was a party-in-a-circle. Auden, who had trouble with plantar's warts on his feet, was wearing bedroom slippers. His face was the soft part of the moon. He entertained our circle at some length talking about a brilliant friend: a master chess player, a renowned architect, fluent in a dozen languages. His friend would not be in New York when Auden returned. Auden wondered then, with genuine sadness over a great loss, to whom he would be able to talk.

Maybe his friend wasn't an architect but something else. I suppose I could find out. There were others listening. I'm not going to ask them, however. I certainly don't want to know.

Now the difference between Auden and the rest of us was only too clear. It was the difference between Oxford (Harvard, if you perfer) and Alfred University (I hope my alma mater will forgive me for its having to own up to me), the difference between learning from Great Books at the Right Time and stumbling along shakily in random corridors of just-discovered libraries—something like a duck on land. When I read the beginning of this sentence on Gerard Manley Hopkins' school days in Paddy Kitchen's biography of Hopkins: "Matthew Arnold, who was Professor of Poetry . . .," my heart skips and then fills with the sheer abundance of such a prospect. For me, a mere prospect, and then only if I imagine myself backward in time. For Hopkins, the real thing. For Auden, in some equally privileged schooling, and then for those who may have sat in turn at his feet, the grand actuality.

And so we come to consider the notions of *more* and *better*. Or *I* do, who am partial to such thoughts. Is it in my interest, for example, to attempt to catch up to those who were steeped in a literary education almost from the start? I once thought it was and went about it.

But it was not. One of the endless rewards of poetry is the wholeness of a life which needs and makes it. Everything is suitable, most particularly whatever does not at first seem to be. There are limits, of course, but in general one can say that it hardly matters which good book one reads but, rather, the quality of attention given it.

I am convinced that the way to learn from the works of others is always to labor to see what is *right* about them. Inevitably, one will have one's quarrels. One can hardly suppress them. Will they block learning? If they arrive first, for most people they will.

Do I know the birds? Some. Do I know anything about trees? A few things. Do I know much about the stork? A bit, mainly from travels in Morocco, but not so much as about the duck, whose every dumb struggle to live and excremental surge against death I walked in the midst of as a boy on eastern Long Island.

I recognize that J. V. Cunningham's personal distinction between verse and poetry holds up in broad terms. (For the sake of discussion, I here amplify and further separate his terms, though in application they overlap.) The writing of verse is a civic, judgeable, rational activity, the result of skill. The writing of poetry is an asocial, unjudgeable, irrational activity, the result of inspiration.

Now "inspiration" has been a difficult word to employ in recent times. It has almost come to mean only a "source," as in, "What event inspired you to write that column, Miss Bombeck?" Yet I understand, at last, that I write out of a complex of need and response that boils over on its own schedule, and that "resembles" inspiration, or at least hot water.

Discovery is everything, the unknown the only place worth going. Verse may be an honorable craft. Well, it is! A glorious craft. Moreover, it is a craft which encompasses, at times, poetry—to maintain here Cunningham's distinction. But poetry is the wider circle, encompassing craft.

It is not so much a question of what knowledge will suffice as it is of what ignorance will suffice. To locate one's ignorance—the stores are great, a little will do—and to head off in that direction—well, that has made all the difference.

The mind has many hands—too many to be satisfied by those little bits and pieces of the world which are paraded before us in the name of art as examples of something complete, completed representations of all of something.

That is why, also, it is so difficult to write about pure happiness. Joyful epiphanies, perhaps. ("I have awoken in Missoula, Montana, utterly happy."—R. Bly.) But happiness at some length, no. Our experience of life does not accord with a simple term like "happiness," whereas "unhappiness" (or "trouble" or "misery," if you prefer) has always, in a world of mortality, its limits. Trouble and pain are, after all, symptoms of life.

Surely poetry is about just that—what life feels like. But there is a trap here for the thoughtless romantic and the unthinking creator of fictions. Just as the conventional wisdom is always wrong, just as every generalization is defeated by each example, so our emotions are schooled in the cliché, the knee-jerk heart-throb, the quick surge of "right" feeling. It takes the attention of the mind to free the emotions; without it, they thrash in the self until they drown—in tears.

What about Auden? "About suffering," he tells us in a great poem, "they were never wrong, The Old Masters." They knew how it goes on without others knowing or caring. That's a sure idea, somewhat exaggerated but beautifully and convincingly illustrated in the poem. Everyone knows the poem, "Musée des Beaux Arts," and rightly so. In it, Auden endorses the perceptions of the painters who gave events—whether the birth of Christ or the fall of Icarus—their "human position." To the perspective of the painters, Auden adds, without ever saying the word, the broad dimension of human *apathy.*

Auden was a moralist. That he altered early poems to accord with his switch from Marxism to Christian Humanism hardly matters. An essentially moral engagement with the world, which is one sign of a great poet, to my mind, is not signalled by schools or churches, and is certainly not signalled by one-cause political positions. Politics is to morality as a rainmaker is to God, or a cloud to heaven. (I'm stretching a bit.)

Randall Jarrell is an interesting writer to mention next to Auden. He was, I think, the best critic of his talky generation, yet he chose to write poetry in a more and more accessible, voiced, intimate manner. For Auden's intellectual distance, Jarrell substituted a deliberate (but not merely reflexive) involvement with the sloppy, the sentimental and the banal. He took the ordinary seriously.

It happens that Jarrell makes reference to a wall of the Sistine Chapel. Specifically, in the poem, "Washing," he likens the look of wash hanging on a clothesline, when the wind has let up briefly, to "the collapsed abject look of the sack of skin Michelangelo made himself in his *Last Judgment.*" The Jarrell poem mentions—no, uses—not only the line of laundry and that remarkable detail from the painting, but also the violence of a sneeze, involuntary circles run by a chicken which has just had its neck wrung, a homey but tough saying and, along with Auden's perception of an apathetic world going about its business, a notion of courage. There is a suggestion of the dilemma of free will.

Isn't the quality of feeling one thing for a person who knows, and knows he knows, and has formulated what he believes, and another thing for a person who comes upon that knowledge, or so it would seem, before our very eyes? Compare the later poems of Auden to the later poems of Jarrell.

Compare Stevens to Williams . . . for *ideas*! It is a literary truism that Stevens is a poet of ideas and it seems to follow for most readers that Stevens is a smarter poet than Williams. "Most people" are wrong again. Stevens' ideas are geometric formulations, artifices that require special glasses. Williams' ideas are farther along, deeper, involved with the physical world—the only evidence we have. In large measure, Williams' ideas are those of a moralist, Stevens' those of an aesthete. Stevens' poems parade their ideas, while Williams' poems just go ahead and use them. In Williams, they are the foundation for proof and disproof and for the work of ideas. In Stevens, they are the whole structure, and so formulated that they are left no work to do. Useless ideas—could there be such a category? Imagine talking all the time about, say, free will and determinism, and never about, say, utilitarianism. Imagine the paralysis of the educated middle class of America when faced with the teleological aspect of utilitarianism, and you see at once who thinks Stevens is brainier than Williams.

As for Auden, he was all the Auden he could be that day in Iowa. He would never be more Auden than he already was. Jarrell had long since published a lengthy essay on his work in which he admired the young, socially conscious, politically paranoid, Old English–paced Auden and suggested that middle Auden was already imitating himself. Perhaps the poet who knows his strengths and knows his severe accomplishments— knows that they *are* accomplishments—has little choice but to serve the master who is himself.

The relationship between old age and wisdom has been exaggerated, certainly, and age's ostensible benefits may not be benefits at all. The poet must protect his ignorance or, like Auden already thinking his way out of that small Midwestern town and back to the City, he will have no one who interests him to speak to.

# The Hours Musicians Keep

My friend Roger called last night, and Dorothy, reading at the kitchen table, gave me a look of bewilderment-going-to-alarm when I held the phone to my ear but said nothing. I knew who it was. I could hear a bass figure in 6/8 time and knew that it was only a matter of measures until a whistle would begin to the tune of that hoary cornet solo, "The Carnival of Venice." If things went well, the whistler might try the first variation from J. B. Arban's version or Herbert L. Clarke's—the arrangement on which I had soloed at the New York State High School Music Festival in my senior year. But there would be no attempt to whistle the cadenza at the start of Del Staigers' fearful version: lip slurs so rapidly up and down that it was rumored that Del Staigers, the redhead, could only play it drunk, and it could be approached by only one high-school cornetist in my acquaintance—my friend Roger.

In college, however, I would sit second chair to Artie Shaw (not the clarinetist), whose father owned a dairy in Hornell and whose credentials included, not only the ability to play Del Staigers' diabolical cadenza, but also to hit double high C, a note my horn has never known, on a cold cornet. He was the closest I would come to the kind of range which was all the rage then and which reached both its zenith and apex in the joint recordings of Maynard Ferguson and Yma Sumac—he of the freak lip with a high range to rival Cat Anderson's, she of the otherworldly Peruvian voice of five or more octaves which could come up from the tombs or shriek like a bird. Was her name really Amy Camus? There were existential rumors.

Music was my earliest way into the world of nighthawks, bohemians (as we called them before the word "beatnik" arrived) and culture. I played from the fourth grade on, eventually owning a handmade Bach cornet bought used from Ned Mahoney, who played second chair to the Goldman Band cornet soloist, the always rapid, sometimes sloppy, one-armed virtuoso, James F. Burke, and an Olds trumpet model named for the legendary Rafael Mendez, who could play high C on a trumpet suspended by a string, and who had once destroyed his embouchure against a swinging door and had taught himself a new lip position for the mouthpiece. In Mexico to end a brief marriage which left me with a son, I would spend half a day searching out a beer garden where Mendez was appearing, only to learn that it was his day off. The trumpet named for him had first and third valve triggers with which to flatten notes otherwise sharp because of the normal characteristics of the trumpet, but I preferred to lip them down, and in fact I preferred the more flexible, warmer tone of the cornet to the colder penetration of the trumpet.

Most young cornet players with a normal embouchure used a Vega 2 mouthpiece, but Roger and I used a Bach 10½C. Its deeper cup produced a deeper tone, though there was a penalty when the player went high. Things could go wrong, and did. In the long run, trumpet players grew barrel-chested and fought their instruments all the way to heart attacks. In the short run, there were sore lips from long gigs (alleviated by the cushion-rim mouthpiece, which resembles an ordinary mouthpiece with a doughnut for a rim), sticky valves (we used trick fingerings to make up for a lack of valve oil, and Roger once soloed on "The Minnehaha Waltz" with a stuck third valve), and a convention that called for the drummers to fire blanks to punctuate the endings of marches—a loud addition said to have been popularized at the University of Michigan.

There were also plumber's helpers to wah-wah the white blues, plastic hand guards to save the silver or gold plating from a sweaty grip, clothespins to keep the music in sight during outdoor concerts, and sometimes a banana to increase salivation in the cottony mouth that afflicts the nervous soloist.

As a soloist, I was always nervous. At my high school graduation, I played Clarke's "Stars in a Velvety Sky," while my cap tassel swung in time. It's the trumpet music of Herbert L. Clarke which one hears, incidentally, behind the action in the movie *Hester Street,* and it was a revelation to me, on first viewing the film, that someone else had noticed the melancholy at the heart of Clarke's lyrical solos for cornet.

Roger and I would drive to New York, two hours west, to take in a Goldman Band concert in Central Park and then go to Birdland or Basin Street or the Metropole. Burke would solo every night that the band played in Central or Prospect Parks, make a token move toward reclaiming his seat, and be summoned forth to play an encore, always something easier— "Dreams of Karen," for example, which was dedicated to Burke by its author, Roy H. Milligan, and which he would play at about one and a quarter times its normal pace. When he was on a run, one could hear the holes in the valves lining up with the openings of the slides with little explosions of spit and breath. Roger and I sometimes unfolded the score to that night's solo across our laps, and one night when Burke chose to ignore the high, optional counterpoint the soloist may play while the band carries the melody to a Goldman solo called "Scherzo," we looked up at him and we thought he smiled down.

At G. Schirmer's famous music store, then at 3 East 43rd Street, we could appraise new solos from the Fischer, Fillmore and Mills music houses, and we would ask to see more and more difficult scores before making a choice.

Going to Birdland to hear trombonists J. J. Johnson and Kai Winding, we were likely to see Miles Davis or Don Elliott too. The stadium dates and big record-distribution routes had yet to weaken the club system for jazz, and the artists came to hear one another and sometimes to sit in. Even then, the beer came only in paper cups, to cut down on violence, and the drinks were hustled to tables little bigger than the napkins. Still, to teen-agers it *seemed* spacious and cheerful. We didn't know shit, but we knew something.

Elliott was interesting to us because he tripled on cornet, French horn and vibraphone. The Modern Jazz Quartet and the Australian Jazz Quintet were new sounds, mixing jazz with the classical. Miles' solos were already ethereal, and he had begun to use a mute on all standards. Nobody knew Cannonball Adderley's little brother Nat yet, but I thought he was terrific. Thad Jones teamed up with bassist Charles Mingus, and, when Stan Kenton made what seemed to be a racist response to *Down Beat's* jazz awards, Mingus published a long poem in reply. A Connecticut station played records by Shorty Rogers in what came to be known as the "cool" sound and, later, the "West Coast" sound when Rogers went off to work for Hollywood. The hottest trumpeter, to my mind, was Clifford Brown, whose records with drummer Max Roach were electric, and who would die young in an automobile accident. The trumpet had a value in those years it would never occupy again in a world of jazz that would never again seem so new, to anyone, nor evolve so rapidly, nor be so richly intertwined with an American lifestyle outside the mainstream.

And what does it mean that so many artists have come to their art by way of another art—writers, in particular, by way of music and painting? I believe I can distinguish between poets who came to poetry from painting and those who came to it by way of music: it goes beyond sound versus image, and is rooted in the difference between the populist spread of bands and group lessons in the public schools of small towns, and the parallel study of painting which, back then, was more likely to be undertaken seriously only by the urban and privileged. I'm afraid I still hear the difference when the band follows the orchestra, or vice versa, at the local junior high, though I hasten to add that I am talking now about childhood influences and not about professional accomplishment, and that there will never occur again, I believe, such clear lines in American culture. For one thing, we now see an increased participation in second-level artistic activity in our country which seems to derive from a feeling that everyone is important and no one is special. It is harder now, I think, to be an outsider unless one draws the lines on a political basis against most of America. It is possible, therefore, that what I, and others like me, took by way of lifestyle and attitude from the jazz world then must now come from the more greatly splintered sphere of racial, sexual and revolutionary politics—in which it will prove increasingly difficult to align a literary majority to judge poets, or to give convincing approval to a handful of the "best." To me, these thoughts follow, as childhood trails middle age, waiting.

I knew I would never be good enough. I was insecure up high, I stayed too close to the chords on solos; worse, I saw notes when I played—the result of the way I had been taught, the only way I could have been taught. I quit the horn by not going to music school, though my trumpet teacher, Chester Osborne—a composer, historian and author of serious books for youth—disagreed with my decision. I quit my musical future when I went to college, though I continued to play for several years: with a dixieland band on the radio, with orchestras, concert bands, marching bands and dance bands. I played the "Trumpet Voluntary" by Jeremiah Clarke, long misattributed to Henry Purcell, on Easter Sunday in a black robe at the pulpit. I played duets with Lyle S. in fundamentalist churches in upstate New York. I jammed with friends in the college chapel. I even took lessons for two more years, and worked up additional solos by Haydn and Hindemith. Meanwhile, I taught myself to fake a popular piano. It was fun making it up, finding ways to make it come out well without being able to do it right.

Flutter-tongue and double-tongue. Pedal notes and shakes. *Schmaltz*, hand vibrato, and Frank Sinatra playing on just his mouthpiece in "From Here to Eternity." The half-valved neighing of a horse. Straight mutes and cup mutes. I played solos, duets, trios, quintets, sextets, with bands, orchestras and combos. I played for fun and money but never to be better than someone else or even to have someone say so. Because of the hours musicians keep, I saw things differently, listened to different radio programs, and had time to think.

Six months ago, sitting in a Roman *piazza* on the outskirts of a fountain, I heard someone whistling "Carnival of Venice." I couldn't see who. If it was corny to identify so quickly, it would be far cornier to play the unaffected bystander. Was he whistling it well, or even correctly? It would not have occurred to me to care. And that's why poets are poets. And that's the name of that tune. And that's why Roger whistles me up twenty-five years later—old friend, Roger.

# Influences

*(The following paper was delivered at the annual meeting of the Associated Writing Programs on April 4, 1981, in Seattle.)*

In thinking about "influence," it is easy to suffer anxiety. I have three possible titles for this paper: "Influence: Becoming Ourselves" . . . or: "Influence? or Dumb Luck?" . . . or: "Influence: The Inescapable."

My wish, whenever poetry is discussed, is to have some poetry at hand. Therefore, I have brought along this short poem by William Stafford, titled "Lit Instructor":

> Day after day up there beating my wings
> with all of the softness truth requires
> I feel them shrug whenever I pause:
> they class my voice among tentative things,
>
> And they credit fact, force, battering.
> I dance my way toward the family of knowing,
> embracing stray error as a long-lost boy
> and bringing him home with my fluttering.
>
> Every quick feather asserts a just claim;
> it bites like a saw into white pine.
> I communicate right; but explain to the dean—
> well, Right has a long and intricate name.
>
> And the saying of it is a lonely thing.

Stafford's poem helps me to remind all of us that teaching is not easy, that its results are not sure, and that it is easily, perhaps willfully, misunderstood. "Right has a long and intricate name. / And the saying of it is a lonely thing."

When writers who teach writing gather, it's natural and healthy to think about the teacher's influence upon the student. Yet, if we are not blinded by pride or guilt, we know that cause-and-effect is difficult to determine, that literary training is the smallest part of a writer, that no student writer should be judged for ten or twenty years, that while many wonder whether or not a thing can be taught, no one is foolish enough to say that a thing cannot be learned (everyone who ever wrote a good poem or a good story is an example of someone who learned how), that much harsh criticism of young writers is self-hatred or hatred of the young disguised as literary criticism, that writing matters to writers for deep reasons having nothing to do with jobs and careers, that Louis Armstrong might as well have been speaking about poetry when he replied to the question, "What is Jazz?" by saying, "If you've got to ask the question, you'll never know the answer," that the teaching of writing is not new and that Basho had thousands of students, and finally that Rilke is right when he says, in the first of his *Letters to a Young Poet,* "Works of art are of an infinite loneliness and with nothing so little to be reached as with criticism. Only love can grasp and hold and be just toward them."

And that's about all I want to say about the influence of teachers on students. It is a subject about which I care and on which I dwell at length, but it is also, to my mind, best left to each person in private. I long ago made my peace with what it is to be a teacher of poetry writing in the vocal, paranoid and competitive world of literary culture.

Another obvious academic aspect of influence is, of course, that of visible influence: one poet, say, imitating, parodying, arguing with, or otherwise being influenced by another's work. We all know seemingly obvious examples. There's Pound's drastic revision of Eliot. There's Pound's own response to Browning. There's Pound's making a pact with Walt Whitman. There's Pound's influence on Yeats. There's Yeats' on

Roethke, who writes, in "Four for Sir John Davies": "I take this cadence from a man named Yeats; / I take it, and I give it back again." There's Stevens' on Ashbery, about whose first book, *Some Trees,* the late Frank O'Hara was moved to say, "This is the most beautiful first book to appear in America since *Harmonium.*" There's the sea-change undergone by James Wright between the books *Saint Judas* (1959) and *The Branch Will Not Break* (1963), apparently the result of reading Trakl, Rilke and Spanish. His famous poem, "Lying in a Hammock on William Duffy's Farm in Pine Island, Minnesota," with its startling last line, "I have wasted my life," is clearly an echo of Rilke's famous, "Archaic Torso of Apollo," which ends, "You must change your life." There is the influence of Rilke's *Duino Elegies* on Kinnell's *Book of Nightmares.* There is the dramatic stylistic change in W. S. Merwin's poetry between *The Drunk in the Furnace* (1960) and *The Moving Target* (1963), surely attributable in part, it now seems clear, to some of the translating he was doing. Everyone has seen the influence of Vasko Popa on one of *his* translators, Charles Simic. And we could easily make a case for many more pairings: Stevens in Justice, Bishop in Strand, Montale in Charles Wright, Kabir in some recent Robert Bly, to name a few.

Still, no one would claim, I hope, that Eliot is only Pound, or that James Wright became Trakl, or that Kinnell simply updated Rilke, or that Ashbery is nothing but Stevens. We know better. We know that, while approach and style in poetry may be influenced by what one admires and even by what one dislikes and wishes to correct, most of what we are and express in literary form is nonliterary in origin. Other texts may influence our style or approach, but they are unlikely to influence much our viewpoint or character.

Surely you all get asked, as I do, who your "influences" are. Taken simply, the questioner probably would be satisfied to know which poets you would walk downtown to buy. Still I've always had trouble with that question because the poets I admire are too many and too diverse to make a telling list.

Today, however, I'd like to fess up just a bit. I'm sure anyone who is paranoid about Iowa City and thinks he or she *knows* would be surprised to learn that my earliest influence was the poetry of . . . Well, I won't say yet. It's not a difficult riddle, really, as you'll see.

I probably began writing poetry from the same impulse that had made me commit earlier to other forms: music, photography, journalism, and before that, even such a seemingly unrelated activity as amateur radio.

Asked in an interview about *his* influences, Bill Stafford said an interesting thing. He said that the voice in his poems was probably the voice of his mother. Well, the voice in my poems has been different voices, depending on my age and the book, but the voice in my newest poems, I can say, is probably the voice my father would have had, had he been an American rather than an immigrant from the Ukraine, and had he done the things I've done. The thinking in my poems comes from such equally nonliterary folk as Van Field, whose call sign was W2OQI; Roy Raynor, W2EBT; Anne Hornbostel, a German lady of enormous spirit; Carl Fracassini, a potter; and many other nonpoets.

I went off to graduate journalism school in Syracuse, where I lasted but a semester. It was 1958. My friend Al Sampson, who like me had experience as a journalist and who, like me, had thought to keep his interest in literature pure by going into some other line of work, and who, like me, was wasting his time in such a place, and the woman who was to become my first wife, would cut classes to read poetry to one another inside a bad Italian restaurant. And do you know who interested us? Ginsberg. Corso. Ferlinghetti. Looking back, I see why. What I see is that I knew even then that the nature of poetry was defiance, bred of genes and character and nurtured by selective attention. I already sensed that the liveliest history of poetry was the history of poets finding ways to put into their poems form and content formerly thought unpoetic—because informal, ragged, controversial, dangerous, crude, vulgar, obscene. The poet was special, and the Beats, flying in the face of the Academy, were more interesting to me than the poets in my classroom anthologies. "Make it new!" said Pound, and "Literature is news that STAYS news."

I never wanted to write like Ginsberg, you understand. I had my own language and viewpoint. But I wanted to assert an equally active engagement with reality.

Since then, I have been influenced by many poets, notably Williams for his mind and the variety of his syntax, William Stafford for his sense of the spontaneous and the forgivable, and James Wright and others for their guts and lingo. But what I *am* goes back to my interest in philosophy, which is, for me, an interest in truth. I need truth. I admire truth-telling. I enjoy truth, even the truth that says that, this time, there is no truth. I find truth in poetry, and try hard to locate it in my own. I do not think, most of the time, that we are likely to find much truth outside of poetry. In that, I agree with Williams. That is why I remain a poet of ideas who believes that most ideas in poetry are not ideas at all but assertions. Without reasoning, ideas remain assertions, vague poetic gestures.

Most of you must surely feel, as I do, like a fish out of water in the Academy. I know there are writers who fit into the Academy very well, who find it a lively challenge to take their Ph.D.s, and who feel good after committee meetings.

Not many, though. The Academy believes in cause-and-effect in what I take to be a simple-minded way. I am inclined to say, with Henry Ford, "History is bunk." History is more likely to be bunk beds, your father's shovel, the guy or girl who said no, the guy or girl who said yes, a popular song you heard as you were falling asleep at thirteen.

So where is "influence" in all this? My tendency is to risk a little autobiography here, to be an example of any of us.

I grew up in a *very* small town on the south shore of eastern Long Island, surrounded by fishermen, duck farmers and potato farmers. The town was primarily Polish, Italian and Catholic, though there was a sprinkling of the rest of us. Almost everyone had an immigrant father or grandparent living at home. Naturally, such people were practical and informal. Community behavior was narrow in range. It was the times as well as the town. Young people did not, as a rule, go to college. An intellectual sort might become a life insurance salesman, or an office worker in another town, rather than, say, a clam digger, farmer or policeman. The military was considered a good way to see the world and improve oneself. Most people's dream of travel was two weeks in Miami Beach. New York City was only seventy miles west but, unless you had relatives there, you went in maybe once a year. In general, those good people found safety in being like others. They had often been in danger.

But there was something wrong with me. I liked the oddness in people. I went looking for it, and found it in strange places. I was a pretty fair country cornet player and playing with "combos," as we called them then, let me rub shoulders with nighthawks. Other nights, I would walk out to the little house that served as the town library, where the librarian—a volunteer from Brookhaven National Laboratory—would undercharge me for the books I inevitably brought back late. I read philosophy but no novels. In fact, I graduated from high school without ever having read a novel on my own and, when the Regents exam asked for a book review, I had to make one up. It was a Western.

Also, my sister got married right after high school. My father wanted her to go to college but my sister wanted to do what the others did—boy or girl—so she got married instead. Her father-in-law, an insurance salesman from East Moriches, took me one Thanksgiving to his attic, where I was introduced to amateur radio. His call sign was W2EBT, which he referred to phonetically as Two Eggs, Bacon and Toast or as Elderly, Bald and Toothless. In those days, it was only very odd sorts indeed who were "hams." Suspected by the neighbors of sending spy reports to Russia (remember the Rosenbergs, who were alleged to have hidden a radio in a coffee table and who were executed for it?), thought curious for going to their attics or traipsing about on the roofs, they were people with rough edges. They were not popular, they had not been kings and queens at high school proms, they had not lettered (though I was careful to letter in several sports, lest I have to prove my manhood twice a week). There was Van Field, W2OQI (Two Ossified, Queer Indians), who lived like a hermit up a wooded path in a one-room house where he did little but build transmitters, power supplies and receivers. I would bicycle to his place and hang around until he could only get rid of me by helping me build my first transmitter. There was Herbie Snell, W2FCH (Two Females Chasing Herbie), who gave me rides to the radio club meetings, all the while philosophizing on the tyranny of clocks (he refused to wear a watch or to have a clock in his car). Herbie supported himself in Aquebogue with a radio repair shack behind his house, in which he kept, naturally, no regular hours, and he was the only man I knew who spoke openly of his love for his wife. You have to understand that I was of a philosophic mind and would extend my thinking from just so tiny an observation. I was, in this way, influenced.

I was also, I am sure, influenced by the notion of common sense which pervaded that small town, as well as by the small towner's natural distrust of complicated language, and by the kind of work I did or witnessed: on the Bay, on the duck farm, in my father's store, and at the weekly newspaper office, where the sports editor let me make up the box scores at 2 a.m.

I should say that it was not the dramatic which influenced me, but the odd and significant. When my sister was more-or-less kidnapped, and my tiny mother went off on a bus, announcing to the family that she was off to find her, and *did* find her—well, that was a moment to deal with but it was not, to me, interesting. Remember, I preferred philosophy to fiction.

Choosing a college out of ignorance, I ended up at Alfred University, a lucky choice. There, in the Design Department of the College of Ceramics, there had ended up, for many odd reasons, refugee teachers from Moholy-Nagy's New Bauhaus in Chicago, and brilliant, eccentric artists from the streets of New York. I knew immediately that they would amount to something beyond careers, and I watched them from a distance. I did not write poems and I wanted nothing to do with the literary magazine. The two people who were literary stars on campus have not been heard from since, though they were brilliant. I do not doubt that they went on writing and, especially, reading. Yet the nature of literary influence is such that poems may copy one another at the expense of truth. I would like to have been born in Defiance, Ohio.

Many of you know Norman Podhoretz's autobiographical book, *Making It,* in which he traces that partly unconscious turning of his back on his roots and language which came along with his being well-schooled and rewarded for others' ideas of accomplishment. In the end, he accepts what has happened to him.

And so he becomes a social critic, not a poet. A poet, it seems to me, takes a step to the side of others early in life—no one knows why—and then just keeps on walking. Along the way, he or she has to answer to the question of influence. The audience usually wants literary answers but the self is not literary.

Thus, when I write about travel, I write about home, because my father was an immigrant and so were most of the fathers I knew as a boy. I write about ducks because I grew up next to duck farms, and broke the necks of sick ones, and saw in them pure examples of a world without intelligence in which the notion of the "victim" was not so clear. For me, it was natural, a first generation American from a small town, growing up during World War II and then Korea, to put together in one poem, as I did, a duck farm and a problem in ethics textbooks, and to believe, as the poem makes clear, that ethics is sometimes a luxury of circumstance, and further to believe, as the poem suggests, that there is in the American middle class a tendency to turn action into theory and to be paralyzed. Who influenced me to think such things? Perhaps it was the image of my father escaping from the Ukraine, riding bareback to Poland, striking down those who held knives and axes to his throat. Yes, I think probably it was such an image, attached as it was to *that man.*

In another poem, I report on my trying to kill a catfish by hammering it on the head. I mention in the poem novels in which a detective does the same to people. Now another poet might never put these two things together, or might see other implications than those I did. But it is natural to me to use such circumstances, as I did, to question our notions of beauty—which are mainly images of stasis and death. You see, I come from a place where the sea never stops moving, where the ocean can move dunes for miles, and where the slick magazines had yet to change the look of people. So the poem, "A Catfish: On Beauty," ends, "That catfish was ugly, I think. / The longer it took, the uglier he got."

Similarly, it is natural to me to begin a poem with the lines, "Whether you sing or scream, / the process is the same," to challenge in it our notions of what constitutes a word, and to title it, "To No One in Particular." If I had gone to Andover and Harvard, would I do that? I doubt it. I wouldn't even think it. In his "Ars Poetica: Some Recent Criticism," in the book *Two Citizens*, James Wright says, "I could tell you, / If you have read this far, / That the nut house in Cambridge / Where Agnes is dying / Is no more Harvard / Than you could ever be. / And I want to gather you back to my Ohio. / You could understand Aunt Agnes. . . ."

Yet we are always trying to go beyond what we have been. I am trying even now to live my life more and more fully, against all odds. To do so, one must want to learn from that which most challenges one. In thinking about this panel, I asked one of the most brilliant of my students about his literary influences. He told me that, whenever he disliked the work of a poet but didn't know why, he was sure to be in love with that poet a year later. Perhaps he is subject to influence as originally defined in astrology: "an ethereal fluid thought to flow from the stars and to affect the actions of men."

Of course we are influenced by everything we read, every remark made in our presence by someone we admire or despise, neuroses such as paranoia and insecurity. Our job is to become more and more of what we are. I have said elsewhere that the growth of a poet sometimes seems to me to be related to his or her becoming less and less embarrassed about more and more. Recently, a student said to me, "We all need a little more courage now and then." That's what I need. If you have some to share, I want to know you. Your criticisms you can keep to yourselves.

# How We Think Back

("*How We Think Back*" was written in 1975 in response to a questionnaire. I picked the poem, "Gemwood," which may be found in the interview by Joyce Renwick at the beginning of section II. Alberta Turner put the questions:

1. How did the poem start?
2. What changes did it go through from start to finish?
3. What principles of technique did you consciously use?
4. Whom do you visualize as your reader?
5. Can the poem be paraphrased? How?
6. How does this poem differ from earlier poems of yours in (a) quality (b) theme (c) technique?

In addition, many smaller questions were posed, some of which may be intuited from my remarks.)

In answering your questions about the origin and evolution of a poem, I have chosen for example a poem which is itself an attempt to follow the mind and emotions backwards, then forwards beyond the present.

The circumstance was this. I keep in a workroom out back—one room under a wild cherry tree—a xerox of my youngest son's hands. Four years earlier, showing him the operations of a Xerox copier, I had had him place his hands—he was five—on the machine. It was just a way of demonstrating the workings of the copier, but I could not throw away the print that resulted. It would always make me sad to look at it.

At five, a child's hands are still fatty with innocence. The xerox showed the innocence, and nothing of experience or the particular: not the fingerprints, for example. I knew this was the obvious reason the print could sadden me.

Still, that shy totem would not have shown up in a poem had not it insisted upon itself, four years later, in a moment when I thought I was thinking about something else.

I had passed through O'Hare Airport in Chicago for the umpteenth time. O'Hare, I'm told, is the world's busiest airport. It is also the one which provides the least to do between planes. Because I live in Iowa City, and must fly to Cedar Rapids to reach home, I often face a long layover in Chicago. Therefore, I have developed a routine with which to pass the time.

Following my routine, I had seen a new item in the gift shop: "Gemwood." I disliked the idea at once: "gemwood" is produced by force-feeding pine trees with dyes, as if the wood of a tree were not enough in itself. The result is a batch of wooden eyes, hung row upon row. "Gemwood" seemed to me an example of one unfortunate meaning of "art" in our time: violation of the natural.

Well, I began with "gemwood." Something of a catty description of "gemwood" was all I intended. That would suffice to refuse it. But the print of Jason's hands looked up at me once more.

What sadness! There was much behind it. That print of a child's hands had been made the summer we had gone to Vermont so that I could teach for Goddard College—the summer my older son's unlikely first pet, a rat, had died unnecessarily.

Now you reading this will probably think a rat a ludicrous pet, and you will almost surely—if your defenses are up—think it silly to feel deeply the death of a rodent. Well, what *did* make us terribly sad, even weepy? Was it the death of the rat, the pain of our son's sudden loss, or both? Does it matter that we know?

I think not. Rather, it matters that we feel. And acknowledge that we do. Writing in my little study, it was enough to acknowledge one's own backyard.

But of course there were other thoughts and impulses that

surfaced. I wondered at the cause of my sadness, but also at the way we think from one matter to another. For a year, the poem was titled "How We Think Back." Furthermore, the "joint effort of man and nature" (the phrase used to advertise gemwood) signalled to me also the inevitable *difference* between man and nature. So too, the past and present came together, as did sadness and joy.

Thus, the poem began, as do so many, because there was present a strong emotion (sadness), tempered and shaped by my attention to occasions and objects. And surely there were general concerns at the time which encouraged the particular combination. For example, I had wanted to write sensible poems to my sons. I was aware that the parent learns too late. I had tried to be a good parent, and I was trying to get better.

One has the literal fact ("gemwood") and the sense that there is more to say, connections to be allowed to surface—not simply to be planned or designed. That is why the poem wanders about, gives and takes back. Its movement is a kind of "hesitation forward."

You ask next about revisions. I remember carrying a draft of the poem—at first, yellow sheets; later, ironically, a xerox of a draft—on trips, finally all the way to Europe. I let it lie, awaiting a clearer perspective. I didn't want to make the poem too shapely. Partly, this was because I had come to desire another sort of movement than my previous poems had shown; but it was also because I wanted the poem to speak as the objects and occasions had spoken to me: haltingly, correctingly, without a posed moment to make famous.

The poem was not to be called "finished" until a year after it had begun. I know now that my practice has been to let drafts sit quite some time, even years, and to publish finished poems long after they are written. Sometimes, my method of revision may be more of a method for acceptance (and then completion) than for making major alterations. I want to be able to accept as much as possible of the poem-in-process: to understand the underlying terms of the poem, the givens, and to make the connections thereby required. In the case of "Gemwood," the poem did not change size significantly from what I had been able to manage during those first days when I had written most of it. I removed one line and added two. Beyond that, I made changes in the service of rhythm, sequencing, emphasis and small clarities. I may have made a change or two in what I took to be dull language.

You inquire, too, about conscious principles of technique. That is, perhaps, the most difficult question you have asked, because almost any answer must remain partial and misleading. I could say that my technique in this poem—and in the poems which were to follow, in some sense, from it—has been to be as much of myself as possible, but without any insistence. This may be a question of tone, which subsumes all technical matters. I wished, as I have already said, to allow the poem to wander with the mind—not without direction, but without preemptive designing. I wished to be colloquial, and to avoid specially "poetic" diction but not abstract words. I wished to write the poem so that it could be read without reference to another text. I trusted my ear, and tried to phrase the sentences, and line the poem, so that it would be graceful, clear and engaging—but not so smooth that it might become a static record of the mind more than it would be an embodiment of process to be participated in anew with each rereading.

Could another writer line the poem differently? Perhaps. Not, however (I hope), without changing it, if subtly. It seems to me that the first few lines of a poem create a relationship between line and syntax, and that the phrasing and lineation which follow necessarily derive from those first lines.

Notice the little transitions between stanzas. The subject matter of the poem changes slightly with each new stanza; with each new stanza, the poem takes a step forward. Yet I was reluctant to permit neat breaks in what was a flow of association, memory and thought. One theme of the poem may be that very flow.

The ending I hope for is the inevitable, earned one. The ending here is not too surprising, but it is also not a simple repetition of all that has gone before. Hopefully, it is the next step, containing all the rest but requiring nothing more.

I prefer the poem to be read silently or aloud, but not with musical accompaniment, though perhaps someone could convince me I was wrong about that. Finally, the eye requires what the mind requires: a helpful relationship between content and style.

And you ask a fearless question as to who I think are my readers. I visualize them as myself, my sons, other parents and sons, and then thoughtful people at large. Rereading is desired. After all, anyone can understand this poem. Anyone can read it and, were we a nation of readers, anyone might.

You ask for an attempt at paraphrase. I prefer to try it on a level more general than that of the poem itself. First, the poem by its very method suggests that association and memory are not always random, perhaps never are. To the contrary, they uncover conscious thoughts and feelings. By its content, the poem suggests (to me) that life is loss; that parenthood includes the inevitability of one's own loss as well as the watching of that sense of life-as-loss arrive in the children; furthermore, that man and nature must be thought opposed unless their "joint effort" is seen to be one of change, ageing and death, as well as of birth.

Such a paraphrase is incomplete in itself in general terms and, specifically, omits the naming, the relationships of events and people, the little telling moves (for example, the one correcting our usual impression of a rat as a pet), and the way in which the feelings are shown to persist through changes of time and place. Of course, the paraphrase also leaves out the music, the language, the organization, and the pacing of line and phrase and stanza. Used improperly, the paraphrase allows us to avoid the poem altogether. In fact, this is the most common use of paraphrase. The paraphrase kit comes with thick gloves, a blindfold, a gag and four corks.

How much do I want to tell you about how this poem seems to differ from my earlier poems in quality, theme and technique? You have asked, but our parents told us, "Comparisons are odious." However, my father used to say, about anyone, "He has to make a living too." Therefore, I'll try.

*Quality.* This poem is as good as many of my poems, better than many, not so good as a few—I think. However, it is as *qualified* as any, which may be what counts.

*Theme.* The fallibility of the parent, the inevitability of the loss of the parent—these themes have been present elsewhere in my poetry, though not before in the context of these circumstances.

*Technique.* The poem reads differently from my previous poems. It signals what I hope to be development rather than mere change, and I recognize that it is nowise the poem of metaphysical convolutions I have often written. It *is* a metaphysical poem, to be sure. For myself, I believe the term *metaphysical* applies to any poem I might want to reread. But this poem takes a different path toward its substance, and walks differently all the way. Compared to many of my earlier poems, it is less neat, less "difficult" or dense, more halting, more sentimental, perhaps more humane.

I told my students that I felt I would be a beginner until about the age of forty. I wrote "Gemwood" in 1975, at thirty-seven, and it signals something near a beginning I now see to have been inevitable yet to have depended on the poems which preceded it—a beginning which would not be rushed. That is why I am specially fond of this little ragged piece of saying, maybe a poem.

# Noun/Object/Image

We are greedy. We want the image to be more than the object, despite how hard it is merely to see an object and render it accurately. We are self-centered. We want the image to be partly subjective. We are proud. We want the image to carry our "vision." We are vain and competitive. We want the image to be *our* kind of image, *our* signature, *our* brick wall.

But photographers can do the object, and painters redo it, better than we. What can we do with it that they cannot?

We can put the object into motion, a motion even more continuous than that in film, where the screen must stay put. We can give the image a non-imagistic context. Hence, the object alone will suffice if deftly placed, and will be treated thereafter as if it in itself presents inside and outside, self and other, here and there. Of course we can also make of the image a place. We can locate there. And we can use the image to objectify our emotions, even sometimes to express them.

Most of the talk about imagery sounds like broadcasts of Army football games of the forties. Mr. Inside and Mr. Outside (Doc Blanchard and Glenn Davis), working together, couldn't be beat. And it's true that a star or two will compensate for one's deficiencies elsewhere. In our country, a so-so mind with a talent for vivid imagery will be praised, while a brilliant mind and ear lacking it will generally be ignored. We are not just TV watchers. We have become TV readers.

Pound's definition of the image—"an intellectual and emotional complex in an instant of time" (*Poetry*, March 1913)—is often reduced in conversation about the image. For all his learning, Pound's heart remained in popular song—Provençal lyrics. He would never have made poetry by squeezing it just from his brain, as have his more esoteric followers.

Pound's image has two parts, and produces an equation between feeling and object. Stieglitz was making such an equation when he photographed clouds and called them "equivalents." The clouds were equivalent to his emotions. No emotions, no images.

Imagism, remember, in reaction to the second-best poetry of its time, published a complete set of principles for tight, dramatic writing. Its advice to show, not tell, was only a part of its program. When it turned into what E. P. called "Amygism" (for Amy Lowell)—poems by poets who imitated the method but lacked emotional depth—Pound got out.

Now the image doesn't work the way we say it does. Take probably the two best-known examples of Imagism. First, Pound's "In a Station of the Metro." Pound finds it necessary to use half the poem to explain what's coming: "The apparition of these faces in the crowd." Only then can he lay before us an image: "Petals on a wet, black bough." The poem accomplishes an image, but not without explanation.

Second, Williams' "The Red Wheelbarrow." "So much depends," he writes, "upon a red wheel / barrow," and then says nothing about what depends on it. The poem argues for Imagism, but its method is rhetorical: the effect of the poem *depends* on the rhetorical beginning of its only sentence and on those expectations which it may thereby establish and frustrate. From the frustration itself arises the point to be made. In other words, though one could argue the propriety and advantages of a red wheelbarrow, it could have been something else.

Are the greatest accomplishments of American poetry those of imagery? I myself think not. Thinking about American poetry (and also about the poetry of young Americans and even about what might be called "Workshop Poetry," good or bad), it occurs to me that it tends to be heavy on rhetoric but light on imagery. Indeed, the colloquialization of rhetoric may be an American accomplishment. The British are better in court but their poetic rhetoric wears leaden boots. The French do more acrobatics but say less. Our idiomatic lingo is heavily rhetorical and metaphorical.

Our practice of Imagism (I would argue that we have been practicing at it ever since the Movement) much of the time has been mindless—the one great flaw in American poetry by which our practice is shown to be limited by an absence of sufficiently considered theory.

Now to your questions. Of course my ideas about imagery have in some ways changed and in some ways remained constant just as I have changed and remained constant. I don't usually think about imagery apart from other concerns. I am fairly certain that a preoccupation with images is characteristic of our technological society and will remain so. I am fairly sure that images in poems have less effect and less value than is claimed by those who are dependent upon them. I know that imagery can be a breeding ground for the fraudulent visionary, the mystifier. I suspect imagery has kept many unthinking poets writing and publishing, but there's always something. Those among us who love Imagism too much are held by its dead hand. So are those of us who hate it. To be free, one must proceed as if writing is an adventure into the unknown. From where one begins, one may see or imagine many images. And later there may be many surprises, some of which may be images. The "so much" that "depends" on each object/image is the object/image itself. In a field, we too are among those objects. The notion that man's brain is superior to a tree will lead to the premature end of civilization. But so will the notion that a tree is superior to a brain. At least the tree, as far as we can tell, is too smart to think so.

Now if we get into the poetry of William Carlos Williams, the most misunderstood, mislabelled and poorly-imitated poet of our time (still!), we shall never see the end of our discussion. For Williams is a poet of syntax and idea far more than he is a poet of things or images. His "thing" poems are mere exercises. His great works are not at all dependent on images. Rather, like most great poems, they are each centered in one image—that one from which the poem derives or toward which it proceeds. The image of the *poem* is vastly more important than the image of the *line*.

My book titles are images, but not always things. Is this possible? The titles are *Things We Dreamt We Died For; A Probable Volume of Dreams; The Escape into You; Residue of Song; Stars Which See, Stars Which Do Not See;* and *These Green-Going-to-Yellow.* Each of them stops short of presenting a single object to which a reader might attach his or her understanding of the whole phrase. In each case the image is bigger than that. To my mind, an object which has been turned on its head or covered with a shroud is still just an object. In such cases, one tends to turn it right-side-up or uncover it in one's mind, thus enjoying the pleasures of the riddle. But, for me, writing is not a riddle, any more than the unexplored polar cap was a riddle for Byrd. Call it a riddle if you like; it was a great space.

In my generation, the best image-makers include Mark Strand, Charles Simic, Louise Glück and Charles Wright. In the generation ahead of mine, one would have to name Galway Kinnell and the late James Wright. In the poetry of James Wright, we can trace the development of what is best in American poetic imagery. In mid-career, by way of Spanish and German poets (notably, Trakl), he develops the crisp, startling, "deep" imagery of *The Branch Will Not Break.* But imagery is not enough, so he puts back more rhetoric in *Shall We Gather at the River.* In the end, in *To a Blossoming Pear Tree,* he writes a plain, colloquial, narrative line, made glorious, heightened and also relieved by gorgeous images—many of them emotional correlatives, not to what has already been expressed outright, or will be, but to other, deeper responses. In such work, Wright refines one of the most powerful uses of the image (to tell us something more, from underneath) and also implies by his continuing need for rhetoric the limits of the image (for the "deep" image, once allowed to dominate the surface of the poem, becomes only the surface).

Images are not the essence of poetry, even for those who make them well. They are only one among many symptoms of a poet's quality of mind and force of imagination. Still, I too am knocked out by them. Who would not wish to have written these lines by Roethke: "Is that dance slowing in the mind of man / That made him think the universe could hum?" I myself think this an image. I also think an image is contained in these lines: "The rain / is too heavy a whistle for the certainty of charity." Those are my own lines, and they have haunted me for years.

The image is bigger than the object. But the noun is larger still. The secrets of the mind take the form of nouns. Those images in dreams which are taken to signify: they are merely the surface of things.

# The Impure Every Time

American poetry has changed utterly in the past twenty-five years. It changed partly because America changed. On the one hand, there was a proliferation of individual styles by the poets of the generation born late in the twenties. This happened mainly in the late fifties and early sixties. On the other, poetry changed because in the seventies we began to speak about it differently. Some women wanted to speak of it differently. Some Blacks wanted to speak of it differently. Chicanos and Oriental-Americans wanted to. Native American Indians wanted to. All kinds of outsiders wanted to. And poets who were increasingly translated into English and published in America spoke about it differently.

I can remember having to defend my practice of "free verse" in workshops. Someone might raise an eyebrow and say, "This appears to be written in free verse." "Oh no," I'd reply, "it's written in sprung accentuals with variant lines." I can remember when a prose-poem had to prove it was poetry, and when it seemed to matter. Now James Wright's wonderful book, *To a Blossoming Pear Tree*, can include a piece of prose (prose? prose-poetry?) about a scoutmaster in Martins Ferry, Ohio, and no one doubts that it is poetry. And I can remember when particular attitudes, even styles, were permitted Oriental poets, Russian poets, or poets of Eastern Europe, say, but were forbidden to American poets.

It's changed because we have gone back to thinking of poetry as something more than a bundle of techniques. Which is to say that we have gone back to emphasizing that there is something more to poetry than accomplishment.

Poetry has content, public as well as private. It has content not available elsewhere. That is why no good poets are dumb. If your uneducated relatives can spot the quality that is poetry, why can't you? Because you've been educated and acculturated away from your instincts, away from your heartbeat and pulse, away from the physical.

While good poetry has to be well written, no one quite knows what it means to write well. Everyone knows that writing well, even in lines, even in meters and rhymes, doesn't necessarily make poetry. It makes verse. Poetry is better than verse.

J. V. Cunningham wouldn't agree. Years ago he published an essay in which he argued that verse was rational, could be judged, and had a civic role, while poetry was irrational, could not be judged, and therefore had no assured civic role. He chose verse, the surer accomplishment.

I choose poetry. I choose the ugly as well as the beautiful, knowing it will all be beautiful soon enough. I choose the unknown (for now), the mystery rather than the accepted solution, the cracked bowl over the flawless one, the voice that has a little spit and phlegm in it, the used shoes, imagination over analysis, Williams over Stevens, the impure every time.

As a reader I don't have to choose between Stevens and Williams. They are equally great. I used to think I didn't have to choose as a writer, either, but I was wrong. They don't merely represent different styles. They represent opposite attitudes, opposing principles, about what the subject of poetry is.

I like to see visible indications of mentality in poems: the poem proceeding intelligently as well as *sensefully*. But I prefer that the subject matter not *be* the intelligence—as it is, I think, for Stevens. Without a greater engagement with the world than one finds in Stevens, language is an accomplished liar. I think Williams is, in the end, a more intelligent poet than Stevens. To write as Williams did, one has to have made sophisticated decisions about the nature of language. Moreover, while Stevens' work is singular, an achievement almost baroque, Williams' experiments and stylistic advances are far more daring and inventive as well as more influential.

We know now that poetry is a quality of imagination and language inextricably bound up with the recognizable world. We know that it's a kind of flying, that it gets up and goes.

The literary career is sometimes a hideous notion. It brings out the worst in critics and reviewers. It develops cliques and antagonistic loyalties when what a poet most needs is to learn from that which most opposes him or her, most disturbs, most confronts. Instead of support, the poet gets knee-jerk hostility from other "camps," and equally reflexive self-imaging praise from friends.

I remember walking across a lawn with Allen Ginsberg in the sixties. A young man called out to him, "What do you think of Creeley's new book?" His tone was clear: he himself didn't think so much of it. Maybe Ginsberg didn't either. But he turned and said, "Whatever Bob's doing, I'm *for* him." A little more of that would go a long way toward a great American poetry.

One of the reasons why America often seems to have no place for great poets of the people is that the critics will always choose Stevens over Williams while Williams is alive. They will always choose poetry which labors to be "poetic," whether by remembered forms or by a nostalgic, privately pained tilt of the head and vocal cords. Ah yes, they say, that's poetry, just as we studied it. The obscure will sometimes get a hearing, for the empty journals are always waiting for material. Hugh Kenner dismissed James Wright's gorgeous book of poems, *To a Blossoming Pear Tree,* essentially because it didn't suggest to him anything to say about it. That attitude makes poetry just an occasion for critical conversation. The use of excerpts from poems in reviews and books promotes the (false) notion that poems are just pieces put together.

Good poems transcend these problems, and we find them. More to the point, the act of writing transcends everything for those of us who need to write. They can take away from you everything but this: the poems you have written, the poems you are writing.

There is a valuable elitism which encourages quality, but there is also an evil elitism which attempts to forbid participation. We see it now in the decrying of the proliferation of poets in America. Some blame the NEA, some blame universities, some probably blame IBM and Xerox, but none think to place the "blame" where it belongs: in the guts and brains of the people who want to write. Millions of people who have played baseball, but not well, know something about it because they tried, and now they go to watch. Is it wrong for people who can't write well to write as well as they can? In the great scale-pan of human vices, a bad poem doesn't weigh very much. We could use a little modesty about publishing, we could usefully bind and gag a few poets who blanket the country with annual requests for paid readings, but then these are not such great vices either. Alas, the coin of the realm in the world of poetry is reputation, and there will always be those who will attempt to steal some for themselves.

I started out to say that poetry is an accomplishment beyond technique. Of course we always knew. Meanwhile, the Academy spoke of technique in one or two ways, the Black Mountaineers spoke of technique in another way, the Deep Imagists in their way, the Minimalists briefly, etc. Do you know why more and better articles about books of poetry don't appear? Because now that poetry is no longer written between the lines, the critics don't know what to say.

The critics have gone off into Structuralism, post-Structuralism, cartographies of misinterpretation, talk about semiotics and hermeneutics—which is to say they have left the scene.

For American poetry this is a time of rapid growth not separate from profound cultural/political/psychological changes. It was probably necessary to get the critics out of town for a while, to have a period when one was seldom being told what it was one had done and could not do. With all the damn talk about the particulars of writing nowadays, it's sometimes hard to imagine anyone doing anything new, but of course there will always be some who don't know any better.

*1 October 1980*

# Richard Hugo

## A Personal Foreword

(*The following piece was written in 1977 to introduce* A Trout in the Milk, A Composite Portrait of Richard Hugo, *edited by Jack Myers.*)

Why would there be so many writers to contribute to this book? I think it is not enough to say that Dick Hugo is a poet or teacher or friend or, sometimes, entertainer of the first order—although he is all of these.

I think it is because he exemplifies for many of us the clear possibility that art is not the sole province of those who are brought up with it, trained for it, rewarded for the mere possibility of it, perhaps even bred for it. The pursuit of consciousness (or higher consciousness, if you prefer) is not a race among thoroughbreds, though one has often been led to think that it is.

He lacks a classical education, though he has afforded himself a lifetime course in people and their stories and in nature. He hasn't a bone of elegant restraint in his body, so far as I can tell, but is impulsive, passionate and playful. All these characteristics get D in the classroom of minor effects. It is as if birdcalls were limited to a little trilling.

Many of the writers in this collection compare Dick's background or lifestyle to their own (though not, of course, in every detail), and I do too. There will always be more of us, and more inside each of us, that is like Hugo than like, say, Eliot or

Pound. We live everywhere, a few in what is assumed to be The City. We have our ordinary pleasures—fishing, perhaps, or softball—though some few may also know how to make a croissant. We hold jobs first for salaries, then for social good, with no thought of special status attached to them, though some few may think teaching a superior vocation or one to be avoided by poets at all costs (nonsense and double nonsense).

And we *identify*, not with the larger-than-life and accomplished, but with the good and troubled (Dick roots for the television detective, Cannon), though some few may see themselves in da Vinci or Sir Kenneth Clark.

Identity is the crux of it. Say what we will, we will become ourselves. After the self-consciousness of the adolescent, after the clever self-saying of young talent, after the desperate swings between rebellion and belonging brought on by our awakening to responses from the outside—after all, we will turn into what we always were. The son will rediscover the father in himself, and the mother; the daughter, likewise. The loved friend, the admired teacher, will surface again in one's ideas and language, in one's *obsessions*.

Dick Hugo, a child at heart (he would say), has written the poetry of a grown-up for a long time. He has not tried to be subtle, clever or elegant. He has written out of his rough identity, identifying with it everywhere: an identity formed out of a feeling for place, the vengeance of time, work, need, suffering and, in particular, the clarity of failure. But always he was going for something more. In lines that drive right into the center of town and wait for the buildings to collapse, he has found out the little bit of spirit within us that is waiting to triumph. For that alone, it is easy to love him.

# Pain and Fear

## *Something about Them*

*(My remarks for the symposium on "The Languages of Pain and Fear," held at The University of Iowa on the afternoon of March 18, 1980, consisted of paragraphs and poems about the limits of our approach to fear and pain. But first I read the comics: two* **Doonesbury** *strips in which the irrepressible Cousin Zonker interviews the immovable Miles Potash. In the first, Zonker asks Potash about his interest in pain and if he creates most of his effects through jogging. "No," says Potash, "Running. But that's a good way to start." In the second, Zonker brings up marathoner Potash's best-selling* **Complete Book of Pain** *in which Potash argues that running is good for the mind as well as the body. "That's right, Zonker," says Potash, "You just can't say enough about pain!" "But surely," says Zonker, "there's a threshold, a breaking point?" "That's right, Zonker," says Potash, "You just can't say enough about pain!" Only after the funnies was I prepared to say the following.)*

We tend to receive language as figurative speech, as metaphor, the more so if by so doing we can avoid apprehending the fearful or painful. For example, if I told you that this morning my wife and I played Scrabble and she whipped me, you would probably assume that she merely won the game.

  Good poetry expresses the otherwise inexpressible. Its turf is the physical world, or may be, but its content is not physical sensation because, while we may involuntarily signal great pain and/or pleasure, and voluntarily talk round it, sensation itself is mute.

Kierkegaard, explaining the situation of the poet, tells of a Roman emperor who arranged the construction of a great brass bull on a spit. It was shaped in such a way and a hole placed in its throat in such a spot that, when two men were roasted alive inside the great bull, the screams of the dying men made, at a distance, a beautiful music. Hence, Kierkegaard was moved to say, "I'd rather be a swineherd in the hut, understood by swine, than be a poet misunderstood by men." To poets, he said, "Your cries make us afraid, but we love your delicious music." The poet Alan Dugan makes quick reference in one of his poems to "this 'life is pain' phenomenon."

There is a yoga exercise which is terribly difficult, perhaps impossible, and which asks only that one sit still and concentrate, genuinely concentrate, on the most horrible thing one can imagine. The mind shrinks from the task.

And so the poems that come to mind today concern the linguistic and psycho-intellectual difficulties in articulating fear and pain.

The difficulty invites whitewashes and erasures, as in this sharp little poem by Emily Dickinson, #650 among her poems:

> Pain—has an Element of Blank—
> It cannot recollect
> When it begun—or if there were
> A time when it was not—
>
> It has no Future—but itself—
> Its Infinite contain
> Its Past—enlightened to perceive
> New Periods—of Pain.

The difficulty likewise invites simile and metaphor, as in Robert Creeley's poem, "The Flower":

> I think I grow tensions
> like flowers
> in a wood where
> nobody goes.

Each wound is perfect,
encloses itself in a tiny
imperceptible blossom,
making pain.

Pain is a flower like that one,
like this one,
like that one,
like this one.

We see in Creeley's simple poem not only simile turned to metaphor, but also two other strategies for attempting to apprehend pain in poetry: accumulation and insistence. Pain is a flower like this one, like that one, like this one, like that one. . . . They bloom in an endless wood.

And the difficulty invites research to the side of language, oblique peeks elsewhere for symptoms if not signs. I'll take a flyer on one by theorizing, or perhaps just wondering aloud, about the growing interest in distance running by people who have no talent for doing it well. Distance running invites pain: David Morris can tell you, and I can confirm it, that the last six miles of a marathon can be gruelling and that even distances much shorter than 26.2 miles can hurt. I don't think runners are into S & M: it isn't that kind of pain, and it's not a show. Yet the simplicity of running, which does away with the complexities of teamwork and the rules of most other sports, makes of the run a gradually lengthening road for pain that is easy to follow, easy to judge, and easy to get off of. It is also, no doubt, easy to get off *on*. In 1968, before the running boom, beginning what would be, I knew, a tortured and demanding book-length series of poems, I opened the series with a poem titled "Homage to the Runner." I should note that I was not a runner at the time. My admiration was directed toward others. From *The Escape into You*, "Homage to the Runner":

The form of this "sport" is pain,
riding up into it, he hurts to win.
These are the moments when death is really
possible, when a man can fit into
his enlarged heart all that is known
or was or shall be pumping fulfills.

The love of form is a black occasion
through which some light must show
in a hundred years of commitment.
By the time the body aches to end it,
the poem begins, at first in darkness,
surrounded by counterfeits of leisure.

Run away. Leave them to ease.
What does it matter you wind up alone?
There is no finish; you can stop for no one.
When your wife cries, you pass a kiss.
When your sons worry, you flash a smile.
When your women wave, you ignore them.

Finally, the question of the limits of language and logic, and
the subsequent question of the modulation in art of the ugly
and painful into the beautiful and pleasing, invite in the poet
second thoughts about good behavior in both language and
life and second thoughts about the audience. Much that hap-
pens to us is accompanied by sounds one finds in no dictionary,
which come up from our bowels or are squeezed out between
taut, twisted ligaments high up in us, and which come out with
a power disdainful of our conventional, prejudicial and self-
deceptive distinctions between the ugly and the beautiful.
Every so often, one has to put the language in its place. I'll
complete my remarks by reading such a poem of mine, a poem
entitled "To No One in Particular":

Whether you sing or scream,
the process is the same.
You start, inside yourself,
a small explosion, the difference
being that in the scream
the throat is squeezed so that
the back of the tongue
can taste the brain's fear.
Also, spittle and phlegm
are components of the instrument.
I guess it would be possible
to take someone by the throat

and give him a good beating.
All the while, though, some fool
would be writing down the notes
of the victim, underscoring
this phrase, lightening this one,
adding a grace note and a trill
and instructions in one of those languages
revered for its vowels.
But all the time, it's consonants
coming from the throat.
Here's the one you were throttling,
still gagging out the guttural ch—
the throat-clearing, Yiddish ch—
and other consonants spurned by
opera singers and English teachers.
He won't bother you again.
He'll scrape home to take it out
on his wife, more bestial consonants
rising in pitch until spent.
Then he'll lock a leg over her
and snore, and all the time
he hasn't said a word we can repeat.
Even though we all speak his language.
Even though the toast in our throats
in the morning has a word for us—
not at all like bread in rain,
but something grittier in something
thicker, going through what we are.
Even though we snort and sniffle,
cough, hiccup, cry and come
and laugh until our stomachs turn.
Who will write down this language?
Who will do the work necessary?
Who will gag on a chickenbone
for observation? Who will breathe perfectly
under water? Whose slow murder
will disprove for all time
an alphabet to make sense?
Listen! I speak to you in one tongue,
but every moment that ever mattered to me
occurred in another language.

Starting with my first word.
To no one in particular.

That completes my remarks. The last word, however, arrived in my mail tray last summer in the form of the following letter:

July 25, 1979

Mr. Marvin Bell
Writers' Workshop
University of Iowa
Iowa City, IA
52242

Sir:

I have been reading "To No One in Particular" in one of your volumes and have been thinking hard on the difference between song and scream. What I want to know is, and maybe you as the author of this poem can tell me, why is it that poetry never expresses fear?

Oh, it expresses anxiety and moral disquiet and metaphysical alarm and sublime terror, but when was a poem ever written out of fear? By fear I mean scared shitless.

Was ever a poet truly frightened as I am now?

Yours,

*Vernon Cudgel*

Vernon Cudgel

# I Was a Boston (Marathon) Bandit
# (On Assignment)

## 1

Like most stories, this one begins in bed—naturally enough, most of us in America having come to consciousness hospitalized. It's a common theory that American men marry their mothers. If it's also a common practice, one doesn't get very far, does one? One need hardly change the sheets.

By the way, this is another article about running. You see, this one begins in bed with a magazine: not *Playboy* or *Oui*, a barbershop's idea of a literary magazine, but *Sports Illustrated*, a snake-oil salesman's notion of athletics. *SI* is as formulaic as any, in between its ads for lung cancer, but occasionally it outdoes itself with a feature piece about an athletic event that happens but once in a while and/or plays to little or no audience.

The good article I'm reading in the winter of 1978 is about a Hawaiian cardiologist, Jack Scaff, who blusters and browbeats his patients into running. For health only, he dangles before them the prospect of finishing a marathon, even *surviving* a marathon. In bed, I am easily deceived.

The marathon, as most people now know, is a run of twenty-six miles, 385 yards. Why that distance? You remember Pheidippides, who in 490 B.C. ran about that far, from the plains of Marathon to Athens to announce the Greeks' victory over the Persians. "Rejoice! We conquer!" he proclaimed, and fell dead. That's how they decided on the distance.

It's important to note here that so-called "mini-marathons" (runs of four to fifteen miles, commonly) are to marathons as a cup of soup is to a meal. The distance is crucial because body chemistry makes the last six to eight miles of a marathon twice as hard as the first eighteen to twenty. Runners speak of hitting the "wall" at eighteen to twenty miles, and generally divide the marathon into halves—of which the first half is the first twenty miles. A half-marathon of 13.1 miles is a lark. A marathon—quick now!—is a vulture.

I am intrigued by the Scaff plan and the Honolulu Marathon Clinic. I have no talent for running. None. Even as a skinny young man, in a school where one went out for all sports just to protect one's reputation, trying to run cross-country I could not manage the 2½ miles without hurting and walking. I was once so far behind the main pack (having spurted vaingloriously past the only two runners as sorry as myself) that I ended up alone. Past this fork and that turn, I saw no one, and began to suspect that I was lost. I asked two small girls sitting on a rooftop. They assured me that I was headed the right way, but not before conferring in giggles. Of course, I knew better and turned back. Wrong again: they had been telling the truth, and it was necessary to run by them once more—studying the ground. By the time I arrived at the school yard, my team members were dressed and waiting by the bus. Then the other school's cheerleaders decided to "encourage" me until, trying to complete the course, I ended up on the wrong side of a fence. A perfect last performance.

Still, I admired distance runners. I was even happy to see in running a metaphor for any long, serious effort, even writing, and when I wrote a book-length series of intense, sometimes tortured poems called *The Escape into You*, I began it with a poem titled, "Homage to the Runner." Its first line reads, "The form of this 'sport' is pain." Get it?

And I had always liked that story about Johnny Kerr, the pro basketball player with bad legs who set a record for consecutive games. Clearly, he played in pain. After he had set the record, he was asked how he could play hurt night after night. His answer: "I tell my legs lies."

So I set out to tell my legs lies. I ran a mile. Then I held onto the wall. I had already uttered a number of lies to my legs, and they weren't having any more.

Somehow, I got to where I could run a mile and stand up, to a mile every-other-day, to a mile-and-a-half, to an hour, to six miles, to twelve, to fifteen, to Oahu, and to the finish line of the Honolulu Marathon on the ninth day of December, 1979. I hadn't made it to Hawaii the first December because I had ended up on a cane during a crucial period in the training. But there I was one year later, barely twenty-one months after that first mile, forty-two and not slender, crossing the finish line with what my wife was to insist was a smile but which the enlargement would clearly show to be a grimace. It had been hot, humid and hilly, and I had done minimal mileage in training, with injuries. My left hamstring had cramped at eighteen miles. My thighs had stopped firing at twenty. When I had finished, a young Hawaiian woman put a shell lei around my neck and asked how it had been. "I've been in hell," I told her. And I had sworn during those last six miles never to do it again.

But there are beds and beds in this life. Beds of pain, beds of procreation, the irresistible beds of printing presses. First, *The North American Review* suggested I run the Boston Marathon and write about it. Then my oldest son, Nathan, moved to Boston. Nathan, now twenty, might be this country's only running vegetarian with a blonde Afro and a repertoire of his own songs. He had gone to Boston to write songs, play guitar and sing, not to take Bill Rodgers for king. Still, it's hard not to be impressed by Rodgers, who comes flying into Boston on his morning runs, doing a five-minute mile easy-as-you-please. Also, it happens that Nathan is a former soccer player, with naturally strong thighs. His idea of running fun is to blow by other runners uphill. The Quadriceps Kid.

The Boston Marathon is infamous for the Newton hills, four miles of hills at about the eighteen-mile mark. Nathan looks forward to going up them. I, on the other hand, would run them backwards if that would preserve the illusion of going downhill. Actually, downhill is harder on the legs. It's just that uphill is harder on the lungs, the esophagus, your ass and your elbow, and the little half-moons on your thumbnails that come from masturbation.

Back from Hawaii, the feeling of pain is replaced by the memory of pain, which is in turn replaced by ideas of memories of pain, and pretty soon I can imagine myself doing better. The key word is "imagine." I concoct a Plan to increase my weekly mileage, to work with leg-strengthening machines, and to do a twenty-mile run each Sunday. This long weekly run is supposed to teach the muscles in the legs to find fuel when the usual sources are depleted. After twenty miles, running is like being in an endless OPEC crisis. Also, my legs are stupid. But I'm going to teach them.

Sixty miles a week. Twenty on Sunday. With my legs, I lift things and push things. But I'm not enjoying it. What with getting to the indoor track in bad weather, changing, stretching, running perhaps ten miles, walking to cool down, stretching and exercising afterwards, using the machines, showering and driving home, my mornings are shot. Afterwards, I want only to load up on carbohydrates, congratulate myself and write in my running log.

But what of the glory, you might be asking. (I don't think you are, but you might be.) Sure, I remember the fireworks in the night sky as 7,000 people began the Honolulu Marathon at 6:30 in the morning. I remember the applauding spectators, the beautiful women along the streets in Waikiki, the theme from "Rocky" playing off to the side at fourteen miles, the cheerleaders at sixteen, the liquid guitar and hula girls at twenty. I also remember the shame of having to walk and run, walk and run, once I hit the wall. Around me, others were as bad off or worse. After twenty miles, all conversation stopped. I passed runners who passed me whom I passed who passed me . . . for six miles, over and over. Some tried stretching to get rid of cramps; no luck. Some had to quit. Some finished only to require a hospital cot and an IV in the arm. Hell, I was better off than many, even better off than some who finished ahead of me, yet I felt lousy. In a nearby tent, one could see the videotape of oneself finishing. I didn't bother to. I knew what it felt like. Why would I want to see what it looked like?

Now, three months after Honolulu, I again began to make that distinction between what it looks like and what it feels like. No one could have done it for me. Until Honolulu, I had often wondered why younger runners in better shape than I settled for runs of six miles, or ran every-other-day, when clearly they could run a marathon. I had figured it out on a hot, humid day in Hawaii, forgot it, and now—faced with losing my life to longevity—was finding it out again.

It seems to me that it seems to others to be something it is not. The notion that one gets "high" while running is nonsense. Just as profitable schools of meditation benefit from the simple fact that sitting still for fifteen minutes a day is good for one, so the running gurus benefit from the simple effects of exercise, which are substantial—and the better ones say so. One doesn't get high. One becomes aware of aches and pain. One doesn't solve problems intuitively or imaginatively, as one might during a night's sleep or during any interruption in a laborious attempt at organized problem-solving. One is too occupied with form, pace, footing, traffic and whether or not one has pushed the wrong button on one's spiffy chronograph.

But by now it has become Nathan's turn. Nathan Uphill. Nathan goes running the Newton hills in the early mornings just to keep himself sane. For one thing, the music business is mostly business. For another, he has to pay the rent by working at a car dealership. He's the flake kept at the cash register; no one would buy a car from him. When an ill-tempered customer takes a swing at a mechanic, Nathan comes to the rescue and, with a strange move known only to songwriting-runners, floors the aggressor. Instant acceptance. Want to get your car fixed?

So he has to find out for himself, and he begins to follow the marathon training program I used—but with a Difference. He runs uphill. He runs two minutes a mile faster than I do. He has longer fingers on his left hand than on his right from bridging the guitar strings. I figure it has to be something.

Now the word that has been missing from this article and

from running books is the word "love." You can come close to it, I'm told, if you run the reservoir path in Central Park in New York City. It's not quite love, but it's something related. Or you can come close to it on the mall near Frank Shorter's running goods shop in Boulder, Colorado, where beautiful youth lounges about in the newest ultra-lightweight synthetic running clothes from Japan, and dresses up only to score cocaine.

It's real love that's got me still wanting to go to Boston, to run some of the marathon route with Nathan, and to see him through to his finish. I can't hope to run it myself. Along with my change in attitude ("Is it worth all this?"), I've had a complete breakdown. The twenty-mile runs were too much. My annual winter sinus infection tore down my entire body. A flu came around. Then there were three days that felt like a stomach pump. Two weeks lost, then three. Only twenty-eight miles one week, only twenty-five another, no running a third. Weight gain. Injuries. There is now no longer any possibility that I can finish the Boston Marathon.

I shouldn't have cared about finishing from the start, I remind myself, for in Boston I can only be a "bandit." Boston accepts, officially, only those marathoners who have run certified marathons in what amount to excellent times (under 2:50 for men under forty, 3:10 for men forty or over, 3:20 for women). They get race numbers. No others need apply.

But Boston doesn't belong only to the people who run it officially, nor to those elite runners who make the news and *Sports Illustrated,* next to the lipsticks and cigarettes. Boston is also for the crowds who line the race routes with drinks and hoses and sponges (Boston has few official aid stations and depends on spectators) and for the unofficial runners who stay behind until the official pack is away. They are the "bandits" who get nothing—no shirt, no certificate, not even an official time.

Nathan, who probably has the ability to train up to a Boston qualifying time, will run it as a bandit, and I will become a bandit too for as long as I am able. When I can no longer run, I will walk and send my thoughts ahead to push him up the

Newton hills. At the end, he's going to hurt a lot more than he now knows.

Because of my inability to run the entire course, I'm going to experience my love for him more than he will his love for me. Once he gets to twenty miles, the run is going to turn into a test and a demand, and a solitary event—so far inside himself that the runner can only make believe that he or she responds to others. Habit and convention make it appear they do, and save them, but they do not. It is this aspect of distance running— profound solitude—that makes it serious and special.

A sense of humor can save us, can teach us; it may even be a symptom of religious feeling or of the spiritual, as has often been argued. But those cut-rate journalists who only *laugh at,* who can make fun of anything, and who make fun of running, miss the mark. There's plenty to make fun of: the language of running (Here are three runners, halted at the corner, "listening to their bodies."), the silly equipment one can buy (sticks to ward off dogs, bragging belt buckles), the hopeless turgidity of training articles in *Runner's World* (do three 440s at 6:30 with 7:30 220s in between followed by 20 percent of the first six until supper), but the running itself, like all physical acts, is its own reason and form, and defies analysis, satiric or straight. Moreover, the effort I put into getting to the finish line in Honolulu was quite as much for me as was Frank Shorter's effort in finishing that race in second place. Quite possibly, for me, more.

And yet . . . while it may be true that the road of excess leads to the palace of wisdom, it seems to me that sometimes one learns from excess only that one has been excessive. Clearly, I am of two minds. And so it also occurs to me that the mixed mind is a result of experience. Those-who-do-not-know know they should not. Those who do . . . ?

Running marathons may or may not be excessive. I may run another. But training continually, one to the next, is certainly excessive, at least for me. Since cutting back my mileage and the number of days I run, I have rediscovered what it means to stay a bit longer in one's pajamas, and to have the time in which to write a new poem. Or a piece like this.

Now you know the background. In four days, it will be April Fool's.

**2**

It is April twenty-first, Patriot's Day. The Boston Marathon always takes place on Patriot's Day, a Monday. Between April Fool's and Marathon Day, I have been twice to Boston. On the first trip, I learn that Nathan has given notice at Peter Fuller Oldsmobile in Watertown and is job hunting. On the second, I learn that he has taken a job at the factory outlet store of New Balance running shoes, where he works with world-class marathoners Vin Fleming and Kevin Ryan, where three-time Boston winner Bill Rodgers may stop in to use the phone, accompanied by Finnish Olympic medalist Lasse Viren, and where employees get two hours off during the day to go running. I sense a deepening commitment on his part.

On the first trip, I get to hear him do a set at a weekend coffee house in Cambridge. In six months in Boston, he has turned from an exceptionally talented young musician into a powerful, driving performer, whose own songs and manner of playing and singing make those who precede and follow him appear to be exactly what they are: just college students. Next to his music, the young musicians with classical training seem merely proper and the school of jazz graduates merely smooth. I'm secretly proud that he has inherited my small-towner's skepticism about everything cultured and collegiate. My best advice to him is not to eliminate the rough edges in his art.

On the second trip, his music and running come together when he does some playing at the Etonic premarathon carbo-hydrate-loading dinner party, held at The Exchange in down-town Boston. Marathoners load up on carbohydrates for three days before the race, hoping to gain something for the last six miles. The chemistry of it is complicated and debated, but most testimony is in favor of a pizza and beer the night before any long run. Good marathoners are light: the room is full of skinnies. The spaghetti disappears quickly. I sit in a dark corner.

From the dark corner I emerge into the warm light of Hopkinton, where the marathon will begin. There is band music, somewhere Heywood Hale Broun is interviewing "unofficial" runners, asking variations of the usual question: "Why would anyone run twenty-six miles, 385 yards, with no hope of winning, perhaps with only a hope of finishing, and with the certainty of lasting pain ahead?" Nathan, his brother Jason (who has turned fourteen the day before and who has come with me to Boston to surprise his big brother), Mary Colbert (with whom Nathan lives and who, like Jason, has the form to run us both into the ground eventually) and I find a lawn in front of a small church near where we suppose the unofficial runners will mass for the start. Nathan is antsy to begin. Everywhere runners are taking on water for what has turned out to be a hot day for a race (seventy degrees; eighty, it is said, on the pavement), putting on vaseline and tape, stretching, meditating and already forming within themselves concise explanations as to why they had to drop out along the way. Even defending champion Bill Rodgers is reported to have lost sleep, to feel lousy, and to give himself no chance of winning.

By such reasoning, I might be the best instead of the worst. The usual reckoning is that, simply to finish a marathon, one needs sixty to seventy miles a week for eight weeks prior to race week, with a month of building up the mileage before that, and a solid base period of running before the build-up. Good marathoners do more than 100 miles a week. With my breakdown and return to common sense, I bring to race day the shoddy total of twenty-six miles a week. If one eliminates the week preceding my collapse, during which I ran sixty-two miles, my weekly average is only twenty-one miles. In the week before race week, I ran but three days, six miles being the longest run.

I know better than to try to go all the way. I figure I can go six miles, maybe ten. But the logistics are complicated, roads will be closed, Mary and Jason will be way down the route with water for Nathan. Hence, our plan has been for me to join

Nathan after he crests the infamous Newton hills, those four miles culminating in what is called "Heartbreak Hill." That will leave four to five miles to the finish line at the Prudential Building.

But now it doesn't seem right to me to follow that plan. I don't want to cross the finish line if I haven't run the entire course, even if it's just to help someone else continue. I don't mind being a Boston Bandit, keeping out of the way of the better runners, starting behind that banner which reads, "The Back of the Pack." But I don't want to cross that finish line meaninglessly. Nathan feels the same, and has thought ahead: if the official finishing chutes are still operating when he comes to the end, he intends to turn off before them. It is important to both of us neither to get in the way, nor to earn false credits.

Little do we know that this will be the race of Rosie Ruiz. As I write this, Rosie has not yet been disqualified nor her fraudulent victory among the women in the Boston Marathon taken away, but I have no hesitation in saying that she could not possibly have done what she claimed. If she had, she would be the greatest athlete the world has ever known. She is a fraud, and every runner knew it immediately.*

Unlike Rosie, I can't see myself joining in near the end. The question remains: what do I do when I have to drop out in the countryside? I put a bandage around two dimes and a twenty-dollar bill and wedge the package into a tiny pocket inside my running shorts. I put on a blue sweatband and sunglasses. And I tell Nathan that I will run the first hour with him and that we will regroup at David Godine Publishers, five blocks from the finish. If not, well, he will hear from me eventually.

The gun goes off at noon. No one near us moves. Then we walk. After four minutes and seventeen seconds, we walk across the starting line. Ahead, the heads of five thousand runners undulate like waves and I recall Gary Margolis' story of seasickness the year he ran Boston from The Back of the

---

*Rosie Ruiz has since been disqualified, and is alleged to have run only the last half-mile of the race.

Pack. It takes seven to eight minutes before we are able to begin running.

The countryside is New England-lovely, the audience along the way is raucous, encouraging and generous. I take water to drink but turn down the hoses, not wanting wet shoes. I take orange slices, swallow the juice and spit out the pulp. I take ice cubes and wipe them along my arms to cool the blood. We go toward Framingham and Natick. In towns, the crowds are thick and take up rooftops, trucks and fields. They crowd in on the race route and the kids line up to slap the hands of passing runners.

As planned, I slow down Nathan for an hour. Most marathons are botched by going out too fast. Then Nathan increases his pace and moves ahead. I wonder how hard it will be for him at the end, and where we will meet. Despite the enthusiasm of the crowds, I have the definite sense that no one along the roadway is planning to carry any fallen runners into Boston that afternoon.

In any case, I want to go farther, at least to make a long run out of it. I owe the *NAR* that much, and I really don't know quite where to drop out. Moreover, I have begun to think of Wellesley College—about twelve miles into the race. The Wellesley girls are well known for forming a seemingly endless corridor (half a mile?; someone claimed it was three quarters of a mile—doubtful), forcing the runners into single-file, while they cheer and sing. "Lord," goes my pagan prayer, "get me to Wellesley."

And He or She does. And I do. And they are.

Someone says it's the half-way point: 13.1 miles. By now, my curiosity is up. I want to see how far I can go. I run without so much as a stop to take water for seventeen miles before I recognize an advancing state of weakening thighs. I know from Honolulu that, once the thighs stop firing, I will be unable to run, hardly able to walk. Mental toughness will be of no use. The legs will be unable to push off, and coming down on a leg will be like coming down on sore, unprotected bone. Downhill running will be a terror.

I walk for five minutes—an experiment. I run two more miles. From now on, I must run and walk, run and walk. My personal goal becomes running the uphills, particularly Heartbreak. I do, passing many others, including one man whose arms and upper body are running but whose gone legs are walking. Indeed, it begins to look as if I can run almost all the way. I don't mind the pain and I begin to increase my pace as I start the last four or five miles of the race—all downhill.

Which is, of course, the last straw of vanity and He or She who got me to Wellesley gives me a cramp in my left calf like you wouldn't believe. A convulsion, a knot heard round the world. I grab a parked truck to keep from collapsing. When I can run again, I can't run much: the calf will not stretch out. I walk a ways, then begin to run. This time, I spot a small block of wood in my path, make a slight move to avoid it, and the right calf produces its own convulsion. I grab a lamppost. Someone offers a massage but I'm reluctant to sit down and not be able to get up.

From then on, I walk. The surprise of my finishing at all is enough to keep me going, and now there seems no point to running through Boston's bus and taxi traffic those last couple of miles. Nearing the end, I run again—feeling surprisingly good, no doubt because of the walking. I run under the digital clock, still keeping time, to the remarkable applause of those who are still keeping watch, at five and a half hours. It has taken me an hour and a quarter to cover those last four miles. There are runners behind me. There are runners stretched out on the pavement for medical help. There are runners in ambulances. I am not much of a runner by this time, and I feel no glory in having finished. But I do feel mildly and oddly satisfied, and I can hardly wait to surprise Nathan, Mary, and Jason when I walk into Godine. I am, today, exactly what an encouraging bystander called me as I walked those last two hurtful miles: a survivor. I take no credit, but a small, clear, intimate pleasure which cannot be put into words.

Nathan has finished in 4:13, feeling the difficulty of his first marathon only at twenty-four miles—ah, youth. Bill Rodgers has won his fourth Boston, and says that the last six miles in the day's heat were gruelling. Don't I know it. Rosie Ruiz claims to have won the female division in a time accomplished by only two other women ever, crossing the finish line without sweat, without salt, without deep fatigue, without sufficient knowledge or training, without having run the 26.2 miles, without the pain of the last six, without the mild shame of having to walk, without having experienced a sporting event no one actually sees, in a confusion of experience and outcome, in a mix-up of medals and moxie, in an utter loss of sense and senses.

If she wants to know what it was like, she can ask me.

# Entry for *The Poets' Encyclopedia*
## *Five-and-Ten*

*Five-and-Ten:* A kind of American store, found now only in small towns considered "backward." Real Five-and-Tens have wooden floors and fixtures, carry a little of everything common but nothing rare or expensive, do not sell medicine or groceries, do not advertise or cut prices, and were largely run out of business by the loss-leaders of large American corporations with the blessing of the American government, which has a parasitic relationship to large business. The Five-and-Ten made its money selling thread, socks and drinking glasses. The register was always at the front and the word *stealing* had not yet been changed to the word *shrinkage*. The store's profits rested on inventory and goodwill. If a store's shelves revealed empty spaces where small items had not been replaced when sold, you could be certain that the store would fail. The name of a failed Five-and-Ten was soon torn down to give a better businessman a chance, but the name of a good store was money-in-the-bank and a new owner would have to pay extra for the "goodwill." A man's father, after several heart attacks, sold his Five-and-Ten and retired, but he couldn't stand it because in those days the Five-and-Ten meant service and the friendship of one's customers as well as personal success. It couldn't have happened in Russia, so the immigrant Five-and-Ten owners often came out of retirement to die in their stores. One owner knew no songs but sang all the time. A dog who was run over by an automobile got well in the back room. The Five-and-Ten, for those who knew it, is like a coloring book on a rainy day, when toy sales boomed. Because the Five-and-Ten sold little things—thimbles, rulers, birthday candles—the distinctions between things still seem important (one might say, primary) to one who grew up handling them. It is possible, therefore, for such a one to believe that language begins in the (mathematical) concept of unity and separation, and that poetry is a way of using meaning (for which the ordinary dictionary is the final arbiter) to apprehend Meaning (for which experience is the source and this kind of Dictionary/Encyclopedia the testimony) and make it known. Notions, "fancy goods," and trinkets. Less is more. Everyone knows what a thimble is. The General Store was friendly. The Five-and-Ten was *personal*.

# II

# The University Is Something Else You Do

INTERVIEWS

# I Try to Feel What It Means

*(The following interview was conducted by Joyce Renwick on March 24, 1981, in Washington, D.C., and is one of a series of conversations between Ms. Renwick and writers who have served on the faculty of the Bread Loaf Writers' Conference.)*

*Tell me about your home town, Center Moriches, New York. I remembered it as "Greater Moriches" and thought, ah, "Greater and Moriches," a wonderfully "American" place to be from.*

(Laughter.) Well, Moriches is an Indian name, but I'm afraid I can't tell you what it means, or even what Indian language it comes from. Center Moriches is so called because it really is the Moriches in the center. There is an East Moriches which is even smaller, and a West Moriches which is smaller yet. West Moriches is nothing more than a stop on the highway halfway out on the south shore of eastern Long Island. And I'm not sure that anyone has ever stopped. There must have been about 2,500 people in Center Moriches when I was growing up. It was a great place to grow up, though I'm not sure it would be the same kind of place now. It is certainly not a place one can easily go back to if one has had the fortune or misfortune of finding out about literature and art and other things that aren't issues there.

*How did you get interested in literature and art?*

I started playing trumpet at an early age, and I would borrow from the town library. In college, I watched the artists. I didn't start writing seriously until after college. Eventually, I ended up in Chicago as a member of John Logan's Poetry Seminar just as the fifties turned into the sixties. That wasn't a college seminar, mind you.

*So it's a rather different life that you have now that you live in Iowa and teach at the Writers' Workshop?*

That's true, in part. I'm certainly a long way from the Atlantic now, and I've begun to hear its call more and more.

Thank heaven for the Iowa River which is a rather nice river that winds right through campus and right through town. There are other rivers in the area. My favorite is the Wapsipinicon, which people call the "Wapsi." On the other hand, it has occurred to me that the landscape of Iowa is—at least the part of Iowa where I live—not much different from the landscape of Long Island, except that there is much more water around Long Island! Indeed, I've been told that the landscape of Iowa—and, hence, the landscape of Long Island—is not so very much unlike the landscape of the Ukraine, which is where my father came from. So maybe he ended up on Long Island because he felt emotionally right there.

*I remember one of your early poems in* A Probable Volume of Dreams, *the elegaic poem, "Treetops," in which your father is duck hunting in your imagination, lying on the water.*

Yes, the poem contains a trick: he is actually in a coffin. It is made clear in a long third sentence in which the reader gradually becomes aware that this is all in the imagination and, in fact, the father is dead. He is floating through the South hunting duck, it would appear, from a coffin.

*Does this mean the South is a kind of underworld?*

In this poem it is.

My father moves through the South hunting duck.
It is warm, he has appeared
like a ship, surfacing, where he floats, face up,
through the ducklands. Over the tops
of trees duck will come, and he strains
not to miss seeing the first of each flock,
although it will be impossible to shoot one
from such an angle, face up like that
in a floating coffin where the lid obstructs
half a whole view, if he has a gun.
Afterlives are full of such hardships.

One meets, for example, in one's sinlessness,
high water and our faithlessness,
so the dead wonder if they are imagined
but they are not quite.

How could they know we know
when the earth shifts deceptively
to set forth ancestors to such pursuits?
My father will be asking, Is this fitting?
And I think so—I, who, with the others,
coming on the afterlife after the fact
in a dream, in a probable volume, in a
probable volume of dreams, think so.

*Was this poem written around the time your father died?*

Oh, all my poetry was written *after* my father died. I had begun writing poetry but I hadn't written much, and I hadn't written seriously up to the time of his death.

*Did your father disapprove of your writing? Or did the emotional impact of his death send you to writing seriously?*

I wasn't writing poetry to any extent while my father was alive. No, he wouldn't have disapproved. He took great pleasure in my intelligence, and had great faith in me. He would occasionally fault me for not working "up to my potential." He thought

I should become a psychiatrist because it required so much schooling. Poet's close enough, don't you think? Did his death send me to writing seriously? I don't know. There's always something. He was probably, for years, the person to whom I was speaking—in the sense that he would be the one to over-hear the poems. I tried to finish the conversation by writing a book's worth of poems to him. Thirteen of them survive, under the title "You Would Know" in the book *Residue of Song*.

*The death of a father, of course, has resulted in poetry for many writers. Mark Strand and Dylan Thomas are only two examples. You have written father and son poems. Is that now a thing of the past? Do you think handling, accepting, integrating the father-son relationship is one of the necessary steps toward emotional maturity?*

Accepting, handling, integrating *any* relationship is a necessary step toward emotional maturity. Or a symptom of it.

*How did you meet William Stafford? I understand that you are friends and are writing a book together.*

Yes, we've known each other for many years. I no longer remember where and when we first met. But the idea for this book came up in 1979 when we were both teaching at the First Annual Midnight Sun Writers' Conference in Fairbanks, Alaska. I had thought about such a thing for years but had never broached the subject to him. As soon as I began to mention it he said, "I'm ready!" Then I went back and thought and thought about it, sitting there trying to write a poem set in Alaska to begin the series. And before I could fiddle with it as was my wont, a poem came from Bill with a note saying, "Well, I didn't know who was supposed to start, so here goes." And we've been doing it ever since. He's wonderful, of course. I have the feeling that he can send a poem back by return mail, and he often does. I can sometimes do that, but most of the time it takes me a while.

*In one essay in Stafford's* Writing the Australian Crawl *he talks about "welcoming the words," welcoming language, and with that stance he will accept anything he writes. He keeps his standards low in the beginning so that he doesn't block himself.*

Yes, that particular approach not only works for him, at times it works wonderfully for everyone. I wish I could be that accepting of my own work, but I really can't be. I throw a lot away. I fiddle with poems a long time before they are done, and sometimes in the end the fiddling amounts to the slightest changes. I may be fooling myself, maybe the poem would have been just as good, or just as bad in its original form, but to my mind the little changes I make, and they often are little, are crucial.

*Do you think there is a certain amount of time that each poem requires?*

That's even more important. My writing methods are in some ways similar to Stafford's. I abandon myself to my emotions, my psyche, my unconscious. I try to say what I don't know I know in the poems. You know, push my way through dense foliage and see where the path is, but not make a path too early for myself because I am writing what I don't know yet. To me, that is the interesting part of writing—even after I have written it, I don't fully know it. And so, the process of revision is more of a process of acceptance. Sometimes it takes me a long time to become the person who surfaced briefly in the poem, time for me to understand the poem and to accept it and to understand what it wants to be. Then I can make whatever changes are necessary. And, as I say, sometimes they turn out to be very minor, but crucial, changes.

*Then do you think that each poet has his own internal time condition that must be met before the poem feels completed?*

Absolutely. Condition *now.*

*Is a poem not only the poem but the reader's thoughts about the poem? Or is it the poet's thoughts about the poem after its completion— thoughts that have been crystallized by the poet so that the poem can be honest?*

Well, all of that. I am partly a poet of ideas—it is not fashionable to admit that. And even admitting that requires some explanation. The ideas that interest me in poetry are not what are called "ideas" elsewhere. Poetry can articulate a certain kind of idea that is not discoverable outside of poetry. This may be wishful thinking, but I do believe it. And that is what I am interested in. But, one doesn't approach such ideas by stating (in poetry) ideas one already has. That is another kind of poetry and one which, for the most part, does not interest me.

*Are you saying that in poetry you are only interested in describing the empty space within the bowl? In Taoist thought this figure or image is used when the idea that you want to express, your unformed concept, is one that can only be captured or encircled by describing the periphery.*

Yes, that seems a good metaphor for a certain kind of poetic accomplishment. Certainly I'm interested in that. But also I think there are ideas that can be expressed in poetry that are extractable and paraphrasable but would not exist quite the way they do, in quite the form they do, without the poem. As I say that, it occurs to me that it would be difficult to prove, but I think I could.

*Have you proved it in your poem, "Gemwood?" You do state ideas here, for instance in the next to last stanza. Here it is. Would you read it?*

Sure.

### Gemwood

*to Nathan and Jason, our sons*

In the *shoppes*
they're showing "gemwood":

the buffed-up flakes of dye-fed pines—
bright concentrics or bull's eyes,
wide-eyed on the rack of
this newest "joint effort
of man and nature." But then

those life-lines circling
each target chip of "gemwood"
look less like eyes, yours or mine,
when we have watched a while.
They are more like the whorls
at the tips of our fingers,
which no one can copy. Even on

the photocopy Jason made of
his upraised hands, palms down
to the machine, they do not appear.
His hands at five-years-old—
why did we want to copy them, and
why does the grey yet clear print
make me sad? That summer,

the Mad River followed us
through Vermont—a lusher state than
our own. A thunderous matinee
of late snows, and then the peak
at Camel's Hump was bleached.
As a yellow pear is to the sky—
that was our feeling. We had with us

a rat from the lab—no, a pet
we'd named, a pure friend who changed
our minds. When it rained near
the whole of the summer, in that
cabin Nathan made her a social creature.
She was all our diversion, and brave.
That's why, when she died

in the heat of our car
one accidental day we didn't intend,
it hurt her master first and most,
being his first loss like that,
and the rest of our family felt badly

even to tears, for a heart that small.
We buried her by the road

in the Adirondack Mountains,
and kept our way to Iowa.
Now it seems to me the heart
must enlarge to hold the losses
we have ahead of us. I hold to
a certain sadness the way others
search for joy, though I like joy.

Home, sunlight cleared the air
and all the green's of consequence. Still
when it ends, we won't remember
that it ended. If parents must receive
the sobbing, that is nothing
when put next to the last crucial fact
of who is doing the crying.

Well, certainly that is an idea there in the penultimate stanza, and it seems to me that those lines could have been made up outside of the poem. But they wouldn't have been made up by *me* outside the poem. All of the poem that preceded it gives those lines more meaning than they would have otherwise, I hope.

*That is what I was thinking. You couldn't have made that statement unless you had the poem to justify it, because we don't care about this unless we have the story that you tell in the poem.*

Yes, that is part of what art does, I think. It gives you the context, and where an idea is concerned, the proof. But you see, in the poem "Gemwood," there are other ideas too. There is an idea stated and a bigger idea implied by the lines, "Still / when it ends, we won't remember / that it ended." Which refers to life, of course. And there is a little social idea after that: "If parents must receive / the sobbing, that is nothing / when put next to the last crucial fact / of who is doing the crying." These are perhaps two obvious examples of ideas in poetry.

*I was considering the penultimate stanza of "Gemwood" to be emblematic of the personal stance you take in your poetry. It seems an example of the mood, the tone of much of your work—a little sadness, allied with acceptance.*

There is a lot of that. I would like to practice, and articulate, and explore in my poems an acceptance which does not have any element of fatigue about it. And that, to me, is very difficult. I mean acceptance, not resignation.

*It seems that your most memorable poems are those in which you have a clear visual object upon which the poem focuses. I remember Emily Dickinson's white dress with the twelve buttons, the hairbrushing in another poem. These visual images make the poem memorable, and then you tie the idea of the poem to the visual object. I was wondering if these specific things were what inspired the poems or if they appeared later as appropriate to the idea? The Emily Dickinson poem, for instance.*

Well, let me give you several answers at once. For every poem there is a crucial image, and that's the image of the experience. I just wrote an essay called "Noun/Image/Object"* for *Field* magazine. I said there something that I believe, and that is that the image of the poem is more important than the image of the line. In other words, imagery that shows up here and again in poetry is interesting and effective, but also the poem makes an image as a whole. The whole poem makes an image, and that for me is the more important image.

Now you asked about the Emily Dickinson poem. I visited her house in Amherst once and was handed—in her bedroom—one of the white dresses she had worn. And since I had always been in love with Emily Dickinson, this moved me, and later on I wanted to write something about it. I wrote one stanza containing a few little but important observations—all of which take place in the house. And that stanza sat there, as

*See pp. 32–36.

many poems I begin do. And then one day I got up very early—the rest of my family was gone, visiting relatives—and it had rained a little and the sidewalks were wet. It was time to take the garbage out, and since I couldn't sleep I got up and went out. It was, oh, maybe six in the morning and as I put out the garbage I realized that padding by me very quickly was a young girl in a white dress, holding her shoes. There was great mystery and romance about it, and undoubtedly—as Jimmy Carter might say—"lust in my heart." I didn't say anything to her, just put down the garbage and went back into the house. Well, later in the day I wound up in my little study out back trying to write. I realized that there really wasn't anything more to say about my visit to Emily Dickinson's house. I mean, sure, I could have made up ideas, but again, those kinds of ideas—the ones that are just made out of nothing—are to me not ideas at all, but assertions. An idea needs to reveal its reasoning to be an idea worth considering, to be effective, to be moving. So then I thought, "What did my visit to Emily Dickinson's house have to do with anything? What did my romantic image of Emily Dickinson have to do with anything?" What it would have to do with would be things that happen in my life. So then came the line that begins the second stanza and the rest of the poem: "Except for you, it were a trifle: / This morning, not much after dawn. . . ." I begin to describe a very small and very quick experience. There it is. There's mention of Emily's dress in there, but really Emily doesn't show up again in the poem.

*Perhaps because we know about Emily Dickinson, we don't have to say anything more about her. Maybe we should include the poem here— perhaps the poem itself is what it means.*

### The Mystery of Emily Dickinson

Sometimes the weather goes on for days
but you were different. You were divine.
While the others wrote more and longer,
you wrote much more and much shorter.
I held your white dress once: 12 buttons.

In the cupola, the wasps struck glass
as hard to escape as you hit your sound
again and again asking Welcome. No one.

Except for you, it were a trifle:
This morning, not much after dawn,
in level country, not New England's,
through leftovers of summer rain I
went out rag-tag to the curb, only
a sleepy householder at his routine
bending to trash, when a young girl
in a white dress your size passed,

so softly!, carrying her shoes. It must be
she surprised me—her barefoot quick-step
and the earliness of the hour, your dress—
or surely I'd have spoken of it sooner.
I should have called to her, but a neighbor
wore that look you see against happiness.
I won't say anything would have happened
unless there was time, and eternity's plenty.

Well, that girl who passed on the wet sidewalk carrying her
shoes becomes Emily Dickinson. So that's what it meant. It's
not that I sat in my study and actually said to myself, "What
does it mean?" It's more like having sat in the study trying to
feel something. And what I felt had to do with what it means.
And that's what poetry is about. At least for me, that is what *my*
poetry is about. That's the way I write. I try to feel what it
means. And what it means has to do with ideas as well as
feelings.

*But it begins with feelings.*

Oh absolutely. Otherwise it would be boring. I mean, I can
work problems of logic as well as the next person.

*Who said, "No ideas but in things?"*

That's a famous remark by William Carlos Williams. "Say it!
No ideas but in things," he said in a poem excerpted from a

long work called *Paterson.* And this has been taken as a kind of credo by many people who misunderstand it, or didn't read all of *Paterson,* or didn't read all of Williams. Because Williams also says elsewhere in a poem something like this, and I might get it slightly wrong: "An empty head, knocked on, still sounds hollow."

Well, "No ideas but in things" is in general a good rule for beginning writers. It's equivalent to the direction to "show, don't tell." In fact, showing by itself without telling gets old fast. And so do accumulations of imagery. Really, this is an image-laden world. It's not just television, it's the posters that are everywhere. Does anyone read a bulletin board anymore? I can remember when people stood in front of bulletin boards and read everything on them. Who would do that now? We are overwhelmed by images, albeit many of them interestingly presented in literature, and in every other art too. Well, by itself, imagery doesn't mean anything. It just excerpts the experience of the world, and a very small portion of it. It's true that we learn in large measure through our eyes, if we can see, but it is a kind of learning that is nothing more than an accumulation of facts, unless other aspects of ourselves enter into it.

I don't want to disagree with Williams, I want to disagree with those people who took that line too literally, because Williams is a poet of ideas. William Carlos Williams is still the most misunderstood and misappropriated poet of our time. Lots of people pay homage to him, but in fact, what they take from him is a little bit of image, and a little bit of cadence and they don't understand that he was brilliant, that his mind was at work in every poem, all the time.

*Wasn't Williams also the poet who listened to people so carefully?*

Oh, he had a wonderful ear for speech, and sometimes wrote poems that were nothing more than exercises in which he represented speech he had heard.

*And his short stories. . . .*

There too. He would pull up the typewriter and type furiously between patients. He wrote quickly, spontaneously. Oh, I can remember a time when people would have thought spontaneity in writing was a sign of carelessness. But it really isn't. It's a different method. And it's a method which I think can produce wonderful results, but only in the hands of a real intelligence. Spontaneity allied with intelligence is a totally different thing than spontaneity allied with stupidity. Sometimes, though, spontaneity can be a way of being deliberately stupid.

*I'm going to take a chance here and be, I think, spontaneously stupid. Would you read a poem? Remember "The Bride in White?"*

Sure.

### The Bride in White

#### I
It is customary to conceive
of the bride in white,
dressed to merit pleasure
and holier than thou.

#### II
"Heh, heh," say the halves of us,
thinking of Samson
and his hairy feats;
and how hairy it must have been
when prophets sang
in their underground religion:

"Speak of Perishing, and You will;
Speak of Hell, and You shall have It."

#### III
Trials have ended in error before,
the dead have been cleared
too late of their lives;
if boys dress for their weddings
like black magic,
why should there be any mourning?

We who have chuckled aloud
during the making of children,
ought to reform.

IV

A crow for a mascot!
We will tell the story of Adam
without embellishment,
just as if we were part of the tale.

*I wanted you to read that just for the "Heh, heh" of the second stanza.*

I don't say that very well anymore. There was a time when I
could say that line. " 'Heh, heh,' say the halves of us. . . ." It was
always tough to say. That's a minor example of how sometimes
poetry exists on the page and not aloud. "Heh, heh." Steve
Martin could probably do it.

*George Starbuck once said you go from "wisecrack to outcry."*

Yes, I used to—once much more than now. Starbuck was writ-
ing about poems that appeared in *A Probable Volume of Dreams*
in 1969. This is for others to judge, but my judgment would be
that each of my books is very different. I think George's de-
scription applied quite well to the poems that he was writing
about.

*Your early work.*

Yes.

*Do you think there has been a definite change in your writing, a midlife
change, if you admit to that?*

Well, a constant changing. I don't know where my midlife will
turn out to have been. For some people, twenty-five is halfway.
For others, forty-five is halfway.

When I have written enough poems so there is a book there
I begin to get interested in other things. I begin to explore

other ways of feeling, even other feelings, other areas of subject matter, other poets. It's not a formalist bent at all, although some people might take it to be that. Secretly, I have always thought of myself as a poet of content. And secretly, I have always thought of myself as a poet with an experimental side. This was much more noticeable when I first began writing, perhaps, than it is now, because the indications were once very clear in the style, which, I might say, was a very difficult style for the reader. I have always thought of that experimental side of myself as having to do with content, not with form, although as everyone knows by now, content and form are inextricable. It's a measure of content and it's difficult for me to explain.

*Certainly you took a chance writing about a rat dying in "Gemwood."*

Well, that's part of it. But it's just a little subversive element. I mention there that we had this rat from the lab with us, and I know what the reader is going to think, so with hardly a pause I say, "No, a pet we'd named, a pure friend who changed our minds." That "no" is there because I can imagine the reader saying, "What kind of pet is *that*? Why should we take that seriously? Would its death matter to anyone?" Well, yes, it did. So this is just a slightly subversive or corrective element. There are ideas sneaking along in my poems, and when I say sneaking along I mean that they are only there for readers who read slowly or repeatedly.

*James Dickey says he sees poetry as "the center of his creative wheel." How do you see it in relation to your life?*

Ah well, wheels run easiest downhill, so that metaphor scares me a little, but I understand it in what might be thought an oriental sense. Then it makes sense. Poetry is a way of life for me certainly. What metaphor is best, I don't know. But, everybody needs a "way of life." It doesn't have to be art, and it certainly doesn't have to be writing. It can be growing hybrid roses, a martial art, a sport. It can be tournament bridge, I suppose, though my experience in tournament bridge in the past indicates otherwise. One of the secrets in life, and in art also, is that if you do anything seriously enough, long enough, you get better at it. And the implication of that is, that if you get better at something it becomes a way of life. It becomes a way of organizing and understanding your experience. It becomes, to use somebody else's phrase, "a momentary stay against confusion."

Writing even becomes addictive. I mean, I get a little irritable, a little more difficult to live with when I haven't been writing for a long time. As soon as I find myself in that study again, and as soon as I write something that I like, or even finish something that has been lying around awhile which I like, I'm much more of a pleasure to be with.

*Do you think that the poetry balances you in the same way that dreams balance a person who doesn't write?*

Absolutely. And the accomplishment is completely personal, in a way almost private. I'm always asked, as all writers are, of course, how much I take the audience into consideration when I'm writing. I always give what must seem to be a very cold and formal reply. I say, "Each of us has to write up to his or her own level—linguistic, intellectual, emotional, psychological—and if readers respond, well, that is a bonus that we cherish." That sounds cold when I say it. The other side of it is this terrific need and pleasure and satisfaction, catharsis, understanding, and whatever else it might be—perhaps even an emotional balancing—that comes from the act of writing.

*And this relates to something Stafford says, that the reader will appreciate your work if he is at the same level.*

Why sure, poetry, like water, seeks its own level. There is no good or bad about it. There does come for each of us a level that is too low to be of interest. And there are also apparent levels of great height which in fact are not even there. What they amount to in poetry is difficulty masquerading as profundity and complicatedness masquerading as complexity.

*Are you referring to complicated form or complicated ideas?*

Complications of idea or language. We are all a little nervous about our limitations, so we tend to grant an automatic respect to what we don't understand. That's probably a good attitude in general, because it may turn out to be something we can understand, and should understand, and is valuable regardless. But, that's not always true.

*Do you think that language is ever really adequate?*

Of course language is not adequate to anything but language. Anyone who works with language knows that it has great limitations. Anyone who works with words knows that there are sounds that are important to us that are not words at all in the usual sense.

You see, truth is important to me in poetry. To say this may be distorting. People may make a mistake if they hear me say this and think, "Oh, he's talking about poetry that is really essays." I'm not talking about that at all. I do think that there has to be some element of truth to poetry.

*You are talking about something other than verisimilitude.*

Well, verisimilitude is part of an appearance of truth. I think I am trying to say that in the hands of a virtuoso the instrument of language can be used not merely to play beautiful music, but also to create false ideas, ideas which are false in logical terms or in terms of how they apply to the world as we know it.

*Studying other languages seems to enlarge our minds and increase our understanding of all language. Doesn't the study of music also help create more honestly expressive poetry?*

Oh yes, even playing a musical instrument is a great advantage to a poet, it seems to me.

*The rests in music are equivalent to the caesuras in poetry, perhaps. But how else does music relate to poetry in your mind?*

Well, music is sound, and it benefits from changes in pitch, pace, tone and rhythm, as does poetry. Also, it takes its significance as sound from silence, and so does poetry.

*Do you feel that there is a certain musical impulse in a poem?*

Oh always. I guess it was Paul Valéry who said that prose is like walking, poetry is like dancing. Louis Zukofsky said that the lower limit of poetry is speech, and the upper limit music. Both these remarks make sense, at least some of the time.

On the other hand, one has to be careful about prescribing, or even seeming to prescribe. The past is really not any indicator of the future, except in the most superficial terms. I'm afraid that I agree more and more with Henry Ford who said that "history is bunk." I think that probably he was right and historians are wrong. The whole history of art and of poetry is a history of people finding ways to put into their art forms style and content which were formerly thought wrong for art, things that were thought vulgar, obscene, inelegant, subversive, dangerous, difficult, obscure, odd, crazy. You see? That's the whole history of poetry. That's not all that's been written, but that's the whole sense of it. Art finds ways to articulate, explore and include areas of human experience that wouldn't otherwise be articulated, explored or included. Otherwise, what's the point?

*Your poem, "Unable to Wake in the Heat," seems to be both an example of a human experience that wouldn't otherwise be articulated and a musical allusion.*

That's true. We like to think that we live our lives in a state of heightened awareness, if not excitement. But much of our time is spent in a condition resembling torpor. Now torpor is not unrevealing. Certainly, there's something beyond.

I can hold up my head, if barely.
Parts of the body reassemble
as in a middle movement of Brahms.
At the porch screens, large ferns
try to brush away the summer spiders.
They go on combing the muggy air
because they are strong and wide,
but the tiger-lilies droop their heads
and the willow, always a leaner,
shakes her long hair in a slow dance.

There is a wonderful hallucination
in this—the consciousness of not waking,
the dimness, the weight of the body.
The head weighs the most, unbearably heavy,
and the eyes are like steel under blankets.
The head falls, finally, to the chest,
the back of the neck numb with straining,
but we know we could go even further.
We hear music far back in our not-knowing.
Our faces relax: nothing odd there.

*Doesn't art also soften the corners of our lives?*

Well, it can, I suppose. Many artists are torn between the desire
to poke people a bit (bring them to attention) and the desire to
give them a way to feel better. These desires can come to-
gether, sometimes, but it's hard to be naive about it. One knows
when one is saying something that's going to be difficult for the
reader to accept. One knows when one is including material
that one's relatives will not like. One knows when one is writing
a poem that will be taken off the library shelves.

The question of poetry's social function, whether it should
have this or that function, whether it does have this or that
function, is a complicated issue, but as an issue it takes a back
seat to the issues that the poet confronts when he or she writes.
I mean the real poet, again, writes up to his or her level and
tries to create something that has never been created before.

*As Emily Dickinson did.*

Sure. Emily Dickinson was a genius, of course.

*I wonder about her isolation and invalidism. Another writer told me that when she herself was writing something that wasn't working, her body tipped her off before her intellect. She'd have a physically sick feeling.*

Well, writing can be frustrating certainly, and I suppose frustration can lead to a bad stomach. For most, writing is a great risk-taking. There are people who write out of their education, out of their background, their upbringing, their discipline, but there are others of us who write out of our ignorance. We put aside everything we know. Well, not everything—but we put aside learning, we put aside as much as we can and try to go forward into our ignorance, feeling our way. I see how this thought might be used against me by poets who believe differently, but I do think I am describing what is true for a great many poets.

*And is this where the risk lies—going into your ignorance?*

Yes. The risks are failure and embarrassment. Worse, success may prove just as embarrassing. Easier and safer to talk about surfaces and to play the parrot, and merely to perform within the lines.

*William Gass said in a* Paris Review *interview that he has a constant knotting in his stomach when he is writing, and he said, in fact, "I write because I hate."*

Ech. That sounds terrible. I feel driven, manic, a little crazy when I'm writing well, but I wouldn't want to say that it feels *bad,* in fact in the end I feel terrific. Imagine yourself lost in the woods—there is a certain pleasure in it, but there is also a certain difficulty and fear—it's something like that, although that seems too calm a metaphor.

*Do you think writers are becoming popular heroes? We seem to need heroes.*

There's always been some of that. There is a tendency on the part of people who don't write to ascribe magical powers to those of us who do. I'm not really sure anymore, but there was a time when I insisted that poets were no different than other people except that they wrote poems. And a part of me still feels that way. But a part of me feels just the opposite: that, in fact, what nonpoets said to me for years is true. That is, poets really are different from other people. At least their going on with their poetry for so many years somehow makes them different.

*I have read that writers don't repress experience as well as other people do, they don't put thoughts and images so deeply back into the subconscious.*

Well, writing does have that function too, as an exploration. If one is willing to consider it an act of discovery, then indeed one deals with thoughts, feelings and language that one wouldn't use otherwise.

*In modern society the hero might be the person who is willing to face himself, to make a psychic journey, to explore an internal spiritual realm rather than go out with sword and shield.*

Maybe among a limited few. I still feel that for most people the hero is still the one who scores the winning basket or catches the winning touchdown pass or beats up ten bad guys. I think that's still true, don't you?

*I don't know. I think many people admire a person who can live a life that is insecure. The writer doesn't know if he is going to gain acceptance, or if he is going to earn enough money to live; he has to make sacrifices in order to have the time for reverie, the time for writing and rewriting. The writer has to be a little heroic to survive.*

I know what you are saying, and yet, I keep thinking of the other side of it, which is the pleasure of being a writer, of writing, and of all the little side benefits that it might bring. If one is lucky enough to keep on writing, or needs to and, therefore, does go on writing, there are so many benefits that it might be hard to think of oneself as underprivileged or desperate.

*What do you consider the benefits of a lifetime of writing?*

Well, leaving aside the "career" benefits (publication, jobs, fellowships, travel, friends among the pros), the benefits are those of expression, discovery, emotional balance, understanding, even sometimes usefulness—and these are plenty.

*Do you have any methods you use to keep yourself writing?*

I believe people can write on a schedule, or at least every day, or every-other-day. Now I don't do that, but I keep intending to. And I recommend it to everyone else, because if you sit long enough, even if your mind is empty, even if you write nothing, even if everything that you write is garbage, even if you pass the time listening to a record, or whittling a toy, if you sit there long enough something will come out that will be worth saving.

For years I pooh-poohed the idea of inspiration, but I'm not sure that, for lack of a better word, the word inspiration shouldn't be used after all. Something just comes over me that drives me out to that little room out back to fiddle and write. Very often the "something" is a piece of language that seems to have an emotional content which is not yet fully articulated, an image for an experience that needs elaboration. Sometimes I just hang around wanting to write, feeling that I want to write, not knowing what's going to happen. I open myself up to that piece of language that might come from listening, looking, thinking, feeling. It might come from anything. There is some mystery about it.

But there is one important aspect of it that is not mysterious, and that is that one writes something, and then one writes the next thing. That is the way writing works. It really doesn't work any other way. People can talk about it in all kinds of ways—in terms of patterns of organization, or what they call "strategies"—but it really doesn't work that way. One writes something and then one writes the next thing. And the next thing, whatever that is, occurs to a person because one's self has a coherence. Bill Stafford has pointed this out beautifully in a number of essays. Of all the things that could have occurred, one did. Now why? The secret to writing the poem may be in making the poem pay attention to itself. That is, when one thing occurs after something else, how did that happen? What is suggested next? Indeed, there may be more than one thing that could have been said, but it will not be an infinite number. And the mistake of the unsuccessful poet is in believing that the number remains infinite. But as soon as the first line or phrase or sentence is put down, the possibilities, while great, are no longer infinite. Of all the possibilities that remain, what is that that occurs to the poet? It occurs for some reason; there is a linkage.

*Do you think a bad poem is the result of someone not making this covertly logical linkage?*

Well, there are many ways to fail in a poem. Imprecision is one way—using words to mean things they simply don't mean and can't suggest. One would think this would never happen but it happens all the time.

I hate to talk about failures. Why does something fail? I throw a good bit of writing away. Well, I don't throw it away, but I don't do anything with it. Sometimes it is because whatever the poem amounts to isn't enough; sometimes it is because the poem isn't a poem: the quality of imagination is prosaic, or the energy somehow ran out. The inspiration—if that is the word—ran out; there wasn't enough there for a poem. There are so many ways to fail.

*And how do you know when a poem is successful? Is it an intellectual awareness?*

No. Well, eventually I will apply intellectual standards. But first, there is a sense of completion, a sense of having used up everything that has been mentioned in the poem, and of everything going together, and there not being anything further to be said.

*Are you saying the poem is complete and you are not abandoning it?*

Valéry, again, talks about every poem being "abandoned" rather than finished, but that is in terms of some vague ideal one has. And the key word here is not "ideal" but "vague." When an ideal is vague, it doesn't really exist. So I think it is just a clever way to talk about poems, and it isn't really true.

*Back in 1966 you had a pamphlet,* Poems for Nathan and Saul. *Was that your first publication?*

Yes, it was. In the same year I published a limited edition hardback book with The Stone Wall Press, a beautiful little book called *Things We Dreamt We Died For,* which included in it the two longish poems that made up that pamphlet. One is called "Pieces" and is mostly about my first wife, and one is called "The Manipulator" and is mostly about my father, who was an immigrant from the Ukraine.

*You've mentioned twice that your father came from the Ukraine. That must be important.*

Well, I like the idea.

*Do you think it made your life, your childhood, different from others'?*

Well, looking back I probably could say, but of course children sort of assume that their lives are pretty much like anyone's, and perhaps it is true, barring physical deprivation. Ours was an Old World family to an extent. That is, there weren't many direct expressions of emotion. But it was perfectly clear that my father loved life and loved us, and he was a wonderful fellow. He would have had to have been to escape from Russia and to live through certain experiences in his life, he would have had to have courage and a willingness to do what it takes to survive. And he was a genuinely moral, helpful person—to strangers as well as friends. He was very well thought of. In fact, the town more or less closed down the day of his funeral.

Those first poems were called *Poems for Nathan and Saul.* Maybe I should explain; it gets confusing. My father's name was Saul. My big son, who was born after my father died, is named Nathan Saul. I have a younger son named Jason Aaron, and just to confuse you more, my mother's name is Belle Bell. My mother's sister married my father's brother. My sister's name is Ruby. And the only other Ruby in our town was a man. And that is the way writing works, you say one thing and then you say what comes next.

*Would you call it free association?*

Yes, but association is never free. That's the secret. And the idea is to discover in the writing what is determinant about the associations, rather than free.

*And as you said, you limit those associations with each step.*

They are limited, that's right. Just as you walk out of your house and you have to go in one direction or another. You may choose to go straight ahead, and now you are no longer going left, right, or backwards. You take five steps and you are closer to something than you were before, and further from something else. It's very simple, of course. Anything can connect. Any two things, or three things, can be connected up if one knows how to pay attention. If one knows how to see through them, not so much think about them as let them think about each other. And that is the sense in which a poem must pay attention to itself. Indeed, as it goes down the page it must give visible indications of paying attention to itself. Or at least for me, that is one of the signs of good poetry.

*What are other signs of good poetry?*

Depth of feeling. Precision of expression. A sense, not of the complicated, but of the complex. Depth of character. Authenticity of language. A higher seriousness—even when the poetry is funny. Probably a sense of original form. Words used rather than mentioned. Maybe other things too.

*Are you using some of your columns from* The American Poetry Review *in the book of essays and interviews you are doing for the University of Michigan Poets on Poetry series?*

I will, I'll use some, probably not all of them. When I agreed to write those essays for *The American Poetry Review* I did so with the knowledge that I would write more or less spontaneously, quickly and informally. My idea was that the column should contain common sense, and that it should be an example. When I began it seemed to me that the criticism and book reviewing of the time were pretty bad. I'm not willing to say that it's any better now. But it seems to me that when one talks about poetry there should be some poetry present. And it seems to me that poetry has content and it ought to be talked about. And it seems to me that the critic ought to be on the side of the writer he or she is writing about, at least at the beginning. And it seems to me that this is very rare now. I wanted the column to be an example of common sense, a method, and sympathy.

I don't know that these columns have had an effect on anyone. I hope that some people have taken something from them. I do "get letters," as they say at the Grand Ole Opry. And I appreciate those letters. But the columns were good for me too. They helped me articulate, even if informally, what I was thinking. Now as it happens, over the years my ideas have developed—I guess I shouldn't say changed—but developed in ways that might require qualification of some of the things I said earlier. But I don't think I said anything wrong in those columns, and so I will collect some of them in that book.

*So if your life is like a poem, you have eliminated some of the possibilities by what you have done previously.*

Oh, yes. By writing one solves certain problems of language and literature and art. One solves some of the problems one can take on and then one is ready for others, whether they are formal or emotional or intellectual. That's true, yes. Each of my books seems to me quite different from the others, and my new book coming out in September will be, again, different.

*And you could only write* These Green-Going-to-Yellow *because you had written your earlier books?*

I assume that's true. But it's always possible that it's just a function of age.

*You talked about common sense, method and sympathy. Something like that combination occurs at Bread Loaf, doesn't it?*

Oh yes, Bread Loaf is wonderful, really. Certainly a part of it is always a landlocked ship of fools speeding ever faster. But there is also an important, serious part. An awful lot of good talk about literature goes on. A certain amount of valuable support goes on. Writers do need courage. We were talking earlier about risk-taking, not only in the individual poem, but in the act of being a writer, of writing poems over a long period of time. And it's true, often, that that's all one needs, a certain amount of courage. Sometimes all one needs are a few new words in one's head, or a new approach.

Bread Loaf is marvellous. It's not just that it is set in such a beautiful place in Vermont in the summer. It's not just that it brings together people who are interesting and who are genuinely interested in something they have in common—a seriousness about writing. It's also that they take it seriously without, I think, being pompous about it. They don't make it more than it is, but they do pay attention to *what* it is. And that's very difficult. Fans of writers often make writing out to be something it really isn't. Some writers, in public, make writing out to be something it isn't. But Bread Loaf is one of those places where enough writers gather together that the very community legislates against taking things too seriously or not seriously enough.

*John Gardner talks about something called "the great conversation," which I take to mean not the individual conversations but the linking of writers through this interaction, the linking of the past and the future.*

Oh, yes, that's right. Whatever tradition means, apart from forms, certainly it is helped by this kind of community, the existence of such a community. However, if you go on writing for enough years you are in your own world when you are writing, and it is a world that no one else understands fully. Other writers can sometimes enter into the world from the side door and make a telling comment, but it is up to you to put these remarks into the places that they should take in that world. Even your best friends are doing something that is really different, after a while, from what you are doing, and you appreciate it in such a way as you would someone who is doing something entirely different. It is as if you all begin in one room together and you see everything about one another and then you each go off with your hammers and pliers and your other tools, and you go off into these sewers which branch off in different directions. After a while you are far enough along in your sewer that you don't see anyone else. You can hear the knocking coming from the other sewers and you know your friends are out there working, and you know that they are doing something similar to what you are doing but it's not quite the same. And in order to meet on common ground you have to go back to that room where you started.

*That reminds me of Henry James': "We work in the dark, we do what we can . . . the rest is the madness of art." To use your figure, Bread Loaf might be seen as getting together in that room again.*

Perhaps. You know what else happens at Bread Loaf? There is a kind of modesty to such a writing community. I live in a community that is in some respects similar to Bread Loaf. I live in Iowa City, Iowa, where, because of the Writers' Workshop there are always a great many writers in town, as well as a great many dancers, composers, musicians, playwrights. And there is something very healthy about that kind of community, artificial as it may seem in one respect, and that is that you really can't pretend you are special in any way in which you are not special. You are a writer, and the proof of what kind of writer you are is in what you write. There is a kind of built-in modesty, a humility which is good for anybody. Before, I was talking about courage. One has to distinguish between immodesty and courage. These are different things.

I actually do have the feeling from my experience that people who come to Iowa City to be around the Writers' Workshop—to teach in it, or study in it, or just hang around it—write better afterwards. And I think that may happen with Bread Loaf. I know it sounds crazy, it could seem Pollyannish of me to say it, but I do have that feeling. I have watched enough people over the years to see what the results are. It is difficult to know about cause and effect but that is what I see.

*Do you think it is more a gaining of courage than learning about the craft?*

I don't know. At Bread Loaf the contributors each sit down with one of the faculty members for an hour's conference. It depends on the teachers—I mean each one teaches in a different way—but I would imagine that in most conferences very specific talking goes on about the particular text of the contributor's work. And in many cases, the teacher says something, or the student may say something, that simply hasn't been said before in his presence. And then the student knows that thing, and he doesn't have to think about it any more. It changes the way he writes.

It is fashionable among artists to pretend that the notion of teaching anyone anything is ridiculous, but I think it is maybe the artists who say that who are ridiculous, because my experience shows that even if one can't teach, one can certainly learn. And for some strange reason, learning seems to go on mostly when someone is teaching.

*Stafford talks about an unnecessary negativeness in contemporary poetry.*

Maybe so. Of course, when Bill Stafford says that, he is being cagey. Bill Stafford is always being cagey. There is a lot of facing-the-facts in Stafford's poems. And there is a lot of dark correction in some of them. He has things to say, but his attitude is certainly not negative. His attitude is one of acceptance; there's a lot of positive engagement. It is an admirable attitude, certainly, in life as well as in art.

There is of course, in poetry, a lot of complaining and self-pity but then again, there is a lot of complaining and self-pity in life, and naturally it would show up in poetry. There can be poems of self-pity which are wonderful because in the end they resist the self-pity, they transform the pity, or they engage so energetically with life that the pity is overwhelmed by something more important. Many things can happen. I do know, however, what Bill is talking about, and of course a kind of banal carping or easy social criticism doesn't interest us for very long.

*You told me that a friend of yours, a novelist, is having a film made of his book and that maybe you will have a part.*

(Laughter.) Yes, it's a possibility. I would love that. However, it's a Western and I'm afraid that he'll put me in a bar scene and I'll be the one who's thrown out the window.

*Maybe you could sit in the corner and wear your hat.*

My "Blue Seal Feeds" hat?

*Of course.*

I do sometimes get into a little minor trouble by not having my hat. Many people know about it because I wear it at Bread Loaf. But you see, I only wear it at Bread Loaf. It stays in the drawer the rest of the year. The original one was given to me by a poet named Peter Sears. We were on one of those clay tennis courts at Bread Loaf and he and I were playing two other poets. The sun was in my eyes. Peter gave me this old, dirty Blue Seal Feeds cap and then decided that it belonged on my head. And I must say that I do have one talent that I am immodest about, and that is that I can wear hats. I'm very good at wearing hats and imparting to them some character, or perhaps taking from them some character, or perhaps being the character over which they sit. In any case, I got to keep this hat and later was given others. I started wearing it at Bread Loaf and it seemed right somehow. A picture was taken by a wonderful photographer who works at Bread Loaf in the summers, Erik Borg, while I was teaching a class. Then that photograph was used by *The American Poetry Review* next to my columns. So people know about it. And they always want to know where my hat is. And the answer is that my cap is in the drawer all year, waiting for Bread Loaf.

*You may disappoint people at the Library of Congress tonight when you read and you're not wearing your Blue Seal Feeds hat.*

That's possible. Well, I'm going to be another character at the Library of Congress. I'm going to wear a three-piece suit.

*Reading your poetry at the Library of Congress' Coolidge Auditorium puts you in the line of another "great conversation," the respected poets who have read there. Does this represent the achievement of a personal goal for you?*

Certainly I'm honored. I'm glad to have the chance. But no. The real goals in writing poetry, if "goals" is the word, are beyond those of career. Still, I was thrilled to be asked.

*Would you be able to keep on writing without this kind of recognition?*

I'm not stone. I can't say for sure. I suppose some response is necessary for anyone. And some responses may count more than others. I'd very much like the poets I admire to know my work, but that has to happen on its own. I prefer it that way. I won't try to make it happen except by writing the poems.

*Earlier I wanted to ask about your music.*

Sure. I played cornet and trumpet for many years, all kinds of music, and I loved it. I don't think I ever would have been good enough. I mean, I was pretty good. I gave it up eventually. I hardly ever play anymore. Also, I was a potter for a while; I was a photographer for a long time. I gave those things up.

My son, Nathan, is in Boston now beginning to make his way in the music world. He's terrific. He's a guitar player, singer and songwriter and has enormous talent, a real individuality to his songs and performances. We'll see. You know, I just think it is a great thing to do when you are young. It's a tough thing to do, too. Talent is only a part of it. Even individuality is only part of it. But I just think it is great that he is doing that. I hope he makes it so I can quit my job and become a "roadie." Carry his equipment. (Laughter.)

I can still play dance music. My lip's not that bad! I was on a television show once, I think it was in Rochester, New York. It was a live show and I was waiting in the wings. A group went on ahead of me and it was a kazoo band. I forget what nationality they were, but I think it might have been Polish. A Polish kazoo band, in costume. And so when I finally got on camera I took out a piece of paper and a comb and started playing a song for the M.C. I'm very good on kazoo. Yes, I especially like to use pages from *Poetry* magazine. It makes a good read. They make good reeds.

*Not only music—and this just might have been fiction—(laughter) I've noticed art allusions in your books as well. I'm thinking of the*

*Impressionistic, Pointillistic cover of* Stars Which See, Stars Which Do Not See, *of course.*

The cover of that book, which is very pretty I think, shows one of the preliminary sketches that Georges Seurat did for his painting, "A Sunday Afternoon on the Island of La Grande Jatte," which hangs in the Art Institute in Chicago. This is just a sketch for a small part of the painting. The title poem, "Stars Which See, Stars Which Do Not See," is based loosely on the painting. I have to say "loosely" because otherwise any reader would know that I've changed one detail. What I should say is that the poem is based on a similar scene.

*The painting points out, as one critic says, the "tediousness" of the Sunday ritual. And you manage to do this also in your poem. Can this always be done—the crossing over of an idea from one art form to another?*

"Tediousness" doesn't seem like the right word to me. The scene is one of calm and propriety, also mild pleasures. One can imagine profound feelings in some of the characters portrayed. What my poem does, in part, is to suggest an undercurrent to their apparent calm and to distinguish between nature as it is and nature as we use it. They look out over the Seine, a calm mirror. "It was probable," says the poem, "that the Seine had hurt them." Finally, a breeze breaks the mirror, "but never the water." Well, you see I've resorted to answering your question about the poem by repeating the poem. The title does some of that work too.

*Do works of art often inspire your poems?*

Oh, I fight against that, just as any poet, I think, fights against writing poems about poetry. But art is part of the world and poetry is part of poetry and so I think it is foolish to make a rule about it. I used to feel that I didn't want to write poems about places that I had been because it would result in a kind of "trip poetry." I still feel more or less that way, but in my new book, *These Green-Going-to-Yellow*, there are, nonetheless, poems which are set in or think back to Morocco, Mexico, Alaska, Hawaii, Cuba, Spain and some other places as well.

*Do you think that old habits keep us from seeing? And that by breaking a habit or a habitual way of perceiving we can see anew?*

Oh, of course. The whole point of poetry and why it should be oneself in some individual way relates to this. I mean, what's the point of writing poetry if it is just a rephrasing of something that can be said and perhaps has been said elsewhere? Or in another form? Or better? Sure, that might be fun, it might even be useful, but not nearly as useful, it seems to me, as exploring previously unexplored territory.

*Might this then, your putting your own personal way of seeing out there, expose in contrast the reader's habitual way of seeing?*

Yes. However, it is important at the same time that the poem think hard about what one's personal way of seeing *is*. Because that can be just prejudice; it can be just unsubstantiated opinion. It can be just disconnected assertion.

*I have been hearing you personify the poem. You say the poem should "think hard." Does this mean you believe it has a life of its own, somewhat independent of the poet?*

The finished poem certainly has a life of its own. I was thinking more of the poem as it comes into being. It's the poet who thinks hard but always within the poem—more and more so as it develops—so that it's as if the poem is doing the work. One lets the poem have its head. How difficult it can be to be sensitive to the possibilities, and to follow along waiting for a deeper content. But trees and plants make their needs and possibilities, even their character, known to good gardeners, and good poets can hold conversations with their emerging poems.

*So the poet presents the poem . . .*

Yes, the poet needs to think about what he or she is saying.
What the poem is suggesting. Why he or she is saying it. What
can be said. What can't be said. Why and why not, where and
where not, when and when not, who and who not, and further-
more, he or she has to do all of this at once.

*Not an easy task.*

Well, in some ways it's the most natural thing of all. The thing
that is unnatural is to become *less* than a whole person. And yet,
unfortunately, we manage that all the time. The idea in poetry
is to be the whole person, to be the whole person all the time.
The whole person doesn't say, "Oh, I won't use intellectual
things. Oh, I won't use art; I won't write about poetry." Or,
"Oh, I will only be intellectual; I won't let my emotions be
expressed. Oh, I will never use rhetoric. Oh, I will disdain
imagery. Oh, I will use only imagery. I will show and won't tell;
I will tell and won't show." No, the whole person never says any
of these things. The whole person hasn't got time to say silly,
compartmentalized things.

*As part of the whole person, do you recognize a symbol system in your
poetry?*

Not a deliberate system. I think one can go through anybody's
poetry and see that some objects show up again and again.
Some recurrent settings, some similar situations come up again
and again. And they may take on symbolic value or they may be
just obsessions. So I'm sure someone could do that with my
work.
    I'm the tree poet! Yes, if everybody gets to be something in
the world of poetry, I want to be "The Tree Poet."

*Your elms, the willows . . .*

Absolutely. In my new book, the title poem, "These Green-Going-to-Yellow," contains a gingko tree. And there's a poem in the book called "To an Adolescent Weeping Willow." The willow in question is in my back yard in Iowa City.

*Would you read it?*

Oh, perhaps I should mention that my father ran a small Five-and-Ten.

### To an Adolescent Weeping Willow

I don't know what you think you're doing,
sweeping the ground. You
do it so easily, backhanded, forehanded.
You hardly bend. Really, you sway.
What can it mean
when a thing is so easy?

I threw dirt on my father's floor.
Not dirt, but a chopped green
dirt which picked up dirt.

I pushed the pushbroom.
I oiled the wooden floor of the store.

He bent over and lifted the coal
into the coalstove. With the back of the shovel
he came down on the rat just topping the bin
and into the fire.

What do you think?—Did he sway?
Did he kiss a rock for luck?
Did he soak up water
and climb into light and turn and turn?

Did he weep and weep in the yard?

Yes, I think he did. Yes,
now I think he did.

So, Willow, you come sweep my floor.
I have no store.
I have a yard. A big yard.

I have a song to weep.
I have a cry.
You who rose up from the dirt,
because I put you there
and like to walk my head in under
your earliest feathery branches—
what can it mean
when a thing is so easy?

It means you are a boy.

*Perhaps the poet always speaks best in his poetry. Do you want to add anything?*

You're right. And no.

# The University Is Something Else You Do

*(The following interview was conducted by Nancy Bunge, of the Department of American Thought and Language, Michigan State University, on September 16, 1980, in Iowa City, and is one of a series of conversations between Ms. Bunge and writers who teach.)*

*What do you want your students to get from your classes?*

A sense of themselves and what the possibilities are for them. And *that* they find out partly by finding out what the possibilities are for poetry. I don't want them to write like me. I don't want them to think like me. I want them to go their own ways and toward that end I want them to be able to read their own work and see what it really is. At any given time one's poetry is a fair representation of what one's life's probably. . . . One always feels, "Oh, that's not me, that's not me, that's not me"; but really, that is you, that is you, that is you, and after a while that gets to be OK. That's the real leap people have to make in maturation. In maturing they begin to accept what they are and to actually work with what they are and to build on that. Now that's what I would like to encourage in my students. Absolutely. And some of them are able to begin that kind of essential work while they're still students. Others don't really get it until a few years later. I get a lot of letters.

*How do you encourage that? Do you have them keep journals?*

I don't require them to do anything, but I don't forbid anything either. I assume they're all men and women of some commitment and of some maturity, as they *are* here; they may not be quite like that everywhere in that they wouldn't be here if they weren't committed to writing.

*Then how do you encourage them to accept themselves?*

Well, I do several things. One is to insist on what the words are saying in class. We try to figure out exactly what's in the poem. It may be of interest to us to know what the poet's intentions were and what else is behind the poem, but we also try to make it absolutely clear to one another what's there in the poem, what does it actually say, what do the sentences say. That's one thing—learning to read your words carefully. And another thing is to encourage them to be not only unlike me when they're writing, but unlike one another and to learn from the work that most threatens them, because the work that doesn't upset them is work that's like their own. Especially when one is young, that defensiveness gets in the way. When a poem is praised in class, it's so easy for everyone else who writes differently to say, "Uh oh, if that poem is good, then maybe the way I write is no good." Then learning stops and defensiveness takes over. So I try to encourage them to be unlike one another and to appreciate every different way of writing and to learn from what seems most alien to them, to read good work widely, to read their own work carefully, and to give themselves permission, permission to try anything, over and over, because one of the great secrets—I hope it's not really a secret, about writing—is that if you do anything seriously enough, long enough, you'll get better at it. Then some teachers try to take credit. (Laughter.)

*Is it a problem that your students have primarily literary backgrounds?*

They don't have backgrounds in other fields, but they have lots of other interests. Many of the students in the Workshop are a little older than they would be if they came here directly from undergraduate school, so that's one thing. Another thing is, they tend to be odd, interesting people who've always had a number of interests. We do try to encourage the students to get out of the Workshop milieu and out of the English Department for some of their courses. We think it'd be just terrific if people took paleontology, karate, and home economics, all of which would count toward their degree. But again, we can't really require it and it wouldn't work out if we did. We just rely on them wanting to know things. Generally, poets do want to know things. On the one hand, it's just wonderful for poets to, say, read books about insects. On the other hand, it doesn't make them experts. Ezra Pound in the *ABC of Reading* tells a story about Dempsey, the prize fighter, during the days when Tunney and Dempsey were both great fighters and people would talk about how intelligent Tunney was while Dempsey was not thought to be too intelligent. And so, Dempsey was asked about a novel that had prize fighting in it and he simply said, "It's not like that." So the person asking said, "Well, I see you're reading a novel about a Grand Duke of Russia. How do you know whether that's like that?" Dempsey said, "I never *wuz* a Grand Duke." And that applies to some extent to people who think that poets should be reading up on insects, say, and then mentioning insects in their next poem. It's one thing to know a little; it's another thing to really know.

*So good poetry is written out of . . .*

Nobody knows. Again, I think it's just wonderful for a poet to read a book on insects, or even 100 books on insects, but . . . when black holes were discovered, there was suddenly a spate of poems about black holes. And these poems, as far as I could tell, never did anything except discover the black hole as a metaphor for whatever else they were going to say. And most of what they were going to say were the standard things: "I'm lonely," "I'm not lonely," "I hurt," "I don't hurt," "I want," "I don't want."

*I guess that's true. I thought that the more people knew, the better poetry they'd write; but you're right.*

In some cases, it's true. Poets do love to learn things that are of use, and one of the best things about being a poet is that one can become more and more educated through one's art without going about it in an organized fashion. It's great to have subject matter and there are some people who have subject matter by virtue of how their lives have gone, in some cases quite horribly. On the other hand, Emily Dickinson's life was not very exciting except in her mind and even Whitman didn't cover the country in person as well as his poems did on the page.

*Is it a problem that more and more people are becoming poets by going to workshops rather than by riding around on steamers?*

On the great scale of human vices, writing a bad poem doesn't weigh very much. In any case, why should only people who can do something well be permitted to do it? That's crazy. If that's true, I should give up running because when I run a marathon, I finish so much after Bill Rodgers or Frank Shorter that it isn't the same event. I like to point out to people that in the Honolulu Marathon last year, I passed Frank Shorter. Unfortunately, I was running one way and he was already doubling back toward the finish line. So what's the point? Who plays baseball in this country? Only the people who are going to make it to the major leagues? And who goes to the baseball games? The people who go to baseball games, those millions of people who attend professional baseball games every year, are people who either played baseball or are attending the game with someone who did; they have an interest in it and they have some knowledge of it because they've tried it themselves. Well, how can it hurt the best poetry for a lot of people to try it themselves? That's crazy. People who are against workshops essentially hate young people. That's all. They hate young people. They don't want any competition. They're elitists in the worst sense.

There's a good sense of being elite which has to do with quality; but when one becomes elitist in terms of participation, that's a horrible position to take. There are academic paratroopers who drop in for a night and blast workshops, then they pick up their checks from the Workshop and they sell their books to the students, and they go on home. Some of us stay right here in the trenches.

*I meant that some people say it could be a problem that more and more poets come out of school and are, consequently, out of touch with the real world.*

Aaww, nobody comes out of school. That's absurd. A few years of college or a couple years of graduate school don't change your character. I grew up in a town where people don't go to college, where most people make their living, or did at the time, from duck farms, fishing, potato farms, and from small town activities. I went off to college wearing a leather jacket with a switch blade in my pocket because I didn't know any better. When I got there, I found out that nobody was wearing a leather jacket; as far as I could tell, they didn't have switch blades. Well now, I don't think my character was going to be changed by graduate school or even many years of under-graduate school then followed by graduate school. That's absurd. My character, even as it develops now, is undoubtedly based on things I do that have nothing to do with teaching as much as on my job, which is teaching. If people who go to the university are out of touch with reality, what happens to people who spend eight or ten hours a day on an automobile assembly line? There's a kind of romanticism among poets that says, "Oh, if you work in the mines, if you work in the factories, you're in the real world." That's nonsense. Nobody comes out of the university; the university is something else you do. Even during the years one is in the university, does one give up all the passions and desires and activities and angers and hates and fears and so forth, that one has, because one is in the university, and start over? It might be good if we could, but we don't.

*In one interview you said that the students' fascination with technical facility used to pose a problem, but that it was going away. Then somewhere else you said that your students had to struggle against a world where no one has any respect for working hard at writing well.*

Well, tendencies come and go in the Workshop. It's hard to judge one class against another. But if one looks back to twenty years ago, when I was a student in the Workshop, one can see that the kind of poetry dominating the worksheets was different from the kind of poetry one sees on the worksheets now. Let me put it this way. The best poets are always the best poets. They're people who have the drive, the commitment, the need, whatever it is, to teach themselves or to learn from me and other people. It's always the second-best poets in whom one finds the regrettable tendencies of an age. When an anthology is published, for example, the reviews are always negative, probably because the reviews are always written by people who aren't in the anthology and who are jealous. When you want to look for a way to put down an anthology or a workshop, it's very easy. You just ignore the best poems and the best poets, and you find, if you can, those regrettable tendencies in the second- and third-best poets. The best work is always so good that it escapes these considerations. It's always original, it's always unique, it's always personal, intimate.

I think a number of good things have happened in American poetry in the last twenty years and those events have influenced the work one sees everywhere, including the Workshop here. I think the old argument about free verse versus metered verse has exhausted itself. As a free verse poet, writing free verse from a long time back, I had to know everything I could know about meter, partly to defend myself and partly to be sure of what I was doing. I'm doing things in poetry which I think would not work well in meters and I don't write metered verse, but I think it's probably a help to a young poet's ear to know how to read metered verse if not how to write it. But there are grand theoretical questions about this. James Wright in the last book he published before his death, a book called *To a Blossoming Pear Tree*, includes a poem about Ralph Neal, the scoutmaster in Martins Ferry, Ohio and it's a poem written in prose. In fact, it's a piece of prose, or is it? Nobody really knows or even cares to know any more. We've gotten past all that. "Poetry," which was for so long a word that had something to do with lines, and for some people also with meters, stanzas and verse forms, has in a sense returned to a more fundamental sense of the word which is very hard to pin down, but which has to do with the quality of the imagination and further, the quality of an imaginative engagement with the world or the subject matter. So someone will say about a piece of writing, "Oh, that's sheer poetry." And it would be easy to laugh and say, "Oh, they're just speaking from ignorance," but they're really not. They're speaking from a heartfelt understanding which is probably more accurate than all those technical definitions we used to apply. So the situation in poetry has changed. And there are many poets in this country, good poets, who still write very well in meters and rhyme who, I think, feel threatened and feel ignored by a young generation which in many respects doesn't know and doesn't care about meters and rhyme. Out of their feelings of being threatened, they have exaggerated the importance of meter and rhyme in poetry and they have then tried in desperate ways, I think, to prove to us that free verse is a kind of aberration and that the history of poetry will proceed mostly in terms of meters. And I think they're wrong.

I also think many kinds of images are showing up in poems now that didn't show up before, partly because of the influence of translation. In the fifties and even on into the sixties, the young poets in this country were bitterly rational. I think now there's less rationality and more passion. We've gained permission for our poetry from work translated from other cultures. All kinds of permission. It always was true and still is to some extent that people would see a poem translated by a Russian poet and they would say, "How Russian!" They'd see the same poem by an American poet and they'd say, "This is just self-indulgent, overly grand." Or they'd see a short poem by a Japanese poet and they'd say, "Oh, isn't this wonderful. How Japanese!" They'd see the same poem next to an American byline and they'd say, "How skimpy! How begrudging! How stingy!" They'd see a poem containing wonderful political ironies by an East European and they'd say, "Oh yes, this is the kind of wonderful poetry one gets out from behind the Iron Curtain." But they'd see the same poem written by an American poet and they'd say, "Oh, how frivolous." So a lot of that prejudice has been weakened by our seeing so much good work in translation.

The poets in the Workshop are incredible talents. Although many of them will quit writing over the ten years after they leave here, they won't quit for lack of talent. They'll quit because they no longer need to. And when I read the theses each spring, I'm really amazed; I would say a good half of the theses are as good as, or better than, the better first books that are coming out that year. They're really that good. It's certainly much better than when I was a graduate student.

*What would have happened to you if you hadn't come here?*

Well, I've thought about that. I got married and had a child very early and then was divorced from my wife and kept the child, so I had to work and make a living and I don't know what would have happened. I was stalling the army. I had an old commission and I knew I was going to have to go on active duty eventually; I tried unsuccessfully many times in many ways to get out of it and couldn't. I stalled them over seven years, but I knew I'd have to go in eventually. So it was crucial to me to find a way of testing my commitment further and producing more work, really being able to think about the writing and do it, and that's what the Writing Workshop afforded me. That's what it affords everybody—a sense of community and a pervasive sense of commitment and time.

*You said that many other programs "have faculty members who feel too good about teaching writing, who feel that it's a credit to themselves, which is, I think, a bad way to feel." What did you mean?*

I think what I meant is that creating the right response in their students takes precedence over raising their standards. Remember *Marjorie Morningstar?*

*Vaguely.*

In the movie version Gene Kelly plays the big fish in the small pond where he is the music teacher, I guess, at an all-girls school, is it? I don't remember too well. Anyway, Marjorie discovers him and takes him to Broadway where, of course, he fails utterly. Marjorie tracks him down and finds him sitting at the piano playing to his adoring girl students just as he had at the beginning. Well, the big-fish-in-the-little-pond syndrome is common to artists in universities. In that regard, the best thing, I think, about Iowa City is that it is so common to be a poet or a writer of any kind or an artist of any kind here that it's impossible to keep pretending one is more special than one is. Everyone knows you fell down the stairs last week; everybody knows that you're human and I think that's healthy. The other half of this, of course, is that one does achieve a certain kind of confidence that one might not otherwise achieve by being paid attention to. That's a terrible thing to say perhaps, but I think it's true.

*Some people I've spoken with say that many writers stop producing when they teach because teaching depletes their creative energy.*

I think there's a very complicated psychological dynamic going on in teaching in that when teachers first begin to teach they really need to be liked by their students. And I think teaching can be a very interesting and strange and rich activity; it can also be endlessly tiring and thoroughly exhausting for the same reasons. It's a little like giving blood except that nobody turns the tap off unless you the teacher decide to turn it off yourself. That's one of the things that teachers have to learn to do—to turn the tap off so they're not depleted of their own blood.

On the other hand, when anyone says that teaching interferes with their writing, I suspect that if it weren't teaching, it would be something else interfering with their writing. I go through long periods when I don't write and I can find many excuses, I can find many reasons for why I am not writing and I can rail against those obstructions to writing, but the truth is that when one really needs to write, one will find a way to do it.

*What did you mean when you said, "The academic life is dangerous to talent not because it is tame, but because it offers too many definitions. The academy trusts language almost without reservation. Writers who matter to us do not"?*

Yeah.

*You agree with that?*

Absolutely!

*What does it mean?*

(Laughter.) Well, it means that language can be misused and the more intelligent the person misusing it, the better they can misuse it. It's not just politicians coming up with words like "deniability," or "protective retaliatory strike," it's also the kind of nonsense that passes for Structuralism, and post-Structuralist theorizing and the sort of high-falutin' talk that goes on now in the name of semiotics and hermeneutics, Mr. Herman Neutics. And it's just nonsense, all that stuff. When language is pushed in a certain way, it loses logic. And I believe that I can go through the essays of the kind of critics I've just mentioned and I can show you where the logic breaks down. But obviously, not many people either can or want to do such a thing. Who would want to waste one's time on that? So they get away with what they're saying. So I submit to you that three-quarters of the people who are writing big books about poetry haven't got any idea of what they're talking about and certainly don't know what they're saying.

*And people are very intimidated by it.*

Yeah. Now in the academy, what you have is people who are older than Auden was when he had a collection of hats and would ride the buses putting on different hats and trying out different opinions out loud to see what people would say. These are people who ought to have passed that stage, but they will still try out anything, and in the interest of discursive investigation that's fine, but students believe it. Students believe it. And I remember when Timothy Leary dropped in on Iowa City one time, not here for any official reason, but just passing through way back when, and a great crowd gathered at his feet in the house where he was staying and he began to explain all the wonders of drugs. And the best moment occurred when a black student stood up and objected and said, "What are you talking about? I come from a place where drugs ruin people's lives. That's the real drug scene. You don't know what you're talking about." And, indeed, Leary didn't know what he was talking about. I think language has to be suspected all the time because it's partial, and because it's vague and because it is language. And I think that the best poets listen to themselves. The best poets always write poems which show visibly that they're listening to themselves and responding to what they're saying and questioning themselves as they go on. They must listen to themselves. Otherwise it's just random chords; slower than automatic writing, but not worth much more.

*In one of my interviews somebody said that there is absolutely no connection between talent and character.*

Ah, that's true.

*It seems to me that you've implied that in order to be a poet you have to have a lot of character.*

"Character" is a hard term to get a handle on. It gets caught up in moral and, consequently, political considerations and no one really knows what it is, but we can see sometimes in poems how character determines the handling of subject matter. The late James Wright had more character in his poems than perhaps anyone in the sense that he made decisions that came out of character. He wrote a poem called "To the Muse," for example, in which he talks to a childhood friend named Jenny who drowned. At the beginning of the poem he sort of brings her back to life and has her come up and stand on the shore with him out of the suckhole where she drowned and he says, "Well, I know three lady doctors in Wheeling, West Virginia. They keep their offices open all night; I don't have to call them. They'll always be there." He's going to take her to one of the doctors and the doctor will put a tube in and drain the lung. Now I'm just saying this in this awful prosy way, but in the poetry it's pretty wonderful. And he talks about what will happen when the tube is put in: she has to walk around on tiptoe and she can't jiggle the needle and stab her heart and so forth. Any young poet could probably write a poem in which he brought somebody who's dead back to life, but then Wright does something that is much more mature and it seems to me comes essentially out of character: he puts her back in the suckhole and he says, "I wish to God I had made this world, this scurvy and disastrous place." He says, "I didn't, I can't bear it either, I know the place where you lie." And he puts her back down in the river because finally he's not God, he's not the agent of creation and he ends up saying, "Come up to me, love, out of the river, or I will come down to you." That to me is an accomplished moment in the poem. Accomplishments that one can talk about in classrooms such as accomplishments of imagery, accomplishments of line and phrasing and rhythm and sound, accomplishments of writing that is, beside all those other accomplishments is this really great accomplishment which one might argue comes out of character which is the decision to be intelligent, to realize that you're not the agent of life and death and that you can't just bring her back to life. Intelligence applied to what the poem is about—that, to me, is worthy and important; poems without intelligence don't interest me at all. Poetry which is just a theme and doesn't have any mentality operating in it interests me less than poetry which makes a turn, or discovery or further exploration in the course of itself. That's along the lines of what I meant by "visible indications of intelligence" in a poem.

*You've said about John Logan and Donald Justice that "teaching as well as they have may have cost them something, but it may also have kept them honest."*

Oh yeah. Oh yeah! Good! It's awfully hard to bullshit your students if your students are any good. So it makes you keep thinking. I change my mind all the time. I hope I don't so much change my mind as I go further in my thinking, but I'm sure I also change my mind and also sure I contradict myself. As you may know, every book of my poetry is different in certain clear ways. Now I hope it's not just change but growth; but that's for others to decide. My ideas about poetry now are very different, not contradictory necessarily, in relation to what I used to think, but very different. I always told my students that I thought I would be a beginner until about the age of forty. Well, I published *Stars Which See, Stars Which Do Not See* when I was forty and for me, that was sort of the end of an apprenticeship, not because I had planned it but because it just did happen to work out that way. And now I have a pretty good sense of what I want to do. I had to more or less shut up, at least publicly, for two years. I had long periods of silence, and I threw a lot away. I knew what I was reaching for, somewhat, dot, dot, dot.

*You said in* The American Poetry Review *that a couple of times you'd gone off places to write and . . .*

Not written. (Laughter.)

*Could it be that your teaching feeds your writing?*

I think that going to work every day helps. Teaching in particular may help because it gets the words stirred up in your mind. You have to use those words, you have to respond to other people's words, so it gets going exactly what one wants to get going in order to write. I myself find having a certain job to do, having a routine to do which isn't overwhelming, is probably better than having nothing to do. I say that with some hesitancy because I hope the university will still occasionally give me nothing to do and I will make up the replacement tasks myself. I've found that the more I do the more I do. Partly I'm that way in general, and partly I tend to write in spurts. This may be just a result of moods, who knows? It may be a result of seasons. We're talking today and it's fall and I love the fall. In the fall, I write poems. I do think that I've cut down on the waste and that I can write more poems, but I think that if that's true for me, it's true because of what I call that apprenticeship until about the age of forty. And I now have a good sense of what it is I want to do and I have a way of doing it no matter what words the poem begins with. That remains to be proved, but I feel that that's true. Rilke worked for Rodin for a while and therefore, he wrote some essays about Rodin's sculpture. He thought Rodin was a great artist, which he was, and I was struck by the way in which he argued for the excellence of Rodin in one essay where what he really leads up to saying is that Rodin had become so engaged with his art and the world, putting those two into some inextricable relationship, that was not only inextricable but continuous and pervasive, he had become so engaged that he could do no wrong. Those are Rilke's words, translated, "He could do no wrong." And that's a condition I think much to be desired.

*He had worked out some kind of . . .*

When he worked with stone, when he worked with his sculpture, it would be art. That's all there is to it. I think there are a few poets in this country who have attained that level of engagement with both the materials of their art and the world as they live in it as artists. James Wright had attained it before he died recently. I think that William Stafford is a poet whose every piece of writing is poetry; whether it's good or bad, it's poetry. Whereas when the rest of us write bad poems, they're not even poems.

*I notice that you think your later poems are more accessible.*

Oh, they certainly are. You can't know *how* much more accessible because I didn't publish the first 200 poems I wrote. I was at one time a graduate student bum with a lot of other graduate student bums here at the Workshop. At the time, I wrote poetry which was absolutely obscure. I can remember Denise Levertov coming to class one time and I had a poem on the worksheet called "Acquaintance/It Happens/Making It Happen" and it was sort of vague and sexual, but it was certainly obscure. There was a line in it that said, "It's obscure as hell," and she read that line aloud and said, "That's exactly the way I feel about it." At which point, my generous fellow students tried to explain the poem to her and probably to me and to defend it. But the truth is that I was writing very obscurely. There are two things that occur to me right now. One is that obscurity is a kind of psychological defense because when a person can't understand you, you're safe from their reactions. Obscurity is in other cases a way of parading one's abilities. I don't think I meant it that way, at least I hope not. I do think it might have been a defense and I did overcome that. The other thing is that young writers, young people in general, have to be told they're talented before they ever take a stab as writers. It's so hurtful in a way to put one's poems on worksheets at first and to get genuine responses from people who are paying close attention, no matter how kind their responses are, no matter how circuitous they may be; one is so vulnerable. And so you have to have a certain confidence behind that; it may be propped up artificially. A person can be essentially humble and yet he or she can seem very immodest in workshop situations, but I think if one doesn't realize at an early age how unimportant an individual can be one certainly finds out. On the other hand, there's a kind of modesty of style that sometimes goes hand in hand with philosophic modesty that is not necessarily good for the poet. For some poets it's the best they can do; but there's a tendency I think among what we might call workshop writers, if there is such a thing as a workshop writer, to adopt a position with regard to style that is not only central but overly immodest. Neruda, for example, it seems to me, is a man of essential modesty, or his poetry, you could say, is the poetry of a man of essential modesty in the way he thinks about himself, but of great, wonderful immodesty in his use of language, particularly imagery.

*I didn't get hold of* Stars Which See, Stars Which Do Not See *until I came here and then I read through the first few poems and didn't understand them, but when I went back and reread them, they all seemed very clear. I've never had that kind of experience with poems before.*

I would guess that it's just because the first time reading through, the other person's mind, if it's somewhat eccentric, you don't know what direction it's going, so each time you're yanked along. After you've read it once, you have a sense of where it's going. I'm just guessing. There were two full-length books in between *A Probable Volume of Dreams* and *Stars Which See, Stars Which Do Not See.* As I said before, they were different from one another. The one that followed *A Probable Volume of Dreams* is called *The Escape into You,* a book-length sequence. Some of those poems are difficult; but they're very intense, almost tortured sometimes. It's a very different thing from the book that preceded it. And indeed the book that follows it, *Residue of Song,* is, as the title might suggest, almost antipoetic. It's full of stuff that is aggressively antipoetic in life, including a poem called "Shit."

*I was going to read all of it, but when I started reading* Stars *I just kept reading that over and over again.*

Did you get all the way through?

*Oh sure, a couple of times.*

Good. I'm glad. I like that book. It's not that I don't like all my books, and I do even read them sometimes, but if I had to, I would be happy to have that book represent the way I wrote at one point for a long time. I like it. It feels good somehow. (Laughter.) But now I have a new book ready; but it won't come out until next September, probably because I messed around with it for so long.

*You've mentioned that your notion of poetry has changed. How?*

It's hard for me to say just how my notion of poetry has changed, partly because it's difficult for me to pin down, partly because it's still developing, partly because I don't want to preempt the poems that will occur by talking about it; but I'm willing to try to the extent that I know. I think one learns to write interestingly, if not well, by abandoning oneself to the materials, the actual materials of language. One discovers content. Like the little old lady who's supposed to have gone up to E. M. Forster at a writers' conference and said, "How do I know what I think till I see what I say?" That's the way poetry works. One didn't know one knew such things. And I do think that's the way young poets should go about it, that they should love language more than they love ideas at the moment that they're writing poetry, because ideas are not only valuable for what they are, they're preemptive in terms of other possibilities. So a kind of exploration and abandonment to the materials is really helpful. I've always felt that. When I was working with clay or with photographic plates and chemicals or cornet, I always wanted to do what the medium could do. I wanted to play in the way the cornet could play; well, that was easy to do because the cornet is a singular instrument. I wanted to use the materials of the clay in making pots and, of course, any potter does really use the inherent qualities of the clay and bring them to the forefront. There's another way which I think is perhaps more appropriate, perhaps only possible to an older person who has written for a while, somebody who has reached middle age, at least, and that is to somehow come at the poem from an area that is prior to language and has to do with imagination and emotion and perhaps the visualization of what it is one is remembering or actually seeing or predicting. It's almost as if the seesaw was formerly slightly down on the form side and on the side of materials as opposed to subject or content, and then it's either more balanced or even slightly down on the side of content. Now this is a dangerous distinction to make because form and content are inextricable even in bad writing and in good writing the inextricability becomes part of the substance. It creates substance, creates content. It articulates things which couldn't be articulated otherwise.

*I'm thinking all the time about the difference between writing poetry and doing academic writing. I've come to think that academics tend to shut off their feelings, or are people who shut off their feelings at an early age.*

That's right.

*They get down to their feelings in convoluted ways. For instance, I'm sure that my obsessions are embodied in the people that I choose to write about.*

Right. Academic writing is more of a process of exclusion. The "problem" is probably the right word for the kind of writing one does for *PMLA* or *Notes and Queries* or *Philological Quarterly* or whatever, or even for the *New York Review of Books*, God help us, or *The New York Times Book Review*, God help us. It is writing in which an elephant can't appear suddenly. But in a poem, an elephant can appear anytime one chooses and one can use the elephant. There's a great deal of preemptive activity that goes on in writing criticism and reviews. There's a lot that is preempted, whereas in writing poetry, I think, one accepts and accepts and accepts as much as possible and then tries to make use of it. And for me the process of revising a poem, except for matters of clarity, has become the process of accepting what's there and learning how to make it all of a piece. And that's one of the difficulties in teaching a writing workshop. It's so much easier to cut a poem down and make it smaller, but better, than it is to see what it was trying to be that was bigger, which can't be achieved by anything that we do in class, but which should be kept in mind if the poet is ever going to amount to anything bigger.

The poet is really giving himself or herself over to the process and then counting on recognizing and working with what emerges during the poem, but even more so, in my case at least, afterwards. So revision is partly a question of recognition of what's there. That makes perfect sense to me because of all those years I put in as what used to be called a "creative photographer." One of the things one does is to snap the shutter and then go study the negative in a darkroom. And there are great photographers who have insisted that the only true way to be a photographer is to previsualize everything, to see it in a ground glass perfectly and then to print the entire negative just as you photographed it. And indeed, I respect that view and often did it that way. But there is another way, and that is to have an intuitive sense of things which carries one into the photographic subject matter and then to work in the darkroom to see what it is one has.

*And poets are more like that.*

Poets do that. That's what they do. Not all of them; there are some people who are very formal and very organized and who succeed in writing wonderful poems this way. But even they are more engaged with the process of their writing poetry than one would normally be in writing essays.

*Is it easier for you to write essays than poems?*

Well, I used to write reviews years ago that were described to me by a friend as very Johnsonian and I did labor over them. Then I quit reviewing deliberately. In fact, I reneged on several commitments. And then I was convinced to write again, and I began to write that series of essays in *The American Poetry Review* and other things, and I decided that I would pretty much write essays when called upon. Whatever the subject given to me was, that's what I would start from. In a sense, it would be very much like writing poems; I would let myself go forward in a conversational way, letting whatever came to mind come to mind, and trying to make a whole out of it. So, I write very informal prose and as I warned a couple of people who've asked me to propose them books, if I put a whole book's worth of it together, I'll probably transcend informality and approach inelegance. But that's the way I want to write. I don't want to give my time over to writing a more structured, elegant, formal, intricate prose. I think there's a lot going on, because of the style I'm writing in, that wouldn't go on otherwise. That's my hope. And it's much more fun this way. It is like once again abandoning oneself to the process.

# "Self" Is a Very Iffy Word for Me

*(The following interview took place on August 18, 1980, at Bread Loaf. The interviewer is Richard Jackson, editor of* The Poetry Miscellany, *published in Chattanooga, Tennessee.)*

*In one of his notebook entries, Roethke exclaims: "Make the language take really desperate leaps." I'd like to put some of your own lines next to that. In "The Self-Made Man" you talk about "a mixture of alphabets, unrolling and unfolding / from all directions." In "To No One in Particular" you say: "I speak to you in one tongue, / but every moment that ever mattered to me / occurred in another language." More recently, in "The Canal at Rye," you say: "The natural end and extension / of language / is nonsense." Now these citations simply codify a tendency in your poetry towards leaps, ellipses, shifts, fragments of scenes and stories—things that make up the grammar and syntax of your poetics. Earlier, the language moved by more intense, local effects like puns, and lately the movement is more a stream of larger elements as in, say, "Birds Who Nest in the Garage." Though the irrational element, the leaps, are still present, there is a greater self-assurance in the newer poems. In "The Hedgeapple," for instance, where the fragmented narrative, the attitudes towards the woman, the discussion of the tree itself, the sense of self-realization, come together in a more expansive way than you could have achieved earlier in the more close-fisted language of the first four volumes.*

This is a good question for me at this time because my language is undergoing a change as you suggest. I did teach myself to write mostly by abandoning myself to the language, seeing what it wanted to say to me. That way, I could find out not only about language, but about my self which was, and probably remains, a bundle of inherent contradictions and paradoxes. Now what poetry can do, what it reveals, is always tied to language, but it also depends on transcending the language, going further than most ordinary language. The lines you quoted reminded me of how often I've distrusted language, how much I have wanted my poetry to express what is inexpressible. How does one get at the inexpressible? I suppose by letting the poem respond to the implications of words and phrases, by shifting contexts so that words and phrases take on an irrational or arational sense.

Most of the early poems use a language that turns on itself to ask whether they can say what it has said, or to question what it means. That listening to itself, responding to itself, in the language of those poems is a way of making the poems whole and less and less paraphrasable. Now, *Residue of Song*, as the title suggests, is an almost antipoetic book, and from there I was able to write the poems of *Stars Which See, Stars Which Do Not See*, which is the best of those books, one where the poems are most opened up. Yet I still think of them as beginner's books. Ever since *Stars Which See*, though, I have been trying to redefine the poetic imagination and its language. Perhaps there's a self-assurance, as you suggest, a willingness to bring in bigger pieces of the world and not have to try to tie every little bit together. I'm embarked on a risky experiment to see how much of poetry can be sensual and imaginative, and not verbal first. That is, how much can the materials of poetry include the preverbal? There is a James Wright poem that contains the line, "I have heard weeping in secret." Without considering the special context of that line, we can say that it touches the essence of poetic imagination. We've all heard weeping and secrets behind doors. The problem for the poet, though, is how to use this elusive material, how to make it part of his sensibility at that moment in that poem. The whole history of poetry turns out to be a history of poets finding ways to incorporate what was thought to be nonliterary or secret material into their styles and content. There is always an undercurrent, the mystery. In the poem "Stars Which See, Stars Which Do Not See" the glassy surface of the mirrorlike water and its promise must break because things are not what they appear to be; there is always something more, different, an additional reflection, a secret. It involves the preverbal realm, and it is this realm the newer poems try to appropriate.

*Your lines have also loosened up, become more spacious. In the light of what you just said about language, how do you conceive of the play between words, lines, phrases, and sentences?*

There has been a lot of talk about the line. One of the problems free verse has had is that many poets feel it should distinguish itself with special effects, particularly in its line breaks. In those cases the line has become too important. If you're just going for effects, for interruptions of the natural phrase to show off what can be done, then perhaps you are syncopating, jazzing, surprising the reader too much. Perhaps you should opt for a more seamless verse. The line length has to hold hands in some sense with the phrase. We should remember Pound's admonition: "As regarding rhythm: to compose in the sequence of the musical phrase, not in the sequence of the metronome." I think the musical analogy is crucial, for I do think there is something called an "ear" and that free verse depends on this ear. It is intuitive. It has to do with responding to different kinds of music and speech rhythms. I like speech rhythms myself, that is, a language which is opposed to what we can only imagine as written. Poems in other words, are not written by word; they're written by phrase.

*This seamless verse reminds me of the way Williams' "Asphodel" strings out its sentences.*

Oh yes, all kinds of sentences, all kinds! Sometimes he had to invent punctuation marks, like the comma followed by the dash. Williams was such a virtuoso with syntax; the line itself means nothing to him; only its relation to syntax has meaning.

*Well, let's talk a little about the relation between language and meaning. There's still a kind of undecidability in your poems—not the early intense questioning, but a playful undercutting. I'm thinking, for example, of "Life" where the letter that is sent out like a poem contains "the spot in which it wasn't clear, perhaps, / how to take my words, which were suggestive, / the paragraph in which the names of flowers, / ostensibly to indicate travel, / make a bed for lovers." The problem is one of referentiality. "Yet what the symbol is to the flower / the flower itself is to something or other" you say in "What Lasts." And in "The Hole in the Sea" there is that "one word" that lies "in the hole of the sea," with a pun on whole, "where the solid truth lies."*

I suppose part of this problem goes back to my suspicion about language. You can't separate language and content. I've always secretly considered myself a poet of content, and still do, less and less secretly. It is curious that so much critical attention has been lavished in recent years upon poets whose poetry has *no* content. I think that sometimes teachers want their activity to be safe from philosophical and other concerns. The perfect tautology, the sweet song of nothing, has always been better received because it is safe. Several poets of my own generation, for instance, write beautiful, jewel-like tautologies; these poets are practitioners of a limited aesthetic. But the rough piece can get at the impure world better. Picasso said, and then Stein picked it up, that "works of genius are always ugly." Part of the problem is that critics don't often see the buried metaphors, the richness, of colloquial language. They don't see the special precision of it, only a folksy translation of what they prefer to be elegantly said. But the colloquial language can hold a great deal of "meaning."

I have the feeling that American poetry can go on writing the same poem over and over again, that many of the vessels we're using just aren't going to save us anymore. It is going to take an enormous effort to break those vessels. For example,

I've greatly admired Wright's *Two Citizens* and *To a Blossoming Pear Tree*, and Kinnell's latest work, but these poets have gotten progressively worse reviews. Wright was accused of being too sentimental; emotional, passionate—yes; but sentimental in the sense of emotion in excess of event? No, I don't think so.

*In an interview in 1966 you said: "I write to make discoveries and inventions, as a necessary strategy to get things said . . . I write to change my life." There's a sense of the self defining itself by speech, by passing beyond itself. I think of Stevens' "The Well Dressed Man With a Beard"—"a speech / Of the self that must sustain itself on speech." What seems important is not the statement but the saying. This leaves us with the strange relation of the poet to his material; as you say in "We Have Known" about poems—"If very little / can pass through them, know that I did, / and made them, and finally did not need them." More recently, in "Haleakala Crater, Maui,"—"I wanted something beyond me." So let's talk some about writing and the self.*

One can labor for years, as Eliot said, to get a thing just right, and then discover that it's not the thing one wants to say anymore. Poetry is often talked about as a grapple with the mind for that very reason; the mind doesn't hold still for anyone. What we have in the end is an exhibit of "passage," as Eliot calls it in the *Quartets*, something that came out on the way to something else. One has to be careful here, careful about the voice, careful not to use this idea as an excuse for bad writing. Half the battle may be knowing who you are at a given time.

When I made the statement, "I write to change my life," I had just articulated many motives for writing, and that one sort of encompassed the others. I think of Auden's line, "Poetry makes nothing happen"—I don't believe that. I believe poetry changes individual consciousness. When I read back over my poems I do see a person who has changed, though it would be hard to say how much the poems changed the person and how much the changes led to different poems. No one can know. I believe, at least, that there's a great benefit in doing anything seriously for a long time, and I'm not sure it matters what. Poetry can become a way of life. For me, writing poetry *is* a way of life, indeed down to my metabolic needs. I can't go very long without writing and not become crabby, hard to live with. I always feel better when I write, when I go to my study out back under the wild cherry tree. It only takes a few minutes before I say, "Why didn't I come out here sooner?" It feels wonderful! It's almost as if now I'd like to reserve the term "poetry" for a quality of imagination which is beyond technical analysis.

*The self always seems at some threshold, always about to fade even as it begins to emerge. In "Trinket" in* Stars Which See *you watch the water ooze through a crack in the pot and say it is this "that gives the self / the notion of the self / one is always losing / until these tiny embodiments."*

It is true that I think of the self as very small, and it is true that I think what can be known about the self it is possible to know mostly by looking outside the self, and not into mirrors. There's an essay by Rilke about Rodin in which he talks about Rodin becoming a great artist whose every moment was caught up in the greatness of his art. When he begins to describe the sculpture in terms of surfaces he realizes what the implications of that are and says—"okay, I've been talking about surfaces, but isn't everything we know about life a matter of surfaces?" Poetry looks at a surface until depth is achieved, that is, suggestiveness and implication. But we look at the surface, the threshold, nevertheless.

*As if the surface were a transparency?*

Yes, as we were saying before, there's always something more. I believe that about the self, too. "Self" is a very iffy word for me, for in a funny way we are self-less. The word has become more problematic to me than "soul." American poetry has been limited in large extent, whatever its achievements are, and they are many and substantial, by two characteristics. First, I think that our technology is translated into a belief in technique in literature for its own sake. Second, there's a terrible burden, which the first characteristic often hides, that the self can expand, optimistically, to legislate what is right for other selves, whether they want it or not. America has always been a country with a vision, even if the vision may have been built on self-deception, manipulation, imperialism, commerce, self-interest, whatever. The vision is always translated into a myth, a moral imperative. It is this sense of vision which defines that American self, and perhaps accounts for a blind faith in that technology/technique which is the means of achieving that vision.

*In "The Self and the Mulberry" you say "I kept losing parts of myself like a soft maple," then decide "That was the end / of looking in nature to find a natural self." But one keeps hearing the children's ditty, and realizes how they define themselves in the group game and in the saying of that song. That tension about the self seems to be the motivating force in the poem, perhaps throughout* Stars Which See.

That's terrific. I never thought of that. Well, I keep making a distinction between what we make of nature and what nature is in its indifference. Nature is not a phenomenon with a consciousness, though we often treat it that way—hence the title, *Stars Which See, Stars Which Do Not See*. We look at the stars and they seem to look back. What are they? They may even be long dead as their light reaches us. We seem compelled to speculate. In the Mulberry poem the distinction is whether we see the mirror or nature itself when we look at it.

*How does a poem like your recent "Late Naps" fit into this problematic sense of the self and its world? Specifically it deals with the soul, though in a comic way.*

It's a poem about going to bed with a bad feeling: one takes a late afternoon nap with a sense of things still nagging, incomplete, done poorly. Anything can cause the bad dreams—"the dreamworks run on an oil so light, / it can be distilled from thin air." One thinks of the soul as laughable, as something that can hover in the air like a ghost, as insignificant but yet mysterious, as something that slips away in dream and yet haunts, nags like those bad feelings. We're weakest when the soul floats up and away, most vulnerable to discontent. The poem doesn't really engage so much the question of the soul as much as a certain kind of spiritual discontent—a spiritual pit in the stomach.

*That sense of the soul going out suggests the notion of the Other. There is, for example, the play of self and Other in* The Escape into You, *of self and divorced self. And in "The Perfection of Dentistry" you see things, as it were, through the caretaker, and "lead his concurrent lives." I think, too, of the recent poem, "Someone is Probably Dead"— "It's stupid to pretend we can be someone else, / when someone else is dead."*

Well, "The Perfection of Dentistry" tries to find a way to see those lives concurring, one life taking place in another. We're all linked that way through imagination. I'm reminded of a poem in a forthcoming book called "A Motor" where the speaker identifies with someone who is up in a light plane and who is probably coming down to go to a hospital for cancer treatment. The poem ends, "Myself in the clinic for runaway cells, / Now and later." The other here involves a possibility in the future as well as a certain sympathetic understanding now. But then there is the other side of the coin. There is Pindar's famous question which I use in the title of a prose poem, "What Are We? What Are We Not?" Rather than finding ourselves in others, there may be no others, no selves.

*The way you use the "you" is perhaps as elusive as this Other. How do you conceive of the Other that is represented by "you?"*

I've tried not to use "you" to mean "one," though I perhaps have sometimes done it ill-advisedly. I'm really addressing someone I know when I use it though the reader may not be sure of whom. "The Canal at Rye," meaning Rye, England, where Henry James lived for a while, begins: "Don't let them tell you." Later in the poem you can figure out that "you" has to be a child of the speaker. Now someone like David St. John writes a poetry that is always fiercely intimate; it seems to depend heavily on addressing a someone as if that person was anxious to be addressed.

*Let's extend this notion of otherness even farther, to other times. To what extent does a consciousness of the past or history enter your poems? In "To His Solitary Reader" you say: "Memory is what we are." In some poems, such as "Virtuoso of the X," history intrudes in images like: "an aroma of gas remains in the showers." At the same time, this is not a cheap or nostalgic sense of the past, but a way of presencing it, as in "Father and Russia" where you repeat "you" as if to presence him: "Now I want you as you were before they hurt you, / irreparably as you were as in another country."*

It may be that memory *is* the sum total of our experiences, but it may also be that poetry includes memory and loss too easily. There's always the danger of nostalgia, a poetic attitude we ought to be a little more careful about—a certain tilt of the head, a certain longing look backwards. Now I did set out to write a book-length series of poems to my father who was already dead at the time. I thought of myself as completing a conversation that never took place because he was a father who didn't speak about many things. It became a sequence of only thirteen poems in *Residue of Song*. I was conscious of the danger of poetic nostalgia. Even the past tense has an aura about it. I like to write more in the present tense, or to write in what one might call the immediate past tense in which things haven't happened so long ago that one has to question "when?" In some ways the poems are about possession. As in the poem where the three people pause for a moment at the edge of the road to look at some hedgeapples. When the lady appears at the screen we suddenly feel as if we are spying, trying to take possession of something. Though we didn't take any hedgeapples, we felt as if we had.

*Your sense of time, generally, is a dynamic one. Time becomes a futural thing, something we have to structure for ourselves. In some sense this is possible, I think, because you think of time as disguise; in "New Stu-*

*dents" you talk about a "shapeless universe disguised as time." It's also a matter of point of view; in "Dew at the Edge of a Leaf" you have the lines: "Everything green is turning brown, / it's true, but then too / everything turning brown is green!"*

I really do believe that time is an illusion. I can conceive of a gigantic scientific breakthrough that would see through time by seeing into material. The idea of space travel today is senseless. You put up a few people in a capsule and they have children and their children do and so on until whoever arrives whenever doesn't know where they came from and are at a place they don't want to be. So, the only way to go from one place to another on that scale would be to defeat time, perhaps through cybernetics, by changing matter. It would be like turning on your TV and actually having the thing before you, not some representation that is always trapped by time. The poem, "Viet Nam," from *Residue of Song*, opens by saying "Viet Nam / is a place you will hear of / 'in the future,' / which is not to say tomorrow merely." When you think of time in terms of a memento or two, a nostalgic memory from the past, something the clock has marked as ended, you reduce time. There is something larger—"Though we know better about time, / we know nothing about peace, / which is a function of time and war." Time is not a form, but a content; it has to do with material.

*And it has to do with presencing that otherness. I was just thinking how often the word "elsewhere" or something like it occurs in your poems. It suggests something of the inexpressible, the secrecy, the otherness we've been discussing.*

Yes, elsewhere. In fact, I almost gave *Stars Which See* a different title—*Poems Which Come From Elsewhere.*

*The elsewhere occurs in "The Hedgeapple" as the place you'd wish you'd gone back to. The refrain, "We should have gone back," keeps appearing at regular intervals. And yet, the poem itself is a going back, a fulfillment of the opening line, "I wish we'd gone back." The else-*

*where is perhaps that preverbal space, but here made present, brought back into the time of the poem. The second half of the poem becomes more authoritative, at least relative to the questioning and subjunctive moods of the first half, almost as if you were going to say, "Okay, this is how it is," and then you end audaciously,: "So: here." You've taken the elsewhere and presenced it, denied, undercut the refrain and opening line. It's like the old gossip who says: "I never should have repeated that story." Of course she has to, again and again.*

Yes, I agree with all you've said, but more compelling is your example. As soon as you say that, I'm interested in it; I want to use that line. That's terrific. What an opening line—"I never should have repeated that story." That to me is where poetry is. How could you not read the next line in a poem that began that way? That works like the opening of Wright's "The Old WPA Swimming Pool in Martins Ferry, Ohio"—"I am almost afraid to write down / This thing." You have to read on. There's so much urgency, so much private power, such a sense of secrecy. Once you've said that line, you've got to write it down.

# If a Poem Is Only Music, What Chance Does It Have?

*(The following interview took place on June 12 and 19, 1981, in the offices of* The Iowa Review. *The interviewers are Lowell Edwin Folsom, David Groff, David Hamilton, Adalaide Morris and Fredrick Woodard. This excerpt picks up the conversation three-fourths of the way into the first session.)*

*When you were putting together* These Green-Going-to-Yellow, *when did you decide that that would be the title poem?*

I'm afraid I have to admit that I thought it would be the title when I wrote the poem. I thought, "This has got to be the title of the book."

*Why is that?*

It sounds relevant for its content, but really I was in love with it as a phrase. It's an odd phrase. I've always liked titles that are odd.

*And it seems appropriate, because in this book you appear to be more content to be in the middle of things. So many of these poems begin and stay in the middle of a situation. They're kind of green-going-to-yellow poems, in a number of ways. And it's a middle life book.*

I hope you're right. That is, I hope it turns out to have been only the middle of my life.

*The poems in the middle section go back to something you used to do a lot but didn't do at all, I think, in* Stars Which See—*titles that move directly into the first line.*

I like titles which offer a little surprise in the space between the title and the first line. One of the surprises can turn out to be that the poem has already begun. Another thing you asked before was how a poem begins for me and, as is the case with most poets, most poems begin from a phrase. Sometimes that phrase is the title.

*"These Green-Going-to-Yellow . . ."*

No, no. There the phrase comes out of the middle of the poem.

*One of the most surprising titles for me is "A Motor."*

I also like off-handed titles, when the poem weighs a lot, somehow. This is a poem that is very serious and goes on for some ways. It begins with the sound of a plane in the air—a motor. Of course, it must have more emotional resonance than that or one wouldn't keep it; and you can come up with as many connotations for it as I can. We all contain a kind of biological motor that can give out. I found a title for an old poem this morning which I would have put in this book if I could have finished it. I changed two or three words and redid the last sentence; and I found a title in the middle of the poem after I had changed one word. I changed "water" to "winter." Then I had the title; it comes over parts of two lines: "Feet in Winter, Head in the Sun." It's a poem in which I'm standing out in the backyard thinking about something that happened when I was a kid. I used to go to Yankee Stadium for double-headers, thanks to an old lady I knew named Jessie Quince who had been a rabid New York Yankee fan. She had once lived in an apartment building with Bill Dickey and Frank Crosetti and a lot of the great Yankees from that time. She worked for my father—she was another odd duck. She was divorced, which was almost unheard of; no one knew a divorced person where I came from. Her house had burned down and so she had put a tar roof over her basement, and she lived in the basement. She had no intention of rebuilding her house; the basement was all the room she needed. She had a coin collection at the time her house burned down. Every once in a while she'd give me some coins, some of which would have been melted from the fire—wonderful. Every year for my birthday, she'd take me to a double-header at Yankee Stadium. And, sometimes, I would stand outside by the clubhouse afterwards hoping DiMaggio or, at least, Snuffy Stirnweiss would come out and I could get an autograph. One day there was a swarming and a worried-looking policeman but it was only—and you must remember that I was a young boy—it was only Humphrey Bogart and Lauren Bacall. But, in the poem, as I stand out back, listening to the gutters rumble with thawing snow, Bogart's face comes back, with all its ugliness, rather than the heroes' faces. So, I'm standing there in the water; it's a three-day-old snow, just melting. So, I changed the word "water" to "winter." Instead of standing in water, I'm now standing in winter. It's mythic.

*But in finding that word, in finding "winter," you were controlled by the dimensions of the first word, rhythmically and in sound.*

Oh, yeah; one of the tricks is to forget that damn first word. You're right. It's hard to substitute for a word a word that contains more syllables. Unless you've made a rhythmic mistake in the first place. Sometimes all it takes is a word or two words or three words to fix up a poem, or one word here and two words there. A great portion of the process of revision, for me, is letting enough time elapse so that I arrive at the point at which the poem has already arrived, so that I can see it and accept it for what it is. Before that, my revision tends to be a strain; it tends to be a violent changing of the poem, which won't work. I have to let poems lay around. Do poems lay around or lie around? I should have been an English major.

*They lay around, naturally.*

Most poems lay around. You guys don't know it, but I published a poem in Kim Merker's limited edition, *Things We Dreamt We Died For*, which is called "What I Did in Paris in the Twenties" and the first line is "I lay around."

*That may be saying more than you meant to say.*

Or I may have meant everything it says. Paris in the twenties was very exciting.

*The most muted aspect of your poetry for me is its music, as opposed to the modulation of a speaking voice. You seem to cultivate an odd duck's way of talking about whatever is around.*

I'm trying to use a voice that *is* a voice, not of the page but of the vocal chords, a voice one can hear.

*I find that particularly evident in this book. I mean, this book seems to be held together by that voice. In every poem, I can hear that same voice telling me the poem, whereas, in* Stars Which See, *I heard very different voices. Even when the pace picks up here, I hear the same voice tell the poems.*

I hope you're right.

*And it has a certain social validity to it; that is, it's not anybody else's voice.*

If that's true, then I'm lucky. *Stars Which See, Stars Which Do Not See* is a pretty book even when it's quarrelling with the reader, or with the self, or with concepts. Its poems are beautiful, even elegant. And I knew that. I'm pleased with its being like that. But the poems I have written since are not pretty in that sense. They have to be authenticated by means of the voice and by means of the physical evidence of the world that each poem offers. If they are not, they'll fall on their faces.

*Was there a period you went through after* Stars *when you were not writing much?*

It's happened after every book. Boy, how I wish it wouldn't. But it happened after this book, too; an involuntary silence.

*Are you waiting for that voice to clear away?*

I think that must be part of it. It's hard not to write a poem that sounds like what you've been writing. I am beginning to write again.

*Do you have steady habits of writing, times of day?*

I wish I did. I think it's good for people to have such habits. I don't. I tend to boil over on my own schedule, an erratic schedule. All I can be sure of is that I love to write when I'm writing. It just plain feels good; I enjoy it. That is, if poems worth saving are coming out. I want the mind to be doing things, somehow, things it can only do in poems. Whatever they are.

*What are they?*

I was trying to escape. You know, Williams says in the beginning of "Asphodel"; he says, "It is difficult / to get the news from poems / yet men die miserably every day / for lack / of what is found there." And, of course, those are ironic lines because the man who's going to die if news can't be found in poems is Williams, in this case, because he's trying to confess something. And he wants it understood and he wants it accepted. In fact, he wants to be patted on the head and told, "That's all right, dear, I love you anyway." But I should add that somewhere else Williams says something about finding truth only in poems. I believe that there's some area of truth that *can* only be found in poems. I really believe that. Again, maybe it's just in my nature to believe that. Remember, I always like things which are instructional, even corrective. I always like things which constitute a moral engagement with the world or, at least, an interest in ethics. So, it may just be in my nature.

*Here we go back to content again.*

It's the crust of the poem; I mean, if a poem is only music, what chance does it have? Music is better music. That the poem aspires to the condition of music is, to me—forgive me—a limited notion of poetry. I think it aspires to something else.

*Off and on, in casual conversation, you have made remarks like, "That's poetry." "That's not poetry." "You can tell that's a line of poetry." "That's prose." I wonder when you're making judgments like that . . .*

Poetry has something to do with a quality of imagination, I think. Now, it can be bad poetry. But, when I say, "That's poetry," or "That's not poetry," I'm making a distinction of genre. Okay? It can be slight poetry. It can be useless poetry. For example—and I know this is heresy—but I think many of the ideas in the poetry of Wallace Stevens, who was considered a poet of ideas, to be essentially useless ideas. That's a whole category of ideas in my thinking: *useless ideas*, ideas which aren't ideas at all, unless you wear special glasses. I think that Williams is a much smarter poet than Stevens. I'll get a lot of letters about that. But I think one of the tests of the intelligence is its ability to extend its labors. And where does one extend one's labors? Into the theoretical world that depends on words or into the world of physical evidence? It seems to me far more difficult and profound to extend them into the world of physical evidence.

*That's what you mean by useful, that the ideas connect with what one calls the world?*

Even as I say it, I realize that the word "useful" isn't quite accurate; but, yes, ideas which are at least engaged, somehow, with the physical world.

*Williams is always talking about things being grounded, whereas Stevens is always working up toward or into the blue.*

But Stevens is well organized, as a good executive would have to be. One has the feeling that, if Stevens had given some of his actuarial tables to Williams, Williams would have messed them all up, in some interesting way, and he would have charged everybody the wrong premiums.

*Or he would have incorporated them into a poem.*

That's right. You know the famous interview with Mike Wallace—of all people—he reads a passage from *Paterson* and says, "That sounds like a shopping list." And Williams says, "It is."

*Then there's the report of the well-digging: "two feet of shale and . . ."*

But Williams knew when to stop. In my opinion, Charles Olson didn't know when to stop. Williams always did something with the facts, but Olson's facts took over his mind, I think.

A poet I admire very much among contemporary poets—and it seems difficult, somehow, to mention his name because he died recently—is James Wright. Everybody will be mentioning his name, with good reason. But long before he died I had become terribly involved with poems of his, in several books, particularly *Two Citizens* and *To a Blossoming Pear Tree*. His whole sense of what poetry is appeals to me a great deal.

*Ethical reasons there too, right?*

Well, yeah, though he isn't beset by as much thinking about things as I am. He feels his way through things more than I usually do.

*But there's a moral edge.*

Oh, absolutely, that's right, yeah; indeed, he even says things in poems which pay homage to his readings in the classics and his readings in moralistic texts.

Yeah, well, two of his friends convinced him it was a bad book; but they were wrong. For one thing, that book contains one of the best poems I know, a poem called "The Old WPA Swimming Pool in Martins Ferry, Ohio," which begins, "I am almost afraid to write down / This thing." It's an incredible poem and it's in *Two Citizens.* And there are others, the "Ars Poetica" that begins the book is pretty interesting, I think. He says something very telling in it. He's talking at one point about his Aunt Agnes who is a sloppy woman, a woman one would not be attracted to ordinarily; and he talks about his uncle who's married to her. "He must have been / One of the heroes / Of love," he says, "because he lay down / With my Aunt Agnes / Twice at least." He goes on like that; and, of course, he's setting you up because, as it turns out, a bunch of boys chased a goat one day, and threw stones at it. The goat goes up into an alley and here's Agnes. Agnes gathers the goat up into her arms and protects it. Well, of course, Agnes was terrific. In the same poem, he says at one point, "Reader, / We had a lovely language, / We would not listen."

## PART TWO

*Marvin, you talked about the influence of Dewey; and I've wondered how seriously to take that. I mean, we've talked about the ethical aspect of your poetry. My memory of Dewey and ethics is that Dewey was a pragmatist. After the First World War, most of Dewey's followers thought that ethical element reflected a permutation of New England puritanism; and yet most could agree that his ethics were those of a practical man, as he moved through various ethical considerations, in education, in aesthetics and so on. So when I come back to the business of ethics in your poetry, having your remarks about Dewey to think back on, I want to know what you took from Dewey.*

*I'll tell you why I ask the question: I find a kind of polarity in a lot of your poetry. That is, you'll take a position and then, very soon afterwards, you introduce the opposite of that position. Later, you attempt to*

*make a synthesis in which more questions are asked than are answered.*
*The moral forces governing your work never seem to add up to an*
*absolute position. Rather, your work offers possibilities, let loose with*
*their opposites, in a game of wit and irresolution, leaving to the reader*
*such conclusions as he chooses to make from a dense and tonally reflex-*
*ive language. While one can take seriously an influence from Dewey,*
*ethics seems to me to be more rigid than all that, seems to me to be a kind*
*of order, the manipulation of which adds up to specific judgments as to*
*belief or behavior. If, then, making judgments in the world really adds*
*up to question marks, how can it be said of your poetry that you, as poet,*
*have worked within ethical parameters? Or are you satisfied that any*
*poem is in itself an ethical statement?*

OK, well, that description of some of my poems seems a fair
description. What carries over for me from Dewey is that sense
of being practical. They used to call him "the practical philoso-
pher." On the one hand, he may have been in part a puritan;
he certainly wanted everything to be useful and to produce a
desired result. On the other hand, he would recommend that
the chairs in classrooms not be bolted, which seems mildly
liberating. So, what I think I carry over—not just from Dewey
but from other people who interested me—was a sense of the
usefulness of ideas. In fact, I came to believe—I think I came to
believe—that ideas which are not useful ideas are not actually
ideas. That sounds terrible because we all know that there is
theoretical mathematics as well as applied mathematics; and,
in fact, as a mathematics student, I was always interested in the
theoretical even to the point of trying to disprove theorems—
all those things that kids do. But it seems to me still that there is
such a thing as a useless idea. I think I was saying something
like this last time. And there has been in my poetry, whether
there still is or not I'm not positive, but there has been in my
poetry a strong argumentative or correctional element; and
I've accepted that. That's something many poets would think a
liability. Perhaps I should too; but it's just part of my nature: I
like things to be useful. I like wisdom in poems, I really do. I
continue to like Stafford's poems for the wisdom in them. I
continue to like Williams' poems for the wisdom in them. And

yet I don't feel that poetry depends on wisdom. There are a few of my poems in which, I think, I make statements having directly to do with ethics; the best example may be a poem called, "After the Ducks Went In."

If I look at poems from *These Green-Going-To-Yellow* and look for ethical edges, if you will, or the edges of ethics, perhaps—I am not sure how to articulate it—and yet . . .

*There are quite a few passages in which you seem to have something you want to say; but I am not sure whether you'd think of this as ethical or not. For example, the second poem in the manuscript, "Haleakala Crater, Maui," where you say "It wasn't perfection I wanted, / with its need for form, hollow / unbroken shell, for all we know." That seems to be making a judgment, more likely about poetry and art than about society and social problems, but that kind of definitive statement appears once in a while in your poems. "I know what poetry is" is another one—remember that?*

Oh, yes. That's in "You Can Keep the Sun Out of Your Eyes with Just One Hand." "I know by now that art / is a part of life, and I know which part / it is" and then there was, in an earlier version of the poem, a colon instead of a period and it said, "The arty part." I swear—I swear it was in there. Somebody told me to take it out, and he was right.

*And then you make, in I think a related line, an attractive statement: "I would hope to hell / not to cover my tracks with elegies."*

Right. Some of the statements that I would regard as having an ethical basis have to do with our acts in literature as writers, even as readers.

*I was going to ask, when you mentioned useless ideas, whether you had a sense of the ends toward which your ideas intended to be useful, some selection of ends that interested you more than others.*

Well, my notion of that is too ideal, I think. You know, one way to change society is to cut off the heads of all the people who are in positions of power; but then, inevitably, the people who take their positions grow heads that are strikingly similar. The other way, though it often seems so theoretical, the other way is to change individual consciousness. If artists, writers, teachers of any kind have anything to do with changing the world, that's the way they do it, it seems to me. Now, you know, we're always talking about how little influence serious literature has; on the other hand, someone arguing with me said, "Well, now, there are some books in the libraries of all people who are in positions of power." I hesitate to think what books those might be nowadays, but . . .

You were on a good investigative track when you asked how much involvement with ethics these statements have, which is sometimes not much, but here's another example. At the end of a poem which begins, "He said to / crawl *toward* the machine guns," the poem says, "I made a man / to survive the Army, which means / that I made a man to survive / being a man." Well, that's a position. Is that a useful idea? I suppose it might be to someone who was, say, eighteen, who was thinking of joining the army and thought he would be more manly for it.

*It's fairly common for poets to devalue the literal statement of what's in their poems. Creeley talks in an interview about the literal statement of a poem not being what's principally of value in the poem, although it may matter. That's such a truism about modern poetry, that you're surprising me, somewhat, with the interest you take in having things to say. Even unto aphorisms. Some of your statements have an aphoristic ring to them.*

Well, I've always been interested in statements. In fact I published and edited a literary magazine years ago which was called *statements*. I chose that title deliberately. It lasted for five issues over five years, and each issue was a different size.

*Do you like aphorisms for their own sake?*

I like aphorisms which are metaphysical. I used some in books, you know. "If you can't get up, get down; if you can't get across, get across"—that's a Yiddish proverb, although it sounds like Zen. Or in an early book, one of the two Yiddish proverbs I used was "Dumplings in a dream are not dumplings, but a dream." I mean, that seems to me a hard-nosed distinction that is useful. But I like those kinds of things. My favorite little tale, I don't know what it is—fable I guess—is supposed to be a story they tell in the Mideast. It's about the scorpion and the frog. The scorpion comes to the frog and says, "Give me a ride on your back across the river." The frog says, "Do I look stupid? If I put you on my back, you'll sting me to death." But the scorpion says, "Why would I do that? If I stung you to death, I'd drown." The frog says, "You've got a point there. Hop on," and starts across the river. Halfway across, the scorpion stings the frog. The frog is going into paralysis and says, "What'd you do that for?" And the scorpion sort of shrugs and says, "I don't know. It's the Mideast."

*I heard a story recently that reminds me of the way your poems work. It must be an old joke because I think I remember hearing it before, but you know, coming in the middle of the interview, I was thinking, "Well, that works just like a Marvin Bell poem works." I heard it as a Texas Aggie joke; it could be anything. There were a Frenchman, an Italian, and a Texas Aggie who had been on a large luxury cruiser and the cruiser had sunk and everything had gone down except for one lifeboat, with these three guys in it. And they'd been rowing for days and they were dehydrated and they had no water and no food and they were tired and they were rowing and rowing in the middle of the ocean. Eventually a little bottle floats up to the boat and they look over and the Frenchman leans over and picks the bottle up, pulls the cork out of the bottle and a genie comes out. He says, "I will grant you any wish that you want. Each of you has one wish, any wish." And the Frenchman says, "Mon Dieu, this is marvelous, what luck, what good fortune." He says, "I wish that I were on the Left Bank at a sidewalk café drinking the best French wine." Poof, he's there. The Italian says, "I wish I were in St. Peter's listening to the Pope celebrating Mass." And he's there. The genie looks at the Aggie and says, "And what is your wish?" The Aggie looks around and he says, "I wish to hell those two guys were back here helping me row!"*

That does put the dilemma all right.

*"I wish to hell those two guys were back here helping me row!" There we are. He may be a little dumb, but my god, he's going to have somebody in there helping him row. That Aggie knows damn well he's not a god.*

That is terrific.

*You said that you like wisdom in poetry.*

I confess that I do.

*And yet you said that you don't think poetry depends upon that.*

No. Wisdom by itself is not enough.

*What is most necessary?*

Maybe I could say two things at once. Poetry is a kind of reporting. Stafford has a poem called "Reporting Back" and that's what poetry is. Now if a poet is like me, he has to report back ideas as well as other things because he can't stop having them. Some poets are able to report back without ever stating ideas directly, without statements of any sort in their poetry. It's not part of their normal way of thinking. So, why are those pieces of wisdom—if that's what they are—in the poem? Well, because that's part of the poet's experience, having those ideas and trying to find a place for them or opposing them to other evidence. So . . . poetry depends on reporting something: you're reporting your feelings, you're reporting the place and the plot, you're reporting your ideas.

*But lots of writing can be reporting, so is there something without which poetry cannot be? Don Justice's phrase for it, his phrase for what just had to be there, was "technical virtue." Then he sort of apologized for using the term but came back to it and said "yeah, I really believe that; without that you don't have poetry. At least not very good poetry." I wondered whether there was something, maybe not calling it that. Maybe something quite different . . .*

Well, that seems like a good phrase. I mean there has to be some . . . poetry has to protect its language as it goes along, I think. "Technical virtue," Don's phrase, seems a good phrase for it. There has to be—I mean, maybe that phrase of his takes in not only questions about what is formal, which we might propose, but also questions about what is moral or ethical. "Technical virtue" seems like a wonderful phrase. If he's not using it today I'd like to employ it. Sure, the poem seems to pay attention to itself, if one is technically virtuous, if one's virtue can be seen in one's technique, that is, and if one's technique can be seen in the virtue that is expressed in the poem—that seems a little more difficult to pin down.

*Your poems seem to listen to themselves intently as they go along. I want to ask about the closure of a poem, where you come to rest. "The Hedgeapple," for instance, ends so perfectly—"So: here."*

I hope you're right. I've been worried about that ending ever since I wrote it.

*Oh, I really like that. I keep coming back to it. As against "So there."*

Right. I guess that sums up a number of the ideas swirling about in the poem. One is that "the language we spoke seemed to make light everywhere / because we stopped to look," so we were lucky—the poem actually says, "We were lucky," the three of us, look: here we had this social interchange going around about this hedgeapple. The good thing that emerges from this has to do with the three of us sharing the experience and even talking about it. The hedgeapple is perfect by itself and doesn't require us. In the end there's another idea and that is about who owns this hedgeapple. "We thought we didn't take her hedgeapple," the poem says, and then right away it says, "We should have given it back." We didn't take it but in a sense we did. We used it, and we didn't include the woman in that act of possession. So I can't give her the hedgeapple back, it's her hedgeapple, how can I give it back to her? And furthermore, I'm no longer there. But I can give her (and you) this that we made out of the hedgeapple, which is now another form of the hedgeapple. "So: here."

*It's a wonderful opening to the book. Because that's what every poem does, right?*

Exactly. That's why I put it first.

*There's a very interesting way in which in that poem the word "light" becomes radiant itself. You begin to collect all the possibilities. Radiance, I mean, it's almost as if the poem is itself a gesture making light of that situation but the light is also reflective of an inner knowledge that the poem allows for the three involved in that experience. "Light" becomes one of your most repeated words in the volume.*

There's a lot of light there, yeah. I don't know if that's because light is everywhere or if it's because I grew up on fairly flat land and now live again on fairly flat land.

*There's also lightness, deftness. That wisdom that we keep talking about could come across as heavy, heavy-footed—but it never does because there's a kind of "making light" in the poetry.*
*Let's return to your talk last time about writing experimentally. I'd like to get you to say more about the nature of your experimentalism and where it's led you.*

Well, I don't want to claim too much, and it's hard to put one's finger on it for sure, I guess, but for me it has mostly to do with content and what is acceptable in a poem and how a poem can think, how it can stop and start up again, what directions—along the periphery of whatever is central to it—it can accept new things from, and so forth. Experiments are tests, right?

And so the poem is, for me at least, a kind of test. It's a test of whatever began the poem, whether an image, a piece of language, a phrase, or a sentence or even a statement. By writing the poem I'm testing what I came with.

*Testing it to see how it can connect with something else?*

To see if it really was something. To see what it connects to. What the context of it was. It's as if a new—I'm not trying to make up metaphors for it now—but it's as if you found a piece of something and were not able to identify it. So now you try to put it in different contexts and run experiments on it to see what it is, to find out what it is.

*Just to tie this for a minute with the ends of the poems, it seems to me that a lot of times at the end of the poem you've taken the piece and put it in a certain puzzle. Now you've found some sort of coherence. The end will often be taking that puzzle piece and putting it in place where it works in one or two contexts at once.*

That makes sense to me, yeah. To find the place where something belongs: as I say, that doesn't correspond to any established meaning of "experimental" but . . .

*One of the questions you must always be asking, then, is how will this poem extend itself? One of the poems I am very fond of is the one called "The Canal at Rye." It begins and makes a change that raises that question.*

I almost didn't put that poem in the book because it becomes so full of statements, so rhetorical and so bald, in a sense, at the end. I do like it—it's not that I didn't like it—but I began to feel scared. . . . But it feels right. The poem says, "Don't let them tell you—/ the women or the men—/ they knew me. / *You* knew me. / Don't let them tell you / I didn't love your mother. / I loved her. / Or let them tell you." Well, now, that's not a poem, that much, so what comes next? I don't think more such statements can follow.

*It's the two opening gambits, though, of a lot of the poems: Statement X, elaborate a little, Statement Y, elaborate a little, and where the poems "make light," is in a third move.*

That's right. Either way would not mean much: let them tell you, don't let them tell you . . . so what? What does all that matter? But I know that when I wrote the line, "Do you remember Rye," and began to describe this wonderful canal that's so thin because the water has receded and the sailboats have to go out single-file in the morning . . . when I said "Do you remember Rye," I didn't know what was going to come next; maybe nothing. But I do implicitly . . . I do believe, in fact, that anything can be connected, and I don't even mean it *can* be connected, I mean that it *is* connected: all things are connected if one can just find the path from one thing to another without going all the way around the world, as it were, without including every possible thing. So I went on with the description for a while; I mean things do progress out that canal. . . .

*So you take the scenic route between two points, not necessarily the shortest.*

Well, not the shortest, but the one that will let you arrive at the right place, or at a place worth arriving at, but not until you're ready to arrive there. Imagine someone being told to "go out and become a man" or "go out and become a woman" and you have to end up in this other town, but you can't get there until four years have passed. It's an old story, of course. But this poem begins to talk about a great novelist who lived in Rye, and of course at the end of the poem, if one doesn't know, one will find out that it was Henry James. Henry James wrote books that are not widely read anymore, at least outside of the university. One of the reasons they're thought difficult, and by some people no doubt unworthy, is that the sentences are so long; and as you know, as James got older and began to dictate his books his sentences got even longer, because it was so much easier to just walk around the room dictating longer and longer sentences. After a while there was no need for the sentence ever to stop. Okay, so "Not many will be reading / his long sentences." And there's kind of an implication, I guess, whoever's being addressed in this poem is being told, "Well, don't let them tell you," or "Let them tell you"—none of that matters; here's another way to think about me.

"Sentence" can cut two ways here. Of course, syntax is logic—that's part of what that means. "There are reasons / not to, reasons too / to believe or not to. But / reasons do not complete an argument. / The natural end and extension / of language / is nonsense." It's true; if language is pushed sufficiently far it turns into nonsense, no matter how sensible it was in the beginning. We see that in certain schools of criticism, we might add. "Yet there is safety / only there," the poem goes on to say; "That is why Mr. Henry James / wrote that way—/ out with the tide"—like those sailboats that went out the canal in Rye—"but further." In language one can go further in some directions than one can ever go in one's physical life. I feel as if maybe I'm squashing it by summarizing it.

*So many of your poems seem to begin in impatience, or a sort of rebellion. . .*

Yeah . . .

*. . . and end with a kind of ambiguity that you can accept.*

Absolutely.

*The gesture is "No, not that" and "No, not this"—BUT—and then a long suspension. They end often in gentleness, with an acceptance of ambiguity. It's as if you work what seems to be a dichotomy into an acceptable blur, one you feel you can live with. It's as if there's been a softening of the mood, from abruptness to calmness, at the end of the poems. That's not the way they all work, but many of them do.*

I think that's a wise remark. I have been thinking lately that maybe I write as if there's a little crisis at the beginning of every poem, and maybe therefore within the poet, I'm not sure. That may be changing.

*The setting of* These Green-Going-to-Yellow *is a much more populous world, a warmer world; the poems are all making connections with other people, and coming to understandings with others rather than the often solitary understandings of* Stars Which See.

There is almost a whole section of this book which contains stories, and for a while I had decided that I would write poems mostly by telling about things that happened. For better or worse, a lot of interesting little things have happened to me, strange little things, like going to Cuba at what proved to be the wrong time, things like that. And I decided to try to put those in poems. After all, one of the secrets of literature every writer knows is that any life will do. It's not necessary to go bathe one's feet in the Ganges and travel around the world and work on a steamer to be a poet, nor is it prohibitive. . . . Meaning is in the small things. That's true, even of architecture.

*One thing I see happening in these new poems that I don't think has happened before in your work, at least not frequently, is that part of the warmth here comes from the way you are continually at play with the reader—"What's the matter? / You don't believe the rain in Paris is red?" "If it happened to you, / maybe you wouldn't know what to say." "I never told you. / There was a woman . . ." or "Don't let them tell you . . . they knew me." There's that "you" that comes so often at the beginning of these poems and is always addressed in a playful way, as if to say that there's something here I'm not about to tell you, but there's something else I* am *about to tell you.*

*Or again that place where you say, in "Things I Took," "Look at stanza one / compared to stanza two. . . ." You step back and say, okay reader, let's take a look at this poem, and let's do a little analysis here; it's kind of interesting, isn't it, the difference between stanza one and stanza two, and what I could have put in one and couldn't put in the other.*

Well, I like intimacy in poems, and I think poems also gain from being addressed to someone, even if the reader doesn't know who that someone is. I think the tone of the poem is helped too, to speak about a smaller thing, perhaps. I like those things; again, to think of the beginning of the James Wright poem that we've already mentioned, "The Old WPA Swimming Pool in Martins Ferry, Ohio," he begins "I am almost afraid to write down / This thing." One can imagine any good teacher saying, "Oh, just cut that stuff out, Jim, and get to it." But enormous intimacy is provided by those lines and, then, you *have* to read on. One of the tests of a first line in a poem is probably, simply, "do you want to read on, or do you want to go out for popcorn."

*There's a kind of trick in these poems that makes you lean into them; it's like* The Secret Sharer *where they have to whisper to each other. The poem starts in a kind of low tone, and you have to lean in to have any relationship with it. One of your more intimate poems, called "The Last Thing I Say," is interesting for several reasons; one is the intimacy of the occasion and the tenderness of the tone. Another, the way it sits playfully, after "The Canal at Rye," where you've said so much about sentences, and then this one turns out to be one long sentence.*

One *hopelessly* long sentence.

*How in the world did you get into that; did you say "I'm going to write a poem all in one sentence"?*

No, there just didn't seem to be any place to stop until the end of the poem. Again, it's just an intuitive sense of things, but once it got going . . . of course some of it's a decision; there are places where there could have been a period, but instead there's a comma. I wanted it all to run together; I wanted many things to happen at once during the moment in which a father closes—in which I, in fact, close my son's bedroom door and say "sweet dreams." Obviously, in any situation in which your emotions are involved you feel many things at once. The sentence is a little complicated.

*You speak in the former poem, "The Canal at Rye," about long sentences, and avoiding long sentences, and then turning back to the sentence, and then you have this sentence poem.*

That's why it's there, sure; also it's "the last thing I say" in section two.

*But not the last thing you say; it's fine having "The Last Thing I Say" not be the last thing you say in the book.*

It was last in the book for a while, but I moved it. That would have been too clever, wouldn't it, if it were last in the book?

*After our first discussion, we were talking and you said that as you were thinking more about where the origins of your poems were, you noted that one thing you hadn't said which you think is true is that the origin of many of your poems is in letters you write to friends.*

Well, to this extent: when I'm writing, I feel like writing. The opposite of that is true, too, unfortunately. And if I'm writing letters to friends—I tend to write fast; I type with two fingers, which allows me to type as fast as I can, and so if I'm writing a letter to someone, I tend to just invent as I go. I mean, once I've answered the three questions that were in the other person's letter, whatever is required, then there's the rest of the letter to be written, and that's an occasion for having fun. So I start having fun with whatever there is to report, or whatever jokes I can make that the other person might like, or whatever. It's the same kind of invention that one is easily seduced by in writing poetry, I think. Sometimes a phrase will come out of it that seems serious, more serious than I meant, or maybe no more serious than I meant, but worth being . . . there's a bigger location for it than that letter, and I want to find that location. That happens sometimes. I'll take phrases right out of essays, and vice versa; I'll put into essays phrases which are lying there on paper that I hoped would hold a poem. The boundaries between genres don't seem any more fixed to me than they must seem to anyone else.

*Speaking of the relationship between poems and letters, this is a good point to move to the book of poems you and William Stafford are doing together, poems written back and forth to each other. Will you talk a little about how that book is constructed?*

Oh, in a very loose way, although sometimes the connections that result are not loose. I had thought about doing this, and not just with anybody but in fact with Bill, for years, but I never had the nerve to suggest it. Finally we were both at the First Annual Midnight Sun Writers' Conference in Fairbanks, Alaska, in June of 1979. Maybe that yellowish light that lasts all night at that time of the year there got my nerve up, or maybe I just hadn't had enough sleep, but we were walking along one day midway through the conference and I sort of mentioned this as something I had once thought about, not quite suggesting it, and he right away took up the idea and said, "Great," so I got home and I tried to write a poem to him to start the series; and I was trying to, I felt somehow required to, use material from there in Alaska. In fact, I may have felt required, without realizing it, to use the pronoun "we," because I kept saying "we, we, we" but the material I wanted to put into the poem didn't have anything to do with Bill; it happened at Mt. McKinley where I went afterward. So I was having a problem with truth; why couldn't I have said "we" even though I was the one in the raft and he wasn't? I couldn't do it. And I still have that darn poem; I've tried to put it in the series over and over, and each time truth rears its ugly head and I can't do it. Now theoretically each poem answers the other in some way, or responds to it, and indeed sometimes the connections are quite clear—there's a little quarrel about attitude or something, how to take something, or there's a parallel plot; my memory stirs his memory, or his memory stirs mine. He has an idea about something; I have a somewhat similar but different idea about something similar. Or a situation that's similar. But sometimes the connections are looser than that, and you have to read into the first poem to see a phrase that triggered the second poem.

My publisher told me that Bill Merwin once suggested something similar to James Merrill, but it never came to be. One has to be able to feel that a project like this is not going to deplete the poems one would otherwise write, deplete the energies. And I feel that I can do both things. Because I feel as if I'm sometimes more than one person. I *know* Bill Stafford can do both . . . Bill could take on *ten* correspondents like this, and still manage his own work.

*Like a chess master, with ten games going on at once.*

Absolutely. His attitude toward writing is marvellous. His sense of the forgivable is just wonderful.

*The correspondence sounds very sustaining.*

I admire his poetry, I admire his way of life, I admire everything about him. I always have. It's in my nature to want to make people into fathers, I think. I have to fight against that, and I certainly don't want to do that to him. But I do admire him greatly; he's a genuinely admirable man, with a life made out of whole cloth.

*He's the person who says in a poem somewhere, "You feel oppressed? Get up at five a.m."*

He's a very interesting man with an extraordinarily unusual mind. I think that, as famous as he is, his work is one of the secrets of American poetry. I think he's famous for a lot of easy reasons, and he's much better than that. His work is experimental—we were talking before about what is experimental—it's experimental in its notion of composition, and it's experimental in its ideas toward the world and how it applies them in the poems.

It may have been Don Justice who said this, but whoever

said it, I agree: work that seems very experimental in style often masks a very conventional mind. Work that seems conventional and off-handed in style often masks an unconventional mind. It's not a rule, but. . . .

*How many poems are going to be in the book with Stafford?*

Well, as many as we have when the deadline draws near. The series will continue; the book will just put covers around a section of it.

*You're not working toward a conclusion?*

Not exactly, but I must confess that when I asked Godine to delay the publication one season I was aware that the series could use another turn in order to be a book. We did have enough poems, but there had been a kind of change after the first eighteen poems or so and now the next change in direction was slow in making itself known. It has worked out very well so far, I think.

*And what direction do you see yourself continuing on your own, aside from the poems to Stafford?*

I have an idea of the kind of poem I'd like to write. I have some sense of what my language is now. There's a line between being fluent and being facile. In any case, I don't have to make as many choices as I once had to make about style, for example. I know what my language is; I might push it in this direction or that, but I know where it's located within me. I would like to increase my range, and of course everyone would like to extend his emotional depth. And everyone has in mind poems by other poeple they would have liked to have written.

*Like "The Old WPA Swimming Pool . . ."?*

Right. I would like to write a poem like "Asphodel, That Greeny Flower." That seems to be one of the great poems—

about as long a poem as I would ever want to write. I don't have any burning desire to write an epic. The only good that comes out of it is critical attention, as far as I can tell. I would rather have written "Asphodel, That Greeny Flower" than *Paterson*. I recognize *Paterson* as a marvellous poem, and *Book Five* of *Paterson* as a lyric poem all by itself. But I still would rather have written "Asphodel, That Greeny Flower."

*And you don't seem to be looking for all-encompassing metaphors, like the city of* Paterson.

No. That, to me, always rings hollow. I would like very much to have written a book like Williams' *Spring and All,* which he wrote in 1923, and which is prose and poetry, the poetry partly illustrating the radical aesthetic idea of the prose.

When I went to Spain for most of a year I took two books: I took a dictionary and I took *Spring and All.* I had a notion of keeping a journal that would result in a book similar in form to *Spring and All* but I never did it, although I probably have the pieces, not just in a journal but in miscellaneous pages gathered over the years. I could probably put together a book that would be similar to *Spring and All.* Maybe I will.

# III

# Homage to the Runner

COLUMNS FROM *THE AMERICAN POETRY REVIEW*

# Prefatory Note

The following eleven essays were published as columns in *The American Poetry Review* under the overall title, "Homage to the Runner." A word about the title: at the time I employed it, it referred to a poem by the same title in one of my books, *The Escape into You.* I was not, myself, a runner.

The first of these essays appeared in January, 1975 and the last in November, 1978, in the order in which they are reprinted here. Three other columns have been omitted and several of those which follow have been shortened.

# The First Column

Any review of American poetry at this time has to take into account the fact that "poetry" still has many meanings. I grew up on the south shore of Long Island among potato farmers, duck farmers and fishermen. I still remember my introduction to poetry as a form of embarrassment. One morning my English teacher (I was a junior in high school) announced, "This morning, we are going to read some 'poitry.'" (She pronounced "poetry" as if it were the source of Hawaiian gruel.) She began to read Thomas Gray's "Elegy Written in a Country Churchyard"—a perfectly good poem. But soon she pulled out her handkerchief and began to dab her cheeks. It was such a sad poem, you see. I wasn't a very good student, and I got up and left. I still type with two fingers because I had to drop typing to transfer to the other English class.

My experience was not atypical. Most high school students are introduced to poetry by way of romance and elevated thought. But self-consciousness is a way of life for adolescents, so that any red-blooded American boy or girl is going to be embarrassed by poems in which the speaker talks to clouds or stands tiptoe on a little hill. For many people, "poetry" will ever after mean "sentiment," "flowery" language, and "inspiring" messages. "That's poetry," they say, about a sudden sentimental effusiveness.

Writers-in-the-Schools programs have helped to change this notion of poetry. In its place, such programs—particularly those in which primary school children are encouraged to write poems—substitute notions of poetry as word-play and poetry as imagination. "Imagination," at this level, means wishes, lies and dreams. Kenneth Koch's work—explained and illustrated in his book called *Wishes, Lies, and Dreams*—is an example of this healthy activity in the grade schools.

It is also an example of that other definition of poetry. Poetry is "creative" language: word-play. Poetry is "creative" thinking: wishes, lies, dreams. When I became a junior in college, it was word-play that attracted my attention to poetry.

I had come across a poem in *New World Writing*. Its author, Neil Weiss, was identified as an ex-seaman. I had more respect for sailors than for poets, so I read the poem. It contained the line, "Fuzz clings to the huddles," and ended with, "We rise and leave with Please." I had never seen language used quite that way, so I asked my Survey of English Literature teacher about the poem's last line: "What does this mean?" "I don't know much about modern poetry," she said. "You might ask Dr. F." When I asked Dr. F., he said he didn't know much about modern poetry either, but he seemed to approve of my interest. When I took creative writing with Dr. F., we wrote short stories.

But word-play continued to intrigue me. I read poems by e. e. cummings and Dylan Thomas primarily because of the word-play in them. It was a while longer before I became aware of poetry as surprising or shocking content. Like many others, I discovered the poems of the so-called Beat Generation. The slang, the profanity, the syntax imitating breathlessness and ecstasy, the apparent defiance of mores, the hostility to institutional inhumanity—these and other aspects of the poetry I was reading convinced me that poetry was the genre for revolt and incantation.

Still later, when I had begun to write poetry with increasing frequency, I discovered the basic lessons of specificity in art: show, don't tell, etc. In other words, the object and the image. At its least, the image was a mental picture. At its best, however, it could be what Pound said it was: "that which presents an intellectual and emotional complex in an instant of time." To many people, poetry is primarily a medium for mental "images."

By extension, I realized that metaphor was a complication of the image and, at its best, a mode of thought; and that, further, there was a way of thinking about poetry in which an entire poem was seen to be an "image" or metaphor. This helped to explain, for example, the hardy resonance of fatigue and the burden of responsibility in Frost's "Stopping by Woods on a Snowy Evening," and of the savory apology for desire in Williams' little poem about the plums, "This Is Just to Say." The symbol and the archetype, I saw, were also forms of metaphor: the first, the fastest form; the second, the "deepest" form.

But images within poems were too numerous and handy to be sufficient by themselves, just as metaphors within poems were usually only figures of speech. (For many people, poetry is figurative language.) Images and figures were a dime-a-dozen; "creativity" was cheap; sentiments were easy; word-play was frivolous. I came to think that what I valued in poems was evidence of human intention, but it was really mentality I valued. Poetry, unbounded by space and time, grounded in the reality of specifics but employing the medium of concepts, could be a form for special thought.

In poetry, thought does not appear merely as earnest, rational thinking, but as something else: indications of mentality. Mentality may take the form of thinking, or of knowing, or sometimes simply of genuine thoughtfulness. It resides not only in logical structures but also in the hundreds of tiny connections within a poem, in precision, in syntax, and in what the poem includes or omits. Metaphor can be a mode of thinking; the archetype, a mode of knowing; even syntax, a symptomatic form of logic.

I had given serious attention to music, photography and pottery, and less serious attention to several other art forms. I had been a journalist and an amateur radio operator. Always, I had been most interested in what each medium could do better than others. What were its special qualities? Well, the special quality of language is thought, not imagery or sound or sentiment or surprise or revolt. Certainly, not causation. Poetry existed between reality and speech, and what was most interesting about it was the way in which it made the trip from one to the other, and back again. It was engaged in the continuous exploration of both. Thought, too, lay in between reality and expression, for it did not exist publicly without expression.

Of course, poetry is not just thinking, or a demonstration of mentality. A poem is not an essay. Rather, the thinking which poetry can do is thinking which is convincing, and which convinces through means other than observable logic. It convinces through testimony, which is why we sometimes confuse the life of the poet with the life of the speaker of a poem, and why we give the wrong sort of attention to poets who try to convince us that, because they are interesting, their poems are interesting.

But poetry convinces better by means other than testimony. We cannot be certain how to define these means, but we are affected by them. That is because, in poetry, means do not exist separately from ends. In other words, form and content can be inextricable. In other words, a really good poem is, to some extent, unparaphrasable. We all say this.

Poetry is *the* art of the mental. Without the mental, poetry tries to re-create the physical, and must do poorly. In his own silly way, Sergeant Kilmer was right. We shall never see a poem lovely as a tree is lovely. A poem is not a tree.

Without a context of the physical, however, the mental is disembodied and unconvincing. The two come together through the imagination. Coleridge reminds us still that the imagination is not mere fancy. Fancy, which derives from our ability to associate (endlessly), is worth something. But imagination, which has to do with penetration, development and structure, is worth much more.

Wishes and lies are fanciful; dreams are not, but more often than not are employed in poetry in a way that is merely fanciful. When American poets change rather than grow, they employ the fancy to do so. When they play the fool or freely associate, when they claim to have a special handle on the subconscious and fill their poems with the "evidence," when they strain for a vision disembodied from the physical—in all these cases, they employ the fancy.

To take intelligence from poetry, to make a rule that ideas, discourse and other mental gestures are not to be allowed in poetry, simply because so many unattached or half-baked ideas used up second-best poems of the fifties, say, is to be prescriptive in a way that cripples the possibilities of the poetic imagination.

Why is good poetry unparaphrasable? It is the wholeness of the poem that makes this so. That wholeness is the result of a special sort of seamlessness. It occurs when a poet's language, emotion and perception are inextricably wed. This is the result, in turn, of what we used to call character. It is not the result of what we now are offered by many poets instead: personality. Wholeness results also from the quality of a poet's mind.

Those for whom cadence and image and surprise suffice often find those elements in the poems of William Carlos Williams. But Williams was better. Ultimately, in his best poems—"The Descent" and "Asphodel, That Greeny Flower," to name a short one and a long one—he was abstract as well as specific, thoughtful as well as responsive, intelligent, profound, and finally convincing in a consequential way out of a fully-developed context. In his greatest poems, Williams, like all great poets, engages questions of morality.

Such poems indicate that good poetry is a profoundly adult art. What the children do in grade school, what the quivering adolescent does in junior high, what the energetic young adult can do with charm and surprise, what the careful apprentice can do by means of image—these are stopovers for better poets.

I know that many inferior poems exhibit a mentality which is superficial or unattached to the natural world, but such poems do not invalidate the profundity of the best poems. Our fatigue with poems of mediocre intelligence need not cause us to lower our standards. Poetry as heightened journalism, poetry limited to image and cadence, poetry as confession and complaint, poetry as collections of interesting junk, poetry as prestidigitation or shock, tiny poems of slight insight (which are not so much poems as excerpts from would-be poems)—such poetry does not engage the possibilities. A poem can be more than any short piece in an idiosyncratic style with some of the transitions omitted. Poetry, even while it honors the physical world, can be a form for profound meditation, response and argument.

The proliferation of literary magazines and presses, the increase in writing courses, National Endowment sponsorship of grade school writing—all can be to the good. But we need not abandon our highest standards to endorse them. It is not true that authenticity is the only goal of poetic expression. It is not true that "creativity" derives merely from being happy-go-lucky, fanciful or intense. It is not true that all writing is of equal value.

In our country, athletics have become a tribal rite, replacing religion. Almost everyone is caught up in athletics at some level; most play. Yet few fail to see the differences among beginners, talented amateurs, and those (professionals?) who are most able, most committed and sometimes inspired. This sort of public awareness is not possible for poetry, however, precisely because good poetry often exists at the thresholds of awareness. That is why culture and art remain separate, though they may occasionally intersect.

Culture means personality; art means character. Art has to do with mystery, while culture settles for mystification. Art hopes for structural unity in a poem, while culture will make do with stylistic unity. Culture is the gossip, the haste, the easy judgments born of paranoia, the poison penmen, the snobbery and aggression of book-jacket blurbs, and the gurus and academic paratroopers—dropping in to say anything for an evening, while avoiding any sustained responsibility to the student or the community.

To say that a good poem is, in part, a singular mental gesture—that it is at its very best, profound—is also to say that it is inexhaustible. One might read it over and over, yet it loses nothing. However well one remembers it, in reading or saying it again one realizes that it is better than one's memory of it.

Once, an intelligent man might have owned perhaps thirty books which he read repeatedly, and from which he derived examples, sayings and lessons. Now, any graduate student owns an albatross of more than a hundred books and doesn't know any of them, and almost any reviewer owns several hundred, about which he may have written or spoken, but about which he knows almost nothing. Could any reviewing of poetry be less serious, thorough and fair than most of what we have to put up with now?

In any case, inexhaustibility is the test for me. I can enjoy any poem the first time I read it. Few, however, last beyond several readings. They are not deep enough. In many cases, a dependence on image or surprise or a too-limited use of metaphor (merely as a figure of speech, a decoration perhaps) makes a poem inconsequential and expendable—even on first reading. In others, the very stylistic idiosyncrasies which have made the poet fashionable seem to legislate against clarity or depth or both. The voices of American poets are often strident and shallow, often frivolous, often self-congratulatory.

Poetry is not an exercise in style, though it is often reviewed as if it were. It is not merely heightened prose, heightened journalism or clever lying.

I do not know what sort of poetry we should write, or what direction(s) American poetry is taking. I believe that poetry is written by individuals, that the most significant and lasting work is usually accomplished outside the circles of culture and fashion, and that the writer who describes what is happening in our poetry inevitably distorts the truth to find a pattern.

I believe that most "progress" in poetry is merely change. I believe that, when we judge, we are more in bondage to culture than we know. I do not believe in gurus or squad leaders or rules. I do believe that the individual poet can grow as well as change, but slowly. I do believe that one's poetry will ultimately be a reflection of one's time and character, and that we begin with shallow characters. I believe that one cannot write for twenty years without finally finding a "voice," and that the search for distinctive voices among young poets results instead in superficial idiosyncrasies of style. I believe that it is style which makes poetry famous, but content which makes it worthwhile. I believe that good poetry is written to the extent that the art remains, for the world at large, mostly a gratuitous effort—and that the important rewards for the poet remain private and internal. I believe that, while the externals of one's life affect the personality of one's poems, they do not affect the character of one's poems. Rilke said it: solitude is not just a cabin in the woods. I believe that the teaching of young poets is honorable work. I am certain that some things about the writing of poetry can be learned, and I am almost as certain that a few of them can be taught. Finally, I believe that good art is made from strength, not weakness.

I have always had a love for poems which begin with ordinary materials and which refuse to compromise the essential truths of those materials. Such poetry involves, too, an uncommon respect for others. The more I read, write, teach and observe, the more convinced I am that poetry's most honorable and helpful function at this time is to insist on the true nature and limitations of given sets of circumstances. When any product of the fancy is considered more or less the equal (because entertaining) of any piece of hard, developed thought, then a corruption of language occurs quite as evil and effective as the corruption of language we have seen in high places in such words as "deniability," "inoperative," "protective retaliation," and "destabilization."

I began as an "experimental" poet. I knew my poetry was "experimental": it didn't make sense. The more I read and teach, the more convinced I am that obscurity and idiosyncrasy of style in young poets is inevitably symptomatic of fear: the fear of saying something apprehensible which others might then criticize for its content. If one says something arty or grand, one is less vulnerable. If one says it only partially, or in code, or fashionably, one is less vulnerable. Sometimes I think that the growth of a poet depends to some extent on his or her becoming less and less embarrassed about more and more. That is why profound care, attention and patience are crucial to poetry and to the (serious) imagination. Real advances in poetic expression occur for the individual after years of solitary work and hard thought, not after a few semesters of "creative" play.

Rilke reminds us that, "Works of art are of an infinite loneliness and with nothing so little to be reached as with criticism. Only love can grasp and hold and be just toward them." In future columns, I would like to write about particular poems which have given me pleasure and instruction.

# What Does Art "Imitate," and How?

What does art "imitate," and how?

Aristotle told us that art imitates life, and thereby created The University of Chicago Department of English. Sergeant Joyce Kilmer said he'd never seen a poem lovely in the way that a tree is lovely, and of course in his silly way he was right. Frank Lloyd Wright, and Ernest Fenollosa before him, said that form follows function, and Robert Creeley gets credit for saying that form is never more than an extension of content. In 1915, the second rule of Imagism mentioned that in poetry, "a new cadence means a new idea." Charles Olson is credited with saying that the poetic line is a function of one's metabolism, and Allen Ginsberg swears that each line of "Howl" takes one human breath.

What does art imitate, and how? Specifically, what does poetry imitate, and how?

Of course, I have some possible answers to the tentative question I have asked, but first I must make a petty distinction between verse that is metered and verse we call "free." In the case of metered poems, we might say that meter imitates our heartbeat—indeed, by extension, the heartbeat of the mother in the perfect world of the amniotic fluids—and at the same time "imitates" in some sense the mathematical ideal, which becomes also the musical ideal, of interval.

But I want to make the question harder by concentrating our investigation on so-called "free verse." Frost, as everyone knows, said that writing free verse is like playing tennis without a net. My friendly tongue-in-cheek variation of this has always been that writing free verse is really like playing jai alai without a net. Free verse can differ so much and so significantly from rhymed and metered verse that the difference may become one of kind rather than of degree.

What does form imitate, and how?

Let me say more about so-called "free verse." No verse is "free," said Eliot, for the man who would do a good job. And we know that expectations established by patterns of rhyme and rhythm—that is, meter—are powerful advantages. In verse which has no regular rhyme and rhythm, there must be other "formal" concerns.

We can name some possibilities: the phrase, the line, diction and syntax, the image, metaphor, the stanza, etc. But these are aspects, after all, of all poetry—"free" or not. In discussing such matters, it is a question of emphasis and frequency. In free verse, pattern and repetition are surprises, and continuing variation is the norm. The formal ideal is something called "organic form," and the presupposition in calling such form "organic" is that it grows naturally, as does a living organism. Form follows function. Form is never more than an extension of content, etc.

But that sort of talk pales in the face of examples. For we all know that singular line division is not sufficient to engage us for very long, nor is peculiar imagery, quirky diction or seemingly unique metaphor-making. And we all know of many poems written to no discernible pattern which seem to us engaging, convincing, consequential and inexhaustible. Often, these poems are written so simply, so straight-forwardly, if you will, so—modestly—that they put into proper perspective our technical obsessions by nothing more complicated than their sheer, sometimes overwhelming, humanity.

Now I admit to a tendency to wince when the talk turns to the "humanity" of poets, and I want to draw a thick line right away between my notion of humanity and the fraudulent critical notion of sincerity which has turned the minds of many reviewers and writers to mush.

The critical notion of sincerity surfaces every few years, and has more than one meaning for those who employ it. Some-times, it means writing without ornamentation. Sometimes, it means writing colloquially. Sometimes, it means writing in the first person. Sometimes, it means writing only about what the author has physically experienced in his or her space- and time-bounded life. And there are always false gurus around to tell us that we can only have meaningful lives if we take this or that job, enlist in or avoid this or that school. More than one poet blinded by intensity has said that he or she didn't care for poems in which the poet's entire life had not been brought to bear on the writing of the poem. Surely, that is self-delusion at best and dangerous advice at worst. It is based on the false notion that art replaces and becomes life. It invites, and at-tempts to justify, the causing of pain to others and, ultimately, suicide. (For contrast, I would mention Denise Levertov's fine essay about Anne Sexton's death and the artist in society in the December–January, 1975 issue of *Ramparts*.)

What's more, few of us will live lives of extreme danger or unusual consequence, in the general view of many others. Few of us will live the life of a Nadezhda Mandelstam. Indeed, like the Chinese poet who foresaw the dilemma in describing what he hoped for his granddaughter, we should probably not wish to live in what will later be known as an "interesting" time.

In any event, I would like to deflate the language with which we speak of our poems. I would like to think of poems we might read together as poems not of urgency but of imme-diacy. I would like us to think of them as poems not of vision but merely of intelligence. Of course, I don't mean "merely." I confess I no longer know what the word "vision," applied to poets, means, if ever I did. I think I understand what a person-al mythology is, and what imagination is, and what lucky prophecy is. The word "vision," however, seems to have be-come for many poets a self-congratulatory term meant to help us pretend that we are more unequal than we really are. One dictionary definition of "vision" is "the work of the imagina-tion." In that case, vision is something we all have, or none of us have, and in either case it is not a useful term. I would prefer, also, not to use the word "inspired" in speaking about poems.

I have always believed, as I have said, that the critical notion of "sincerity" is, in any of its recurrent forms, invalid and beside the point. I would prefer to speak of the "modesty" of poems. The poems which survive for me are essentially modest . . . in attitude. They may not be modest, may even be outrageous, in diction, in syntax, in range or subject matter, in ability and willingness to teach, or in other ways, but they are modest with regard to: (1) the necessity for evidence; (2) the necessity for form.

The first necessity means that content must be based in reality—probable, possible or actual—no matter how made up the metaphorical landscape. Coleridge's distinction between the "fancy," which is essentially frivolous because merely associational, and the "imagination," is relevant again here. The second necessity means that works of art do not exist except as *art* first, no matter how far into "life" they may take us.

It occurs to me that the notions of "sincerity" and "modesty" in poems are too close not to be related. I insist, however, on their difference. Sincerity may be present without modesty, but modesty may never be present without sincerity. Sincerity may derive from passion, whereas modesty always derives from wisdom.

Going perhaps uncomfortably further, it is modesty which allows a writer to hold in mind opposites, apparent contradictions, at the same time, and to resolve them within a poem.

Such poems—poems of wise humility, if you will—often make uncommon good sense by paying attention to the ordinary. When they do, they seem uncommonly genuine expressions. They are in special touch with life and accept it. They are not self-congratulatory, they are clever at times but not self-consciously or pridefully so, and they do not distort reality for the sake of the poem—either by investing it with a drama it does not contain, or by pretending it is "cooler" than it really is: they do not pretend that the amount and kind of life portrayed in the poem means either everything or nothing.

At this point, I would like to point to a poem by William Stafford—not one that's likely to be anthologized often. It appears in the collection *Allegiances,* available from Harper and Row.

### With Kit, Age 7, at the Beach

We would climb the highest dune,
from there to gaze and come down:
the ocean was performing;
we contributed our climb.

Waves leapfrogged and came
straight out of the storm.
What should our gaze mean?
Kit waited for me to decide.

Standing on such a hill,
what would you tell your child?
That was an absolute vista.
Those waves raced far, and cold.

"How far could you swim, Daddy,
in such a storm?"
"As far as was needed," I said,
and as I talked, I swam.

Writing about another of his poems ("The Farm on the Great Plains") for a 1962 anthology, *Poet's Choice,* Stafford said that he could "confront and accept something of my portion in writing: an appearance of moral commitment mixed with a deliberate—even a flaunted—nonsophistication; an organized form cavalierly treated; a trace of narrative for company amid too many feelings. There are emergences of consciousness in the poem, and some outlandish lunges for communication; but I can stand quite a bit of this sort of thing if a total poem gives evidence of locating itself."

Here is a small clue to what art imitates: "an appearance of moral commitment." We mustn't leave out the word "appearance." Does it mean that it just seems that way? Or does it mean that the moral commitment appears, shows up, makes itself known? Might I hazard that the choice was cagey, perhaps honestly modest, but that it means the latter—that moral commitment makes itself known in the poem.

But Baptist preachers aren't often poets. When I say "moral," I mean "of, relating to, or acting on the mind, character or will." Do you like that definition? It's the most tentative one I could find—the last offered, in my Webster's Seventh. You see, I didn't want to go to any heavier dictionary for this discussion of the uncommonly ordinary. By "moral commitment," I *don't* mean didacticism. Consciousness and a sense that there can be right and wrong in human behavior will do it. Indeed, a true-seeming view of human nature seems to me sufficient evidence with which to impeach the poet on the grounds of uncommon virtue.

Stafford makes other gestures in this poem which keep us on the ground and at ease. Lines one and two of stanza three are, I feel, disarmingly straightforward. And they put us on the spot, which is what morality always does. Now it is true that these lines are each trimeter lines with reversed first feet and that the poem as a whole is mostly trimeter—sprung trimeter. It is likewise true that the language is casual, off-handed, colloquial; and not caught up in complaint or congratulation.

Certainly, it's a minor accomplishment just to be able to get into a poem such an apparently "unpoetic" line as, "How far could you swim, Daddy, / in such a storm?" Of course, the history of poetry is to a large extent the history of the accommodation of manner and substance hitherto thought to be unpoetic or even antipoetic. Wordsworth's language, after all, was thought to be too "common" in its time; and it wasn't long ago that Whitman's was thought vulgar. The vulgar and the controversial are large parts of poetry—the writing of which, in its insistence on clarity and individual perceptions and, ultimately, individual decisions, is always a subversive activity. Even Miss Dickinson was probably wisely advised not to print many of her poems during her lifetime because of what could be anticipated: an angry reaction to her seeming informality. (The lunge for prose-poetry in America at this moment seems to be a desperate attempt to incorporate the seemingly unpoetic, but it has so far taken the form mostly of clutter and comedy.)

Apart, however, from the petty thrill I get at just seeing in a poem such a common question, commonly phrased, it's that last stanza which makes this poem one of uncommonly good sense for me. "How far could you swim, Daddy, / in such a storm?" asks the daughter. And the speaker's answer is both cagey and seemingly straightforward. Surely, it is the sort of reassuring answer the speaker in this poem senses the situation demands. Yet it pretends nothing. "As far as was needed, I said, / and as I talked, I swam." How far is "needed?" The implication of this poem is that nature will decide what is needed. In the realm of *human* nature, *we* can decide what is to be *said*. There is a great deal of difference, and the poem refuses to blur the difference.

What does art imitate, and how? An appearance of moral commitment? The distance between speech and action, between nature and thought? What our gaze should mean? Standing on such a hill, what would you tell your child?

Good poems refuse to blur essential differences, even as they seek what is common in the seemingly disparate. A general impression of "sincerity" or passion is a poor substitute for this ability. It is just such a defiance born of intelligence which reveals what we might call "authentic" character. Authenticity goes far beyond an appearance of sincerity.

Given unlimited space, I would reproduce a variety of poems to illustrate further. One would surely be John Ashbery's brilliant poem, "Illustration," which appeared in his first book, *Some Trees* (Yale, reissued by Corinth). Indeed, Stafford and Ashbery seem to me two poets who consistently risk uncommon mental gestures in poems. In the work of both, what was formerly thought unpoetic or antipoetic is absorbed into poetry time and again. Next to their best poems, the flash of neo-surrealism is little more than poetic vaudeville: clams playing accordions, etc.

"Illustration" is about a suicide, but it is neither an expression of hysteria nor an attempt at total (and false) identification with the tragic heroine. Rather, the poem is about one's distance from the event. We might, says the speaker (after a girl has jumped to her death from a tall building), have felt and acted differently. We might have cared more. But she was only an "effigy of indifference." Solely of *our* indifference? It would be easy to say so. But no. The indifference which the poem speaks of is the indifference in nature. The final illustration in the poem is of a tree losing its leaves at the approach of winter.

> But she, of course, was only an effigy
> Of indifference, a miracle
>
> Not meant for us, as the leaves are not
> Winter's because it is the end.

The young girl who plunged to her death, that is, is no more ours than are the leaves which fall to winter the property of winter. To believe otherwise would be to deceive ourselves quite as much as those well-intentioned bystanders who thought they knew what she wanted, offered it to her, and in so doing became merely part of the ceremony she desired. "I want to move figuratively," she had said, "as waves caress the thoughtless shore." But it is not the thoughtlessness of human nature which those lines speak of anymore than winter is a blunder of physical nature.

What does art imitate, and how? "Illustration" imitates, in its diction and syntax, in its plot, in its weaving philosophic discourse, in the necessity it finds for illustrations, the distance from that event to the mind which survives it, and the process by which apprehension of the physical becomes the mental.

Here are some other examples of poems of ease, attentiveness, and unusual awareness and "modesty." One is *"¿Habla Usted Espanol?,"* from James Reiss' book, *The Breathers* (Ecco), which spots the distance between the language of a child's reassuring imagination and the more practical and allegedly "useful" definitions which accompany the child's loss of innocence and security. Another is "Willy Lyons," by James Wright, available in his *Collected Poems* (Wesleyan), because the poem makes a crucial distinction between the speaker and the lives and arts of his uncles (now dead), and between himself and his weeping mother. Although by resorting to mythology the speaker allows for the possibility of "the other world," he recognizes also that, if the other world is unknown to the grieving mother, it is equally unknown to him. A lesser poet would have claimed to know.

Wright's powerful poem, "To the Muse," is another example. In this poem, the speaker brings back to life a childhood friend who drowned. But he does not allow her to go on living in the poem, as many poets would have. Rather, he pulls back. He is not, he realizes, the agent of creation. He is more like the frightened garter snake that he and the drowned girl caught long ago—writing his poems and listening, just as the snake moved its tongue in and out. He can be the agent only of his own death. That is why he says, at the end of the poem, "Come up to me, love, / Out of the river, or I will / Come down to you." As he wouldn't, he has said at the outset, lie about the pain he would cause the dead girl in bringing her back to life, so he does not lie finally about his own powers.

To recognize one's limits in this regard may be an important basis for moral commitment. What does art imitate? Neither the agency of life, nor the agency of death, but the coming into consciousness of the presence of the moral agency.

(At this point, I simply want to note, for anyone who might be interested, that at another time and in another place I used the following poems to further illustrate that level of poetic awareness which manifests itself in a refusal to compromise essential differences or the human condition, a willingness to apprehend one's judgments and reconsider, and a refusal to take credit or to freely condemn others: Randall Jarrell's "Washing," "Next Day," and "The Truth," Alan Dugan's "Elegy" ("I know but will not tell . . ."), "Portrait from the Infantry," and "To a Red-Headed Do-Good Waitress," and Gary Snyder's "Hay for the Horses." Other poems by these poets could have been used, of course, or poems by many other poets. A look at these, however, will not misdirect the attention of anyone who wishes to continue the analysis, or the praise.)

Of course, I have been trying to do two things at once in this essay. First, I have been asking, What does art imitate, and how?—the implication being that the usual answer, that art imitates life, is insufficient and misleading because it is not life in its physical immediacy that art imitates, and because art is itself a part of life. Does life imitate art sometimes? Is the difference between art and life that you can't do anything about life?

"How" art does whatever it does we can answer. Every poem is another answer. But it is more difficult to say just "what" art imitates. Art, like life, needs no purpose to come into being. Its destiny, like man's, is its character. And it is a part of life we can have nowhere else in life. The title of a new book I saw advertised notwithstanding, life is not the ultimate poem any more than a poem replaces life. The green of a pine is all we will know of green. All we will know of the dark is sleep's forgetfulness. Time is all we will know of the end of time.

Second, I have tried to draw a thick line between fashionable notions of sincerity and that authenticity of speech and writing which derives from attention, wisdom and conscience.

In asking what art imitates and at the same time discussing the sensible and the genuine, I have tried to merge two long-opposed doctrines.

Aristotelian notions of imitation are part of classical poetics. Plato had condemned art because, in its imitation of characters, it gave the young themselves the opportunity to imitate the low and the base. But Aristotle defended poetry against Platonic condemnation by saying that poetic imitation is of plot, rather than of characters; that it is a valid representation of the actions of men according to the laws of probability and necessity. By plot, Aristotle meant not a sequence but a structure of events, firmly welded to form an organic whole.

Whereas the notion of imitation is central to classical poetics, it was of little interest to the Romantics, for whom imitation was felt to be out of keeping with the new spirit of spontaneity and self-expression. For them, sincerity was a genuine correspondence with, or expression of, the poet's state of mind and feelings, from which the poem derived its vitality. The Victorians, however, gave sincerity a moral twist. To Matthew

Arnold, the touchstone of great poetry was "the high serious-ness which comes from absolute sincerity."

So what does art imitate? Specifically, what does poetry imi-tate? One tentative, general answer is that it imitates a quality of authenticity of thought and perception; that is, sincerity. Put another way, sincerity might be thought of as—to use Stafford's phrase—"an appearance of moral commitment."

The poetic notions of imitation and sincerity cross where we recognize the distance between physical reality and mentality or speech. To pretend that that distance does not exist is to be a vagabond among poets. You can cross the country, but you won't get anywhere. Nor will fancy, the ability to associate, travel that distance. Only the imagination can get from one to the other, and about that our knowledge is limited to ex-amples.

The line is that, in a poem, anything is believable. But that is not true. In a poem, anything is *provable.* There is a difference.

Finally, here are three Yiddish proverbs which bear on the questions of truth, reality and sincerity: (1) Dumplings in a dream are not dumplings, but a dream; (2) For example is no proof; and (3) If a horse had anything to say, he would speak up.

# Looking Away from the Self

There is a wonderful quatrain by Antonio Machado, first
brought to my attention by Robert Bly, which goes:

> People possess four things
> that are no good at sea:
> anchor, rudder, oars
> and the fear of going down.

A wonderfully disarming piece of advice. But only because
we know that he doesn't "mean it." After all, normally one
would argue the opposite: that these are precisely what one
needs at sea: an anchor to maintain position; a rudder to set
direction; oars for propulsion; and even a healthy fear of
going down to encourage safety. But no, says the speaker, one
does not need these things "at sea." The sea in the poem is a
metaphor (the "sea" of life?), and the advice the poem offers is
one of abandonment to the medium. That is, "Why go to the
same islands all the time? Why see the same sights, have the
same thoughts, the same experiences? Why not," suggests the
poem, "abandon yourself to the medium and see new places,
have thoughts, as Williams put it elsewhere, 'heretofore
unrealized?'"

In this little poem, the medium is the sea. In poetry, the
medium is language.

There has been in the last few years a lot of loose talk about
the subconscious in poetry. Some poets have believed that they

could go directly down into the subconscious. The result often has been poems filled with associational catalogs which have had no context or unity other than that which a very specific title (often localized, often cumbersome) insisted upon, or poems which, when rational, have created a standardized inventory: wings, jewels, stones, darkness, silence. In straining toward greater contact with the subconscious, these poems have shown more and more conscious manipulation and less and less depth.

Could it have been any other way? I think not, and the little Machado poem suggests to me also that it could not. Rather, the aesthetic process functions through a kind of abandonment—of oneself *to the materials*. To simply abandon oneself is not enough. To "abandon" oneself *to the materials* is not to encourage the fancy to endless, random association, but to give all one's attention to the meanings of a word, and the implications of a line, without regard to one's preconceptions. Most of us probably became serious about writing poems because of the thrill of discovery which can follow such abandonment.

We all know that self-consciousness breaks down the smooth functioning of the mind and body, and prevents concentration. The Zen art of archery is based not on detailed technical instruction but on enabling the archer to become "one with" the materials, and thus unthinkingly fluid. "I *am* the arrow. I will fly into the heart of the target." Poof! Bull's-eye.

It works. We all know it works. We have seen, a thousand times, the athlete who, given extra time to think, fails the easy play, and the athlete who, under sudden pressure, makes the extraordinary play as if by instinct.

Forms of meditation and hypnotism invariably use an outside element to begin the "descent," if that's what it is, into the self or subconscious: a mantra, the flame of a candle, a mole on one's hand, whatever.

Though it may embarrass us to say so, we all desire such states as "heightened consciousness," "greater understanding," "wisdom," etc. The lesson of art, and the lesson of the Machado piece, is that one is more likely to approach, embody, or articulate "heightened consciousness," "greater understanding," "wisdom," etc. by writing about one's writing table, one's thumb, or a rose, than by writing about . . . "greater understanding," "heightened consciousness," etc.

That is because the way to encourage the subconscious to make itself known in the poem is to ignore it.

Left alone because the poet is concentrating so intensely on the externals of language and perception—the look of a leaf, a special congruency of syntax and enjambment—the subconscious will float upwards as always, right into the poem. And it will reveal itself in the most ordinary presences—charging them with emotion and significance—rather than in the deliberately strange. The strange, by itself, simply remains strange . . . until we lose interest.

When a person begins to write poems, he or she usually believes that he/she has something to say—something important and/or dangerous: "I love you," "I hurt," "I need." Later, that concern may be altered by another: what the words themselves can say. The notions that one should show rather than tell, that there are "no ideas but in things," and of the "objective correlative," for example, are all ways of favoring the language over the initial "idea" of a poem. Nothing counts in a poem, says Pound, save the quality of the emotion. And he may be right. Yet we learn soon enough that there will be no clear emotional set to the poem if the language is not first used carefully. There will be no meaningful set of connotations unless the denotations are clear and connected. Pound also said, "Make it new." But what is "new"? At first, everything is new: subjects, words, poetic landscapes and furniture, metaphors. But what remains "new"? One might distinguish between "connected" and "disconnected" (or "unconnected") poetry. What keeps a poem "new" (i.e., "fresh") is a fine web of connections: thought, implication, emphasis, etc. The old ideal seems true still: that of a poem like a spider's web, the whole of which, when any part is touched, trembles in response.

We are right to attend to the language as we do. Yet there is another side to all this. Those of us who go on writing after those first adolescent expressions of need and loss fall dangerously in love with the materials. For one thing, the materials are new to us and help us to discover thoughts and feelings we hadn't known or planned. For another (though we do not always know or admit this), there is an emotional safety in the codified language of poetry.

Here is a simple, perhaps silly, example. If one begins a poem, "I opened the window halfway," anyone can understand that and, given the overwhelming tendency of literary and academic people to be critical, anyone can take the writer to task for it. It is far safer to say something grand or arty about, say, the half-light. But that's not the way it was once when we were solely among people who, like us, knew nothing about poetry. Reading the line, "I opened the window halfway," our uncle would be likely to say, "Oh yes, I remember that window. We never could raise it completely."

Is it possible to come full circle, if you will, and to derive from the materials of poetry a special clarity? Is it true that poetic wisdom, as wisdom in graphic design is supposed to, shows itself in simplicity? I believe that the answer to these questions is yes. There are major examples everyone will think of: Frost and Williams, for instance, and Whitman. And there are many others.

The "problem" is that the young poet wants to, and needs to, try everything, and to abandon himself/herself to the materials. A dozen years later, perhaps, those poetic possibilities will have become second nature, if he/she is lucky and talented and diligent, and then the subversive possibility that one did have something to say after all will make itself known again. With luck, now one might say it—because it will be the result not only of greater experience but also of a deeper, more seamless language. I don't believe that a poet can write for twenty years without finally sounding like one person rather than like *any* person.

We can assume that this "problem" was less a problem when one was given by the Age certain rules for the writing of poetry. One followed them or one didn't, but one didn't have to thrash about for years among the endless variety of good poems written as "free verse." Will our reviewers understand this? I think it is a mistake, for example, to review a first or second book of poems by a twenty- or thirty-year-old in the same way that one would review the fifth book by a forty- or fifty-year-old. To rush young poets into the most telling and fragile parts of themselves in the search for "significant" or astonishing or "relevant" content is to exhaust them the way today's major league managers deliberately burn up their young pitchers because they know there are always more where those came from.

Not all of these poets would agree, perhaps (nor is this list exhaustive), but from reading their poems over a period of about fifteen years it seems to me that the work of such various and superb poets as Robert Creeley, Alan Dugan, Donald Finkel, Anthony Hecht, Donald Justice, Galway Kinnell, Philip Levine, John Logan, Robert Lowell, James Merrill, W. S. Merwin, Sylvia Plath, Anne Sexton, George Starbuck, Mark Strand and James Wright all show markedly this movement from a willing "tilt" toward materials (and sometimes received attitudes and opinions) to a language not so much "under control" as embedded in the whole person. There are other kinds of examples among our best poets. I believe that Robert Bly had that wholeness in his first book, *Silence in the Snowy Fields,* but didn't trust it, and seems now to be finding his way back carrying the treasures he picked up elsewhere. William Stafford seems always to have had it, and Robert Duncan, but then they were allowed/made to develop their art more in private than were others.

One of the reasons some of our best books of poetry of the past few years have received little critical attention is that it is difficult to say much about art that is this mature without erecting a critical scaffolding on which one risks looking silly and too busy. Wright's *Shall We Gather at the River,* Kinnell's *The Book of Nightmares,* Justice's *Departures,* Strand's *The Story of Our Lives,* Creeley's *Words*—these and others, in my opinion, have been badly reviewed and sometimes ignored for this reason. Other books have been come to late—Merwin's *The Moving Target* and Finkel's *A Joyful Noise,* for example—for the same reason.

But the great example of a poem so wise and lucid and

graceful all at once that it is difficult to speak about is William Carlos Williams' "long" poem, "Asphodel, That Greeny Flower." What is there to say, to account for beauty and rightness, about a poem which begins simply:

> Of asphodel, that greeny flower,
>     like a buttercup
>         upon its branching stem—
> save that it's green and wooden—
>     I come, my sweet,
>         to sing to you.
> We lived long together
>     a life filled,
>         if you will,
> with flowers. So that
>     I was cheered
>         when I came first to know
> that there were flowers also
>     in hell.

I suppose one can lay the historical–critical groundwork by talking about Williams' notions of the "variable foot," and the "triadic stanza," and perhaps "the American idiom," but that all seems petty and peripheral. And it is. Indeed, the lines are predominantly iambic and the idiom not especially colloquial.

And one can specify the interest the language itself can hold for us, being simple yet not quite ordinary. The syntax of that first sentence, the somewhat old-fashioned use of "save," the placement of the words "long" and "first," etc.

But I would suggest that there are two more important aspects to these first sonnet's worth of lines, and that they are central to the accomplishment and beauty of this great poem. First, there is the crucial maneuvering *away from the self*. The poem will be spoken to someone else throughout, and that person will remain as important throughout as is the speaker of the poem. Indeed, this love and marriage poem is predicated wholly on the need to speak to a wife.

Second, there is that off-handed yet telltale reference to "hell." Why should the speaker be cheered to learn that there are also flowers in hell? This is clue enough, though soon after the poet will say:

> There is something
> > something urgent
> I have to say to you
> > and you alone
> > > but it must wait
> while I drink in
> > the joy of your approach,
> > > perhaps for the last time.
> And so
> > with fear in my heart
> > > I drag it out

Facing death, honoring propriety, there is something coming—an "apology," in the sense of explanation, but an apology/explanation so full, so whole, so universal, so *moral* (Williams himself speaks of a "moral odor"), that it will take 1,046 lines in three "books" plus a "coda" to say it, and not once will the poem rush or loiter.

Self-consciousness and the rush to judgment by young poets who believe they have "something to say" are always preemptive and usually fatal. The petty and insular notion one has of the self at such times, and of its seeming importance in poetry, is a giveaway. Far better, then, that the poet abandon himself/herself to the materials. Such an "abandonment" should not be misunderstood as an obsession with technique. It is, rather, an instinctive awareness that the materials of the art, if honored by attention, are better paths into the self, the emotions, the subconscious—have more to say for now—than does the conscious mentality of the young writer. Yet, given support, the poet who has abandoned himself/herself to the materials will find his/her way back to the essential self with a wisdom and clarity perhaps not otherwise obtained.

It is tempting to suggest, at this point, that the self is better thought of as very small, and best identified and given value through attention placed almost anywhere else. Contemporary American poetry has become tiresome in its relentless search for the self, and in its repeated "discovery" of individual sensitivity and vulnerability. One recalls that back home, "self-importance" was a term of belittlement.

Hand in hand with poetic self-consciousness and self-importance has gone the assumption that the poet is a person of special insight or sensitivity. It may be true, but more likely the only special quality of a poet is that he/she writes poetry. If luck and labor may indeed lead to insight, perhaps this ought to be expected to take a while. Someone asked the great Japanese potter, Hamada, how long it takes to make a pot. His answer: a hundred years.

In any case, it is tempting to suggest that technical wisdom comes through an abandonment of the self, at least partially, to the materials of the art, but that emotional depth comes through an abandonment of the self as a subject of attention.

I love the much-anthologized little poem by Robert Creeley, "I Know a Man," partly because the speaker—a worrisome, philosophical sort who doesn't even bother to get his friend's name right and who admits he is "always talking"—is brought up short. "The darkness surrounds us," he philosophizes, "what shall we do against it?" And his friend replies, "Drive . . . look / out where yr going." What better answer to the self-obsessed—to both the driver and the endless philosopher.

Then there is that wonderful poem by Stafford, "Bess," such a simply written piece, about a librarian who is dying from cancer but still on the job. "In the last year of her life," reads the poem part way down, "she had to keep her friends from knowing / how happy they were. She listened while they / complained about food or work or the weather. / And the great national events danced / their grotesque, fake importance." After some lines about her constant pain, the poem continues in this way: "But she remembered / where joy used to live. She straightened its flowers; / she did not weep when she passed its houses. . . ." This poem, though very different in many ways from the Creeley poem, does something the Creeley poem also does: it redefines the self in terms of its littleness, its unimportance, the pettiness of our complaints, and the futility of our abstract philosophies.

Many of the late Randall Jarrell's most moving poems are those written in the voice of a child or of a woman. It is no good to say that he *is* the child, or that a male poet is more "feminine" than most men (and a woman poet more "masculine" than most women). The real point to be made is that, by turning his attention to others, the poet was able to assume a "central" position with regard to both content and language and yet retain an almost unnoticeable tension in the language. One could argue also that, by looking away from the self, he was better able to articulate the self.

One is reminded of Yeats, arguing in "Adam's Curse," that the poet's difficult labors are to make his/her lines seem but "a moment's thought." And one is reminded, further, that he was laboring to say this to Maud Gonne.

Most readers know the great "laundry" poem by Richard Wilbur, "Love Calls Us to the Things of This World," and some know the excellent "laundry" poem by James Merrill, "The Mad Scene," but fewer know this fine little poem by Jarrell. Laundry hangs out in it, and Michelangelo, and chickens, and together, amazingly and quickly, these make a statement about circumstances and the self. The poem is titled "Washing," and this is its last stanza:

> But as old hens like to say,
> The world isn't chickenhearted.
> The washing inhabits a universe
> Indifferent to the woes of washing,
> A world—as the washing puts it—
> A world that washing never made.

If in America we are more willing now to consider the notion that we are not so all-important as once we thought, then perhaps this notion should come down happily into our poems—to whom, after all, we have always tried to be true, even when we had nothing to say.

*23 April 1975*
*Sitges (Barcelona)*
*Spain*

# Students and Teachers

I was lucky. When I went looking for a poetry-writing class, I stumbled upon John Logan's. This was 1960, in Chicago. Logan taught for Notre Dame, and would bus ninety-five miles from South Bend to teach in the Downtown Center of The University of Chicago one night a week. His second book of poems, *Ghosts of the Heart,* was out, and he was writing the poems which would go into *Spring of the Thief,* but I had no idea who he was. There was one especially interesting student who talked about a home town I imagined too far away, pig- and corn-filled to be visited: Iowa City.

But I was lucky. Logan was a patient, generous critic. And he read so beautifully. When he read our poor poems aloud, we felt that we mattered and that in each of our poems we had managed to sing (or cry?) for a moment.

His approach was like none I had known. He talked roundabout the poem, often alluding to myth, fiction and science rather than to other poems. I am sure that sometimes we thought he was stalling, or going-on, but then we would see that he was trying to help us to locate the real subject of each of our poems. He wasn't embarrassed to speak of beauty, or desire, or to treat the secret content of our badly written poems seriously. In this way, he taught us to recognize the implications of what we chose to include in our poems, and the uses of metaphor. Shown a poem baldly stating vague emotions, he would suggest that the poet had not yet found the metaphor for the experience.

Now this is very different from agreeing with, differing with, or even articulating the surface content of a poem—the apparent substance, anything stated as message or preachment or philosophy. I'm saying that I was lucky, I know now, to stumble right off onto a poetry writing teacher who: (1) loved language, and (2) understood the special content of poetry to be a matter of implication and suggestion rather than one of conscious plan or preconception.

How different is such an approach from that which likes or dislikes our poems because of what is "said" in them. The instructor who prefers a poem because it protests injustice, or because it is written about a painful personal crisis, or because it admonishes us to read poetry—such a teacher is a fraud or an innocent.

From Logan's downtown class, I joined a group with no academic affiliation, though it called itself the "Poetry Seminar." We met regularly in the offices of Jordan Miller's Midwest Clipping Service. Logan was our master. Among the students were Dennis Schmitz, Bill Knott, Naomi Lazard, Roger Aplon and William Hunt. One of the best poets, perhaps the best, was Jim Murphy, who is now dead.

We weren't always intensely serious. Turning my poem on its side, Jessie Kachmar would say that it looked like the skyline of Chicago. Since the Chicago skyline beats the New York skyline six ways from Sunday, I liked the simile. Oh, it was probably a comment on the varying lengths of my free verse lines, too. Other times, the class would agree that this or that maneuver in a poem was very "Bellian." That was OK. We had words for the characteristics of each of us, and these served to make us reconsider our mannerisms.

The point is that we all knew that poetry could be meaningful, and that the writing of it could be a serious, sometimes very difficult, task. Therefore, it wasn't necessary to *pretend* to be serious. My impression of people without a sense of humor is that they are *pretending* to be serious. Worse, that they are pretending to be *concerned.* In reality, such people rarely help anyone. That, of course, is a personal view. I suppose I'm saying that earnestness and seriousness have no necessary relationship. That's all. (The first person who writes to suggest that I'm promoting frivolity is instructed to stop pretending.)

Well now, why was John Logan able to help us to appreciate the music of poetic language, and to reveal to us the implications of our choice and handling of a "subject?" I believe that it was partly because he had read the so-called New Critics, as well as critics before and a great many good poems.

There is a clichéd view of the fifties around. It's supposed to have been the time when "nothing happened," when the president was a windup golfing doll, and when those who made love did it badly. Not true, friends. Like all views rampant among the *intelligentsia*, that one is based on stereotyping, misreading, fragmentary perception and—to be honest—a fear of the uneducated masses, rooted in self-doubt and self-hatred.

Now I don't really care to go into this very far. I have no interest in modifying anyone's view of the fifties, or of the sixties. Whoever believes that the poetry of the fifties was "closed" and the poetry of the seventies is "open" is either playing an adman's game or trying to avoid looking at the poems. It would be correct to say that more of the poetry of the seventies is written as so-called "free verse" than were poems of, say, the fifties. Beyond that it is not possible to go without distorting the truth. Indeed, it would be possible to argue that "formal" verse has often been the container of wild minds, that our best "free verse" poets are those who began as "formalists" or reveal the formalist's intense engagement with "measure," and that much of the "free verse" being published today reveals minds engaged exclusively with clichés and stereotypes, and other forms of received opinion.

The standard question is, "Can you teach creative writing?" One possible answer is that maybe nothing can be taught but anything can be learned. Everyone who ever wrote a good poem is an example of someone who learned how.

But what luck to begin with a wise and generous teacher! Where I teach, many of the graduate students come from having been the stars of undergraduate writing classes elsewhere. Thus, they have also been, often, the apples of their teachers' eyes. Often, these students are not teachable for a semester or a year. Sometimes, they never are. Having been praised for accomplishing certain tricks, and thereby writing above their heads as undergraduates, they think to improve by accomplishing the same tricks, but better. By now, it is a truism where I teach that some of our most imaginative and productive students arrive by way of schools where there was no poetry-writing class. Because they arrive without preconceptions or large egos, they can be set free among all the possibilities.

And so I arrive back in Iowa City, where I never thought I'd be, and where I live and write this. From Chicago, on Logan's advice, I went to Iowa City to meet Donald Justice. Like Logan, Justice has to be one of the very best teachers of poetry writing, though he seems very different in approach.

Or is he? At first, it seemed that he was. Justice read aloud differently. Whereas Logan practically hummed the sounds of the poem, Justice read for gradations of tone, subtle inflections of speech. Logan's poems are personal and insist that the reader see just how personal they are. Justice's are, or pretend to be, impersonal (or universal).

In class, Justice did not speak much about the content of our poems—either that which was obvious and intended or that which was suggested and perhaps unintended. Instead, he subtly rubbed our noses in the inconsistencies and contradictions which fancy allows into poems (and which imagination, in contradistinction, unifies), and located for us the often unintended and unrealized formal assumptions we were making. His one rule was that there are no rules, but conversely, he was not about to allow us to claim intuition when we were following rules without knowing it—often by imitating the fashion of the time or by appropriating empty mannerisms.

Now the interesting thing for me is how alike these two very different poets were in their approach to student poems. Logan sought out our hidden subjects; he wasn't deceived for a moment by our ostensible concerns. His understanding of the subconscious was so much more profound than the hokum and scarum we get from those who will accept anything in a poem so long as it seems strange. Justice sought our hidden forms and strategies; he wasn't deceived by our claims of intuition or fine tuning, or appeals to personal taste.

How damn lucky I was. At the time, most of the Poetry Workshop students were a bit older than other graduate students. Most of us had done other things. We were a most unacademic lot. Some of us spoke as if we were anti-academic. But we were all opposed to stereotypes. Logan had said in an interview that he thought pigeonholes were for pigeons, and we weren't about to collect, or be, the pigeons. (We underestimated the desperate need some critics have for labels.)

Logan had also said that he knew of no good poet who had not at one time or another been a member of a literary community—whether in Iowa or Chicago, or at a café in Paris. There had been some serious yet good-natured poets in the two Logan-led groups in Chicago. In Iowa, likewise, the group included Catherine Davis, Mark Strand, Kenneth Rosen, James Crenner, Al Lee, Charles Wright, Michael Van Walleghen, and many other excellent poets.

These people could speak intelligently, and with generosity for the poet, about any poem on the worksheet. Because they took poems seriously, they also had a sense of humor. No one was in a rush to publish. Nor did anyone feel that publication validated one's efforts. In any case, one wasn't likely to have a better reading of one's poems elsewhere. These people, too, had been taught by the so-called New Critics to read a poem closely. They knew that, while one's hunches and guesses might be of value in a secondary reading of the poem, first it was necessary to read the poem as it was. If it were desirable to go outside the poem to understand it, the poem would tell us to do so. Sometimes, it did. The charge today against the New Criticism is that it kept us from locating the poem in the wider world of influences from which the poem had come. But the New Criticism, so far as I can tell, never precluded such efforts. Rather, it served as first lessons in attentive reading—without which, it must be said, one might remain the wooziest of romantics and the most vocal of illiterates.

Those classmates of mine were better conversationalists

about poetry than most students (and teachers) are today. Today's student, with rare and wonderful exceptions, has swallowed a clichéd view of the whole period when the so-called New Critics were calling our attention to the text of the poem. Many have been suckered by cheap social psychologizing, or self-indulgent critical impressionism—literary activities which honor the critic and treat the poet as a skinny fool in the wind. (I hasten to note that, while most students in my classes honor the poem by their attentions, my teaching situation is not typical.)

Still, there are those who honor poetry by their efforts at criticism today. Richard Howard, who wrote for a time for *The American Poetry Review,* loves poets and poems, and himself attempts in his criticism to locate the unstated motivations for this or that poetic manner—an individual search that has much in common with Logan's teaching as I remember it, but which is duplicated nowhere else in contemporary criticism. And there are others who, I think, right or wrong, care for poetry.

We need more who do. Wouldn't it be nice, for example, to have on our hands another Randall Jarrell—a man of taste and sympathy, who wore his learning lightly in his essays, and whose easy criticism was accessible and humane and never far from the essential *simplicity* of poetry? It is no accident, of course, that Jarrell got better and better as a poet as he went more and more for plain but moving speech. His last book was his best.

So now the New Critics are the "old critics." In the American drive for idiosyncratic style, we have done them a disservice. That is, because they turned our attention to the text of the poem, we tried to make the text stranger, more interesting as a text, worthy of their critical labors. At first, this produced the second-best poems of the fifties: the empty sonnets, the nostalgia and irony and local detail that, in the hands of the second-best, became mannerism. Then, it seemed to get better.

I say it seemed to get better because, in the sixties there was a flowering, if you will, of poetic styles. Who could have said where the Beatles would go from *Abbey Road?* We should have known: nowhere. They would break up. Their stylistic assumptions proved apocalyptic. And who could have guessed where those American poets then in their late thirties and forties would go in ten years? How overwhelming was their collective accomplishment to those of us who read their poems in Chicago and in Iowa City!

But now one looks back and sees the germs of self-destruction in so many of their aesthetic decisions: decisions which were exciting for a time but which turned to the dead ends of mannerism and self-righteous preconception. I don't intend to name anyone. These poets are to be honored for what they have done already. And every one of them still alive is always a threat to write powerfully and meaningfully at any time. Nor does my analysis comprehend anything like an entire generation, but only some of the more famous whose extreme aesthetics produced second-rate imitators—among whom, in some cases, were themselves.

Two who have not opted for change over growth, who have affected no idiosyncratic styles, yet have developed strong individual voices rooted in character and experience, are my old teachers, John Logan and Donald Justice. It is no accident that both are poorly anthologized and have friends rather than followers. They have that in common too.

From their teaching, I deduced that both Logan and Justice had read and mastered the New Critics, and that they understood that criticism had to remain after-the-fact, and not be played to. At the same time, they knew that poetry is an art, and that "art" is part of "artifice." Their early books showed that they were interested in writing well. Not strangely, but well. The strangeness would come from inside, from the individual quality of the poet.

It may be telling that both are poorly anthologized. In Logan's case, many of his best poems—for example, "Spring of the Thief"—are too long for the usual compromises of anthologies. But there is no reason for the anthologists to keep reprinting "The Picnic," a poem of adolescent discovery which simply can't keep company with his best work. In Justice's case, one can get awfully weary of seeing "Counting the Mad" and his little poems in the fashion of WCW reprinted time and again. His second and third books, *Night Light* and *Departures,* could provide new stars for anyone's anthology. If anthology editors didn't limit their careful reading to other anthologies, Logan's poems would come from *Spring of the Thief, The Zigzag Walk* and *The Anonymous Lover.*

Of course it has long been true that anthologists tend to reproduce other anthologies. This is part of a larger phenomenon by which reviewers tend to reproduce previous opinion and readers are seduced by labels. So much is published in America that we can be tempted to "check off" books and authors rather than to read them. Because of the way in which I ordered the poems in my first two books, I could tell whether or not a reviewer had read the whole book, and at what speed. Few had not skipped and scanned.

No praise; no blame. No matter. Certainly, for the poet, no second thoughts. One has one's reasons and standards, not plans. To have studied with men or women who, like Logan and Justice, honor one's reasons and (as only the best teachers do) *see through* one's first imitative surfaces of form and content to the deep possibilities—to have been so lucky is to have received a "charge" that one honor the expressive *art* of poetry and show the possibilities to anyone who is interested. Not everyone is. Again: neither praise nor blame. Poetry, like water, seeks its own level. But it is for those who need the *art* of poetry, rather than the mere activity of writing imaginatively, that I write these columns. So long as I do, I can remain a student.

It is not easy to be a student. But it is so much easier than being a teacher. For the overly ambitious misunderstand the teacher and go off half-baked. The best students, and the best teachers, seem to me humble in the face both of the circumstances of our world and the imaginative possibilities of one's art. It is difficult to know who is going to be a fine poet ten or twenty years later, but it is rarely going to be the current star—local or national.

There have been, and are, many good teachers of young poets. But there are fewer and fewer who have taught as well as long. Logan and Justice are exceptional among poets who teach because the student who learns from them is in no way bound to a complete set of aesthetic assumptions. Although each has had his student imitators, neither has encouraged them, and they have been few. (I would place in the second rank of writing teachers those who write well and teach hard but whose students remain examples of the teacher.)

I can't say what John Logan or Donald Justice, or other good poet-teachers like them, will write from here on. Teaching as well as they have may have cost them something. But it may also have kept them "honest." Poetic b.s. and clutter will not survive the attention to a text—the honest-to-goodness easeful and careful reading—required of the responsible teacher. And they have survived the temptations of idiosyncratic style and hysteria which overcame so many of their generation, so that it is open to them, as it may not be to all, to write as well as ever, or better.

Let me put it one last way. The Imagist credo stated it: in poetry, a new cadence means a new idea. Whitman corresponds to that notion; so does Williams; so do many others. More recently, however, the stylistic changes have been smaller and the new ideas mere refinements or fragments of old ideas. If most recently the most interesting "developments" in poetry have been those of imagination, then the poets most able to range freely in the new territories may be those who formerly stayed in the center.

# The Content of a Poem Is Not the Same as Its Contents

One wants to, sometimes needs to, talk about it, yet speaking about poetry is risky. These columns are meant always to direct attention toward poems, not away from them. What was astonishing about the little Williams poem, "The Red Wheelbarrow," when it was first taken out of the context of his book of prose and poetry, *Spring and All* (first published in 1923), and printed by itself? "So much depends," it said, "upon / a red wheel / barrow," and then substituted a somewhat extended description for any explanation of what it is that "depends upon" what was there pictured. To the readers of the time, that poem must have seemed an incomplete sentence.

Williams knew all about the importance of position in grammar. From the first, he would charge a sentence and pull us forward by holding the verb until the end or near it. Later, he would run sentences together so that some words were ambiguous as positioned but meaningful in either case, and so that the grammar of the poem was itself a comment on the subject matter of the poem. Compare his description of the Brueghel painting of Icarus falling (the second poem in the series, "Pictures from Brueghel") with Auden's poem on the same painting, "Musée des Beaux Arts." The first is kinetic and imagistic; the second, meditative and descriptive. There is no point in ranking them. They are as different as their authors, perhaps more so.

Or take a look again at the first of Williams' "3 Stances," a poem called "Elaine" (also from the collection, *Pictures from*

*Brueghel*). In "Elaine," the grammar of the poem catches up many things: the movement of the young girl, summer, awakening sexuality, perhaps even an old man's cool longing. Just as all these things are contained in the summertime leap of the girl, so all these things are caught up in suspension within the poem, until the grammar and the poem come to a resolution at the end. A poem is a thing made of words, said Williams, and he emphasized the word *made:* "When a man makes a poem, makes it, mind you. . . . It isn't what he says that counts as a work of art, it's what he makes. . . ."

So, if a poem is made, why should we fear injury to it when we speak about it? We do fear it, if we have any sense at all. Even those of us who are trained and paid to speak about poems fear it, even those of us who love some poems and want to give others the chance also to fall in love.

How many kinds of love are there? I know about a few of them, enough to know that "love" is not "like" raised to a significant power. Or, if it can be, there is still a kind of "love" which is not that. There is a kind that has no rational basis, and is subject to no one's will to have it otherwise. That kind transcends such concerns as "understanding," in the usual sense of the word, and "forgiveness." It may feel like "salvation," but it is salvation only in its own world. In the world we all share, it may be irresistibly destructive. It most surely belies our analysis and any description of any part of it but its symptoms. So he left his family and fortune to live with her? So she bolted from the altar to go to the desert with another? Those are symptoms, and they tell us little of the essence of such feeling. For that, we go to works of the imagination, perhaps a Shakespeare play about star-crossed lovers, or George Meredith's scarred sequence of poems, *Modern Love.* I have myself written a more-or-less unread book about such things, and literature and art abound with similar efforts. They are all, of course, failures—some few glorious. In a "tough-talking" credo of a sort, the speaker in an e. e. cummings poem begins with the lines, "mr youse needn't be so spry / concernin questions arty" and ends with, "a pretty girl who naked is / is worth a million statues."

How many kinds of poems are there? I know about a few of

them, enough to know that "poetry" is not "prose" raised to a significant power. Or, if it can be, there is still a kind of "poetry" which is not that. There is a kind which—whether rational, irrational or arational in its symptoms—derives from no rational basis, and most surely belies our analysis and any description of any part or aspect of it. So he wrote "about" this or that? So she flushed her lines right, or counted syllables, or spread on a "field" of composition? One rhymed, another didn't. These are symptoms, and they tell us little of the essence of the poems. No wonder that there are so many poems about poetry, so many paintings in which the artist or another painter appears, etc. No wonder the best teaching is tangential, the best lessons riddles without end. Journalists know what reality is; so do advertising men, zealots and literary gurus. For the rest of us, it is hard to find the truth in large amounts.

Here is a little Williams poem we overlook. It is from his *Collected Later Poems*, and is called "The Dish of Fruit":

> The table describes
> nothing: four legs, by which
> it becomes a table. Four lines
> by which it becomes a quatrain,
>
> the poem that lifts the dish
> of fruit, if we say it is like
> a table—how will it describe
> the contents of the poem?

How would you "summarize" such a poem, or "paraphrase" it? Shall we say that it suggests that the form of a poem is not all that there is to a poem, and that a poem also has content in no way described by an analysis of form? Shall we say, also, that the poem suggests that it is impossible to fully apprehend the content of a poem by describing what is *in* the poem?

Or shall we admit that, insofar as the question the poem asks is rhetorical, not to say double-faced and somewhat mystifying, it is not to be answered—not at all a question in the usual sense? And shall we go further to see in the poem a creation of metaphor, and an accumulation of circumstance that never did exist before? Is the poem a lesson by example in the reading of a poem? Does the poem tell us, as another poem which contains fruit and speaks of poetry tells us, that a poem "should not mean / But be."

Shall I say, at this juncture, that the most useful "paraphrase" of this poem in a classroom seems to me to be something like this: The content of a (good) poem is not the same as its contents. Not only is the whole greater than the sum of its parts, it is not to be described by itemizing those parts.

When we talk about poems in the classroom, it is not wrong to build a scaffolding from which to get closer to various parts of a poem, so long as we remember to take down the scaffolding when we are through. Probably our last critical act in discussing a poem in the classroom ought to be to destroy that critical scaffolding—by examining its assumptions and methods, by invalidating it in the face of the poem. Bad critics erect a permanent scaffolding from which to dismantle the poem.

It is a question as to whether the gift of poetry is, for the poet, a blessing or a curse. John Logan has written a marvellous poem, "To a Young Poet Who Fled," in which he recalls the story of the emperor who would arrange to have men roasted alive in a brass bull, so designed that the screams of the dying men, at a distance, made a beautiful music. This, says Kierkegaard, is the condition of the poet. Thus, reasons the philosopher, he would "rather be a swineherd in the hut, understood / by swine, than be a poet misunderstood by men." What sort of criticism dares to stand up to poetry written out of such needs and cries? If not "merely" formalistic, what kind that does not belittle the poet and reduce the poem? Let the critic look in the mirror while he or she answers.

Or, if poetry is made from peace or from ecstasy, my question remains. How are we to honor it yet speak of it? In "An Introduction to Some Poems," William Stafford writes: "Look: no one ever promised for sure / that we would sing. We have decided / to moan. In a strange dance that / we don't understand till we do it, we / have to carry on." That's the first stanza. In the third, he writes: "We find it an awful thing to meet people, / serious or not, who have turned into vacant / effective people, so far lost that they / won't believe their own feelings / enough to follow them out." And here is the fourth stanza and two lines of the fifth: "The authentic is a line from one thing / along to the next; it interests us. / Strangely, it relates to what works, / but is not quite the same. It never / swerves for revenge, // Or profit, or fame: it holds / together something more than the world. . . ."

That is why poets get nervous when asked how they do it, or even why. Their evasions, in essays about their poems and in remarks to what we call "live" audiences (are readers dead?), take several forms. One is the nose-in-the-text version, probably the most useful, perhaps the most honest as well as modest response, in which the poet tells us how to read the poem by showing us what it says and in what order and in what way. Another is the, "Aw, shucks" disclaimer, in which the poet reckons that inspiration is everything. Another is the background story—irrelevant if it wasn't in the poem to be known in the first place, but often fascinating and appearing to cast light on the poet's needs.

Even simple questions about technique often present tautologies for the poet. How to respond at all? In an early poem called "Near," Stafford begins:

> Walking along in this not quite prose way
> we both know it is not quite prose we speak. . . .

I have said that the most useful, perhaps the most honest, response by the poet to groups of readers is the one that looks again at the text. Even though there is so much more to say about a poem or, rather, a poem is so much more. Pound faces this problem in an early chapter of his *ABC of Reading*. Looking for a place to start his description of the best poetry, he tries out two. The first is a statement by Dante: "A Canzone is a composition of words set to music." The second is a statement by Coleridge or De Quincey (he is not sure which) to the effect that "the quality of a great poet is everywhere present, and nowhere visible as a distinct excitement."

Now Pound elects to begin with Dante, in this case because

he wishes to begin with what is undeniable. But he doesn't reject the other statement. To the contrary, what he says, in a disarming pairing of sentences, is: "This would be a more dangerous *starting*-point. It is probably true."

I think it true. For example, though I once said in print that I wished my poems to be "both surprising and inevitable at every turn," I now believe such a distinction to be false. The Coleridge or De Quincey statement holds hands with my feeling now that inevitability in poetry subsumes surprise—that, indeed, there is only the one lasting surprise: that of inevitability, the thing said rightly for all time at one time. But I recognize that such a statement—the one Pound uses, or my own—represents, not just attention, but values. It would be foolish to attempt to elucidate such a statement at the beginning of, say, an undergraduate course in the reading of modern and contemporary poetry. One might get back a sympathetic response in discussions and in course papers, but it would only be an echo: the self saying it to the self.

Given our colossal ignorance about life and the world and the elaboration of genealogies over the centuries, it is possible that we are always falling most in love with those who are, unknowingly, distant flesh and blood to us. Science fiction? Perhaps. Yet surely we go among poems in this manner—or as if, say, through an art gallery, picking and choosing, caring for one canvas, disdaining another. If the collection is first-rate, chances are that we are responding to whatever we need at the moment. It is not just our level of "understanding" or "sophistication" that is involved—but memories and needs much deeper. Returning to the gallery (or anthology), we might make different choices next time. Indeed, we will.

Even the simplest of poetic terms is infinitely variable to the poet. Here are two simple examples and corrections. First, Pound's definition of an image. Is it that an image is a visual imagining? Is it that an image is an object in a poem? Is it that an image is something descriptive? Not at all. An image, said Pound, is "an intellectual and emotional complex in an instant of time." That is a far cry from "Show and Tell."

Here is a second example. This one is taken from Williams,

who also did not mean to suggest a simple-minded rule of composition by his famous line in *Book One* of *Paterson:* "Say it! No ideas but in things." In *Book Two,* he amends it to read, "No ideas but / in the facts." And in *Book Five,* Williams—that master of lyric thought—writes: "You can learn from poems / that an empty head tapped on / sounds hollow / in any language!"

For the poet, life is better with poetry ("through" poetry?—the nature of reality and perception is an ongoing mystery, though there is no necessity that we "solve" it). That may be all we can say. We can go on and on about uses of poetry, kinds of poetry, definitions of what seems to matter to us in good poetry, values in the reading or writing of poetry, etc. On the other hand, when I don't write for any length of time, I feel dissatisfied, then despondent, even tired. I find fault with small matters, and sometimes turn cranky and difficult to live with. But when I am writing, all is right with some small part of my world; perhaps one should say that all is right with one entire, if small, universe. Publication isn't the issue: I publish little of what I write, circulate poems to magazines infrequently, allow finished poems to lie around in ragged form for months (sometimes years), and do not feel the same thrill when a poem is published that I do in writing it. In fact, I don't feel as great a thrill from publication as I do from rereading one of my poems in which, through rereading, I rediscover a perception or emotion in a context that makes it convincing or telling. I think that I am typical in this regard. To alter slightly a Yiddish proverb: With poems in your pocket, you are wise and you are handsome and you sing well too.

Writing to Kappus, Rilke said, "This above all—ask yourself in the stillest hour of your night: *Must* I write?" The implication is that, if the answer is no, one should give it up.

That's a severe prescription. We can make it less severe, and more generally applicable, if we further define "must" in terms of the quality of survival one needs or wants. Regardless, Rilke's advice takes account of the central fact about writing: that the motivation behind it may or may not be related to the general effect of the result. Art doesn't need a purpose to come into being. In the presence of poetry, the believer in poetry may feel at times that it is not the reader the poet loves. Here is a little poem about this by Jack Gilbert, called "In Dispraise of Poetry," from the collection *Views of Jeopardy:*

> When the King of Siam disliked a courtier,
> He gave him a beautiful white elephant.
> The miracle beast deserved such ritual
> That to care for him properly meant ruin.
> Yet to care for him improperly was worse.
> It appears the gift could not be refused.

If at times the motivation of lovers or poets is not to be discerned, so not judged, it is still true that this can be a license for hokum. I admit this. In our age, most communication uses the method of juxtapositioning. The film cut, the abrupt transition or absence of transition, the associational mode of thought—all are so easy for us to follow that it is difficult to imagine it were ever otherwise. Even a first-grader in our TV-, film- and newsmagazine-laden society is extremely sophisticated in "understanding" the current methods.

Moreover, readers of poetry have no difficulty accepting the psychological makeup of the poet as a factor in perception. When Eliot wrote that the evening was "spread out against the sky / Like a patient etherized upon a table," the critics were confused. Does the evening sky actually look like that, they wanted to know. How subjective it seemed! And that was the point. Whether or not the evening sky looks "like that" often or to many of us, it can be seen that way by a mind as filled with ennui, if not despair, as is the mind of Mr. J. Alfred Prufrock. We no longer have any difficulty understanding this.

In fact, we are so trained, if not sophisticated, in the current methods of style and perception, that it is possible to forget that the use of such methods once presented issues and required conscious, artful decisions. Associational thinking and linear thinking are both "linear" at some level, but the emphasis makes a difference. Presented with most or all of the steps in linear thinking or viewing, we can understand and judge with confidence for ourselves. The training we require, if any, is—

once again—merely that of attentiveness to a text and sometimes the ability to research a word or a reference.

Most of the poetry that one reads in literary magazines today, however, more readily employs associative thinking, keeping the poem spare by leaving out paths of perception and thought and including in the poem only the stopping points. Sometimes, we can make out, after long attention, what must have been the now-invisible path. When poetry "leaps," we usually cannot. (Actually, the notion of "leaping" poetry—which is written in leaper's colonies—requires a subdivision: that of "leapfrogging" poetry, in which a perception, once used to jump over, can no longer be seen in its place but has come around in front to be used again.)

So we come again to the matter of trust. The reader must have it. And we come again to the complex notion of "sincerity" in poetry. Without the appearance of "sincerity," the poem will not command the reader's trust. In a previous column, I tried to link the notion of sincerity in poetry with "an appearance of moral commitment" (a phrase by William Stafford). I say again that sincerity in a poem does not seem to me a matter of style or voice or biography but of perception and the ways in which the poet travels between the physical and the mental.

The problem exists also for the novelist—more so, I think, insofar as the novel insists on itself as a first-hand report. Dorothy Bell tells me that she has had difficulty at times believing the narrator of a seemingly autobiographical novel when he or she has made factual errors. In one such book, the female narrator mentioned the long, winding tendrils of an avocado plant and the easy, conventional birth of a second child to a woman who had borne her first by Caesarean section—as if this were common. Avocado plants don't have tendrils to send winding, and a woman who bears her first child by Caesarean section until recently, and in most cases, would have had to bear future children in the same way. These were small matters in a novel, but they hurt the book's credibility nonetheless; for how could the reader trust the narrator's analysis of other people's actions and motivations when such factual matters had been set wrong?

Still, the imagination is not subject to such double-checking—even less so, perhaps, to the extent that a poem "leaves out" the physical world and linear thought in favor of associational thought and a surreal inner landscape.

Perhaps that is why so much criticism of poetry is personalist or merely appreciative today. Luckily, for the poet, the poem is not written to be judged. Afterwards, the poet may become a "first reader," and judge too. But first there is that wonderful feeling that comes with the writing—once it is underway. For me, the feeling builds as the poem goes on. There comes a point when the poem seems to cohere—to shape a range, a direction, and a set of movements for itself in terms of singular language. At such times, I know for the first time that what has been written so far can become a poem—can be finished, or made into a whole wherein the poet came upon something and the reader can too. At that point, the feeling within me is so charged that I find it impossible to sit still. My whole body bristles, and often I must get out and walk about before working further on the poem. I have seen indications that this sort of metabolic charge occurs for others, too. Sometimes, a lesser "charge" is a prerequisite to starting a poem. How often, it seems, one begins to write after a brisk walk: the revving up of the metabolism seems to encourage perception, particularly the special observation of the physical.

For the poet, writing is better than not writing. For the poet—who must first engage himself or herself—writing at all means writing up to the level of discovery: linguistic, rational, psychological, emotional.

The question poets ask one another more than any other is, "Are you writing?" It sounds meaningless, but is not. When a poet "is writing"—whether or not he/she is writing a poem that very day or week or month even—the world is one sort of place. For the poet who does not feel he/she "is writing," the world is very different. Is one world more real than the other? Who can know? The poet prefers the former. Does anyone know why one person arouses another to love? The poet prefers arousal. Here is a wonderful poem by Donald Finkel about the making of love and poetry. It appears in the collection *A Joyful Noise.*

*Hands*

The poem makes truth a little more disturbing,
like a good bra, lifts it and holds it out
in both hands. (In some of the flashier stores
there's a model with the hands stitched on, in red or black.)

Lately the world you wed, for want of such hands,
sags in the bed beside you like a tired wife.
For want of such hands, the face of the moon is bored,
the tree does not stretch and yearn, nor the groin tighten.

Devious or frank, in any case,
the poem is calculated to arouse.
Lean back and let its hands play freely on you:
there comes a moment, lifted and aroused,
when the two of you are equally beautiful.

And the poem is a dance. Does one ever really know why one dances when and as one does? The dance is also an escape, no doubt, from whatever is not the dance. There is a poem about this, too—a charming and winning poem by William Stafford, included in the collection, *Someday, Maybe.* It is called "The Escape," and in it the very lines of the poem speak to us about the act of reading the poem. "Every life is like this," we are told, "carried on while some inane plot / tries to intrude. How lucky we were / to find each other and make our escape. . . ."

Finally, one must answer questions about the identity and quality of poetry the way one would answer such questions about jazz. You'll know when you hear/see it. If one has to ask the question, one will never know the answer. Etc. To my mind, attention and relaxation are one, and all that one needs.

There is the traditional story in which the Zen master presents a student with the *koan:* "What is the sound of one hand?"

The student, according to the story, snaps his fingers. "No, no," says the master. "Go to your room for a week and meditate. When you have been enlightened, come back." In a week, the student returns to offer a lengthy statement on the meaning of existence. "That's stupid," says the master. "Return to your room for a week. When you have been enlightened, come back." In another week, the student again returns, this time to fall to the ground and play dead. But the master kicks him, saying, "No, no, no. Go back to your room for a month and meditate. If, at the end of a month, you have not been enlightened, kill yourself."

The story concludes by saying that, on the third day, the student was enlightened.

# Language That Makes a Difference

Consider the return to religion of the soul without the body?

It is a time in which poets no longer insist on evidence of art, or even of human intention. It was Yeats, that painstaking laborer whose practice was to manage a few lines in several hours and who labored so hard and long at a poem that he was able to make poems by versifying prose, who told us, in "Adam's Curse," in which the young poet is preening for Maud Gonne, "A line will take us hours maybe; / Yet if it does not seem a moment's thought, / Our stitching and unstitching has been naught."

Why is Yeats a great poet? It is always fun to ask a Yeats scholar that question because it is so much more difficult to answer than the same question asked about, say, Stevens, Williams or Eliot. Yeats' mature style is not nearly so individual as that of most of the great modern poets who wrote in English: Stevens, Williams, Auden, Eliot, Frost, Pound, Crane, Cummings, Thomas, Moore, Dickinson, Whitman or Hopkins, for example. Of course, Yeats is a great poet in part because of the scope and precision of his arguments and the number of forms and genres in which he wrote well. Etc. But that does not explain why any single Yeats poem seems great. I think certain poems by Yeats are great because Yeats took a central position with regard both to content and form, yet labored sufficiently to create from the form and content a third thing—inextricable, unparaphrasable. It may be that his very willingness to make poetry from plans laid in prose kept him in this central position. The result is that his poems remain also in the emotional center, with which the emotions of most readers overlap.

Over the years, Yeats' belief that the hard labors of writing good poetry should disappear into the ease and grace of the poem itself has turned into a trust in spontaneity and found materials—spontaneity itself being another method, perhaps the modern replacement for labor, of finding. In *Book Five* of *Paterson*, Williams reports for us an interview with Mike Wallace, in which Wallace quotes a bit of Williams' poetry ("2 partridges / 2 mallard ducks / a Dunganese crab / 24 hours out / of the Pacific / and 2 live-frozen / trout / from Denmark") and adds, "Now, that sounds just like a fashionable grocery list!" And Williams replies, "It is a fashionable grocery list." *Paterson* makes room for all sorts of prose and found language. One continuous effort in modern poetry has been this effort to make room for all sorts of found items—from the Sanskrit used by Eliot to Williams' grocery list and Olson's anthropological histories. At their best, poets have not merely made room but have woven the found pieces into the fabric of the poem. Marianne Moore, whose method of writing syllabic lines of greatly differing lengths (the count of each line remaining the same from stanza to stanza) enabled her to make poetry from such scientific and literary excerpts as often appear in the works of lesser poets as prose, insisted on the difference in the original version of her often-anthologized poem, "Poetry," when she wrote: "nor is it valid / to discriminate against 'business documents and / school-books'; all these phenomena are important. One must make a distinction / however: when dragged into prominence by half poets, the result is not poetry. . . ."

It has always seemed to me telling that Williams closed his effort at a long mythic poem, *Paterson*, with an extended lyric. Indeed, *Book Five* is surely the most lyrical book of the poem and hardly seems to pause for its few interruptions of prose. By then, I believe, he knew that prose is not poetry and subject matter is not art. Accordingly, while there are many superb poems in his *Selected Poems*, and wonderful passages in *Paterson*, the reader who would read his most profound work must turn to *Pictures from Brueghel and Other Poems* and read to the end.

Regardless, Williams teaches us again, by his example, the truth of the Yeats statement that poetry need not show the labor of composition, and may be the better for not showing it. Williams was the genius of one sort of direct language, Frost the formal genius of another, Stevens the genius of a third, and there have been others.

But when we look for the deep influence of, say, Stevens, we find many who are superficially influenced but few who show Stevens' purity of diction and severe clarity. Among those who do, I would name John Ashbery (in all of his best poems), Donald Justice and Mark Strand. If we look for the influence of Frost, which is really the influence of Hardy, we find again the superficially influenced but few who show Frost's clarifying mixture of speech, meter, proverb and detail, though there is surely one: William Stafford. If we look for the influence of Eliot, we find the superficial influence of "Prufrock" and *The Waste Land* before we find contemporary examples of the clarity of thought and simplicity of language brought to perfection in *The Four Quartets.* Nor is this phenomenon limited to the apparent influence of poets who wrote in English. Those who claim the influence of Sappho or Martial often show only the ability to be lusty and wise-ass. The inheritors of Spanish surrealism seem to have turned the mysteries in such writing into mere mystification. Those who have learned from Rilke often turn his conversations with God to mere friendship and his great heart to spite and despair, though it seems to me that both James Wright and Jon Anderson have gone ahead with care and understanding.

As for Williams, who believed so fervently in a sense of "measure" while writing what we misleadingly call "free verse," his influence shows itself mainly in the flat language and lack of measure in the work of all those who learned from him only the pleasure of the local. There are some who learned more, among whom are Robert Creeley and David Ignatow.

Despite Creeley's statements of indebtedness to Charles Olson, I have never believed that it was Olson's poetry which influenced Creeley's. The evidence is not in the texts. Olson's friendship and intelligence were crucial to Creeley, as was his suggestion that Creeley listen to his own speech. But where the good work is concerned, I believe that the influences are Latin and Williams. Anyone who reads Williams' *Collected Early* and *Collected Later Poems,* and also reads that marvellous book of Creeley's, *For Love,* will see this for himself/herself. The syntax is Latinate; the philosophic purity and precision (*rooted in language,* as always) is Williams. Influences notwithstanding, the result of course is Creeley.

Our trust in what we call "free verse," in spontaneity, in the importance of almost any detail, and in the rightness of common language lead us to seek more than ever a certain appearance of artlessness. The appearance, however, remembering Yeats and Moore, is not the fact. The question arises as to how minimal one's artfulness must be, or can be, if one hopes for a poem not only authentic and widely accessible but special and inexhaustible. This is really a philosophic and aesthetic dilemma, which I shall return to later.

I would say that David Ignatow's best poems, which I like very much and which seem to me to show the influence of Williams (or perhaps the same influences which affected Williams—working, ways of thinking and experiencing), show the minimum. Here is a little poem by Ignatow:

### And That Night

A photo is taken of the family
enjoying the sunshine
and that night someone sneaks up
from behind in your flat
as you sit reading the papers
and clobbers you. You never
find out why or who, you just
lean back and die.
The sunshine is gone too,
the photograph gets into the news.
You bring up a family in three small rooms,
this crazy man comes along
to finish it off.

It would be possible to look at a poem as small as this one and see no art at all. That would be a mistake. For, although this poem by Ignatow is about as flat and quick as can be, it is far better than the flat poems of second-best regionalism which now dominate our little magazines. To speak about its art, to stop down its time, may seem a bit much, but here goes.

For one thing, the line in this poem has an identity which goes hand in hand with syntax and speech. The first line is a syntactical unit (containing smaller syntactical units, to be sure). It is a pleasure to find that the next line extends the sentence. Having extended the first sentence to two lines, the poet extends the sentence a lot further. But the way in which line three runs over to line four is different from the way in which line one connects with line two. The poem does not allow itself the lethargy of lesser poems in flat language. When a caesura occurs in the midst of line six and again in line seven, the effect is definite and singular, both in terms of varying our formal expectations and in sticking to the subject. But, having made two lines in a row like those two, the poem ends with six consecutive lines which are larger whole pieces of syntax, as were the first three lines of the poem. In other words, the line counts for something here—just a little, to be sure, but enough to matter. In the end, the lining is what makes that three-line final sentence so simply moving.

And the diction of the poem seems simple enough. Yet there are things to notice. Little things that one might think do not matter, but which make all the difference. In line one, referring to "the family" in that way is workingman's language, and is ever so slightly different in its emotional coloration from "our family," or "my family" or "your family." To say that the family is "enjoying the sunshine" in line two is also to use a telling phrase. It is the diction of the forties and fifties and goes along with Sunday "visiting" and "having company over." Rich people "bask" in the sunshine, or "luxuriate in its golden rays." Poor and middle-class people go out to "enjoy" it, and at *home*. Indeed, the family in this poem lives in a "flat"—in fact, in "three small rooms." "Clobbers you" in line six is worth noticing. In young poets' young poems, "clobbers" might become part of a poem which made a point of using slangy words, thus emptying them all. Here, however, it seems a natural, accurate word. To see the eighth line as worthy, one might have to imagine some other ways of saying "lean back and die." The absurd ease of those words is, in this poem, better than the other ways you might imagine.

Is anything in this poem imaginative in terms of the physical? Line nine is. Line ten quickly says it just the way we might: "the photograph gets into the news," and indeed it is an event to be noticed when one's photograph "gets into the news." Said here flatly, it makes the absurdity of it all that much more precise.

Finally, there are those simple and moving last three lines, colloquial at every turn yet never fancy. To "bring up" a family, "this" crazy man, and "to finish it off" are pieces of the language of a speaker we neither doubt nor dismiss. Looking back to the title of the poem, we might now notice the way in which the title belongs to the middle of the poem and what it now suggests about the middle of a story coinciding with the abrupt end of a life.

I realize that I have chosen a very small poem to be deliberate about. I did so deliberately. For I believe that no one will ever read or write poems better, nor will poems ever mean more to a life or a community, by our talking of "deep images," "projective verse," themes, arguments, symbols, myths and the like, unless there is concern first for the precision of the word, the phrase and the line.

Poetry is language that makes a difference. One way to examine the quality of what appears to be straightforward language is to see what difference it makes to rephrase it. About the good poem, one thus discovers that the language is not so ordinary after all. Similarly, one way to see whether the lining of a free verse poem makes a difference is to recast it into other lines. About the good poem, one finds that it makes a difference. I would go further to say that, if an image in a poem could be any of a dozen other images without making a difference, then the image is worth little and the poem of such imagery just another piece of writing without the capability of creating or recreating precise observations or precise thoughts or precise emotions. However much such writing means to its author, it can never mean anything so particular or deep to us. Eventually, it will dissolve, even for its author.

An object in a poem, or an image, or a comparison makes a difference when it is *used*—not just in one line or one stanza, but over the whole of the poem. If the poet's attention turns from it for a while, it will still be part and parcel of the fullest meaning (and often the very conclusion) of the poem. Otherwise, we are being given that light form of diversion known as description. Descriptive art and accumulative art (this latter from the surrealist junkyard—spare parts for random adventures) are to the art of poetry what magazine illustration is to the art of painting.

In this respect, it is to the poem's credit that the sunshine of line two reappears (by its absence) in line nine, the photo from line one reappears in line ten, the murderer from lines three and four appears again in line twelve, and the newspapers from line five reappear in line ten. That may be a greater number of overt connections than one can expect to find in many surrealist epics. The irony in the appearance of the family photograph in the news, which occurs only because the head of the family has been murdered, is a form of artifice. Saying in line nine that "the sunshine is gone too" is a form of artifice, recognizably so because we realize that the sunshine is not gone at all, of course, from the world of the living. The sunshine remains, too, in the photograph. Saying in lines six and seven that the victim never finds out the "why or who" of the murder (of course!) is a form of artifice.

I don't believe for a moment that David Ignatow necessarily thought out these things. Indeed, his is an art of apparent artlessness in the extreme. It takes its formal aesthetic definition in contradistinction to poems of a more elevated diction, poems of regular rhythms and regular rhymes, poems of strange objects and startling metaphors. Moreover, as I stated at the outset, in choosing this poem I deliberately chose a poem of minimal "effects." If there is as much to notice as I have about the writing in this poem (and there is more), how much must there be to notice in other good poems which do not derive from such a consciously skeletal aesthetic.

The question is what is the minimal amount of artifice necessary to a good poem, but the question cannot be answered. That is because, in asking it, we make it seem as if artifice were an overlay, something one adds to a poem. It seems that Yeats sometimes did it. If others could also, I do not believe they could do so in free verse.

Rather, a language which is precise and economic and therefore interesting derives from perception, and perception from character, and character from experience and intelligence and training, and it is therefore indistinguishable from what is being said, indistinguishable from both the kind and quality of perception—of observation and of thought.

In the late fifties and early sixties, we saw a number of our best poets turn from metered and rhymed verse to free verse (though not all by any means). Some renounced their earlier poems or teachers. At the time, we were concerned for a body without a soul, a poetry without spirit. If the terms grew smaller—if spirit, for example, was reduced to mere emotion—still we knew that craft was no substitute for art. In the late sixties, it became routine for reviewers to dismiss well-written first books of poetry as so much technique. Meter and periodic rhyme were by themselves signals to some to dismiss such poems as exercises in ornamentation. We have now a horde of young poets of energy and imagination who can neither read properly, nor fully understand, the poems of a Richard Wilbur, a James Merrill, or an Anthony Hecht, nor follow the "meter-making arguments" of Yeats, Stevens, Hopkins, Dickinson, Hardy, Frost or Roethke.

Nonetheless, we had always hoped for a wider audience for serious poetry, and if that depended on a new and visible emphasis on the essence of poetry—the genius of its arguments, the power of its subjects, the depth of its emotions— then a loosening of the technical restraints which so intimidated readers was acceptable. The virtue of such a loosening up was proved time and again in the new work in syllabics and free verse in such books as Allen Ginsberg's *Howl* (1956) and

*Kaddish* (1961), Frank O'Hara's *Meditations in an Emergency* (1957), Robert Lowell's *Life Studies* (1959), Charles Olson's *The Distances* (1960), Robert Duncan's *The Opening of the Field* (1960), Denise Levertov's *The Jacob's Ladder* (1961), Alan Dugan's *Poems* (1961), Anne Sexton's *All My Pretty Ones* (1961), David Ignatow's *Say Pardon* (1961), Robert Creeley's *For Love* (1962), Robert Bly's *Silence in the Snowy Fields* (1962), Kenneth Koch's *Thank You* (1962), William Stafford's *Traveling Through the Dark* (1962), W. S. Merwin's *The Moving Target* (1963), Louis Simpson's *At the End of the Open Road* (1963), John Logan's *Spring of the Thief* (1963), James Wright's *The Branch Will Not Break* (1963), John Ashbery's *Rivers and Mountains* (1966), Donald Finkel's *A Joyful Noise* (1966), Gary Snyder's *A Range of Poems* (collecting three previous and two new books in 1966), Donald Justice's *Night Light* (1967), Galway Kinnell's *Body Rags* (1968), and in other books by these and other poets.

For those of us beginning to write poetry (about the act of writing, it was still common to say that one was *practicing* one's art), the American poetry of the sixties seemed insurmountable. If those poets were so good already, each in an individual style, how much better would they be—how much more expansive and penetrating both—in another ten or twenty years?

Many of us learned to write by reading these good books and some which followed, along with the works of Williams, Pound, Whitman, Eliot, Stevens and others.

But prosody was not an issue. Our attention was fixed on other aspects of the work at hand: the depth of new imagery, the diction, the syntax, the ironic or visionary attitude, etc. If the poems we were reading were in fact well-written, they seemed effortless or natural extensions of personality, and we quickly took for granted such elements as rhythm and organization in these well-written poems which contained so much else.

Now it happens that these good poets knew meter backwards and forwards, and had studied form and composition, though some pretended otherwise. In most cases, they had published first books of rhymed, metered verse. Their free verse did not forget that English remains a stressed language whether or not you choose to count the stresses, and that their placement makes a difference. Their free verse—check it for yourself—in most cases owes much to the accentual-syllabic line with its usual metrical variations.

In the eleventh year of my "teaching" for a graduate writing program which brings together, year in and year out, an astonishingly various, gifted and interesting group of young poets, I believe that excellence in the writing of poetry derives from genius, character, and professional humility. I am also convinced that it will take an enormous amount of character for any young poet to become as good in his or her own way as was a Williams or a Stevens or a Whitman or a Dickinson, or even as good as the best poets in this country now in their late forties, fifties and sixties. Everything legislates against it.

For one thing, anyone who starts out to learn how to write will likely be held up to scorn for it. Where once a reviewer might rightly call a well-written first book "promising," the new reviewer is likely not to know much about meter or composition, nor to care. He or she is more likely to be looking for instructions for living—responding to those which seem right on whatever day of the week it happens to be.

Nonetheless, I believe that the young poet is better off to concentrate on artifice while his or her character builds. Character will assert itself in any event. But what chance for special accomplishment has the poet who has no interest in language? Fame notwithstanding, the answer is none. In poetry, precision and perception and thought depend on language that makes a difference. Let the young poet, and the teacher too, look at the individual poem. But first let them look at the stanza. And before that, at the word, the phrase and the line. To quote Miss Moore, "There is a great amount of poetry in unconscious fastidiousness."

Or doesn't it make any difference? It's true that our imperfections are only temporary. To write these articles, I have to believe that the metaphor of eternity is useful, even crucial, to our every little act.

# Learning from Translations

I want to write this time, as informally as possible, about the influence of poetry in translation on contemporary American poets. I write from the point of view of one who is inexpert in foreign languages and does not translate, yet who now responds more to the work of some foreign poets in translation than to the work of many fine American poets. Moreover, this would not have been the case a few years ago when, like almost everyone, I was caught up in the virtuosity of American poetry—its personal voices, intimate subjects and individualized methods.

In beginning this article, there are three things on my mind: (1) an abiding feeling that American poets often act like tourists when reading foreign poets—stereotyping them and granting them methods, subjects and tones of voice which we deny ourselves; (2) a sense that, because so many poems do matter to us even in translation, the term "poetry" requires a working definition larger than any of craft—including that which I employed last time ("Poetry is language that makes a difference."); (3) a superb new anthology of translations into English: *Another Republic*, "European and South American Writers," edited by Charles Simic and Mark Strand, to be published in August [1976] by The Ecco Press.

Clearly, the influence of foreign poetry on contemporary American poetry is nothing new. In particular, Spanish surrealism and French surrealism have influenced, for better or worse, a great many American poets. Usually, the talk about such influences centers around the poetic imagination. But the influences have been, preponderantly, those of image and metaphor, of images as secret corridors to the subconscious. So accepted is this emphasis that the poetic term "imagination" is in danger of being reduced in scope to image, metaphor and archetype. Because the influences are mainly of limited methods—in particular, of imagery—the poets most widely translated and most imitated were for a while those who seemed flashiest.

In the last few years, however, there has been a great increase in translation of poetry—good translation and hack translation both. Alas, we all know of writers who will translate from any language on assignment, and whose translations of poetry sound either like prose or exclusively like the translator's own poetry. Nonetheless, such work is prerequisite, it would seem, to first-rate translation, and there is now much first-rate work available.

And much of the new translating has been from poets less flashy and less famous than those chosen first. In much of the work just now becoming available to us in the form of first-rate translation, we find an easy power we long for. Compared to the work we have been discovering in other countries, much American poetry of the past decade sounds tortured, naive, self-righteous and cacophonous. For cultural reasons and their psychological consequences, we have not permitted ourselves the range of emotion and speech of an Akhmatova, an Amichai, a Cavafy, an Alberti, a Drummond de Andrade, a Milosz, a Ritsos. Indeed, given the poetry of a Ritsos or an Alberti, for example, an American poet would be far likelier to be taken by the imagistic imaginations of each than by the quality of their discourse and emotion.

In the world of poetry, much American poetry seems provincial. We have been technocratic in our internalization of subject matter, easily adopting the imagistic tendencies of others but refusing a place in our work for the fullest range and variety of human expression and emotion we permit elsewhere.

I am tempted to venture some loose questions. For example,

have you ever felt, as a reader, that a Chinese poem praised for its provincial simplicity and clear lines would be, were it suddenly identified as an American poem, dismissed as thin and simple-minded? Might not a Hebrew poem admired for its profound tone of religious sorrow, were it identified as an American poem, be written off as church verse or the conventions of literary Judaism? Have you wondered whether a Greek poem respected for its historical scope and conversational intimacy, were it identified as American, would not be set aside as the work of an academic stylist? Would not the marvellously subtle political allegory and irony in a poem by one of any number of Eastern Europeans, were the poem identified as American instead, become a target for critical sarcasm for using a device "of the fifties" and playing it safe?

As I said, it may be that foreign poetry translated into English gets a more sympathetic reading because, without knowing it, we accord to poets in other countries a freedom of expression we deny ourselves. Obviously, such blanket sympathy sometimes serves to apologize for mediocre work by those whose political trials we would influence, or whose culture we envy, or about whose past we feel guilt. And it is true, too, that we permit ourselves easy critical sympathies for mediocre work when we think that it is very "Chinese," or very "Greek," or very "Spanish," etc. Nonetheless, I am here concerned with a book of excellent translations of excellent verse, and it occurs to me that the sympathy we accord foreign poetry (in place of the contempt too often directed at American poetry) not only enables us to see just how good these poems are, but also is itself requisite to the best work that we can do.

In an interview in the Winter, 1972 issue of *The Ohio Review*, one of the editors of *Another Republic*, Mark Strand, talks about a new international style with which, now, the anthology he and Charles Simic have edited is concerned. This international style, says Strand, "has a lot to do with plainness of diction, a certain reliance on surrealist techniques, a certain reliance on journalistic techniques, a strong narrative element, etc." Later in the same passage, Strand says, "And I think we read other poets in translation, oddly enough, for content."

*For content.* Is content as important as "form" in its largest sense? Can we read poetry for its content? I would answer yes. Of course, formless poems form no clear content either. But I do believe poetry has content and is not just form. It's not in my nature to believe otherwise. Moreover, I believe that as readers, we value, if secretly, the content of our favorite poems.

*For content.* Is it possible that our sympathy or generosity or charity toward poems in translation comes about because we are reading for content? *Something* accounts for the freedom of expression we reserve for others.

We allow Yehuda Amichai the ease with which he titles one of the poems in *Another Republic* simply "My Mother Once Told Me" and begins it, "My mother once told me / Not to sleep with flowers in the room. / Since then I have not slept with flowers. / I sleep alone, without them." We do not denigrate the diction of this poem for its flatness. Nor has the critical notion of flat diction any relevance here. Is that because, inasmuch as we are aware that we are not reading the author's precise words, we read *for content?* If so there is an ironic lesson about range, ease and voice in what we may fail to realize is the very method of Amichai's poems. Here, then, is a whole poem—simple, clever and moving as translated by Assia Gutmann—by this Hebrew poet who is neither self-conscious nor too proud: "A Pity. We Were Such A Good Invention":

> They amputated
> Your thighs off my hips.
> As far as I'm concerned
> They are all surgeons. All of them.
>
> They dismantled us
> Each from the other.
> As far as I'm concerned
> They are all engineers. All of them.
>
> A pity. We were such a good
> And loving invention.
> An airplane made from a man and wife.
> Wings and everything.
> We hovered a little above the earth.
>
> We even flew a little.

Think of the demand we make of American poems today, particularly of "political" poems, that they be "up-front." Such a demand has been translated, in practice, into poems of angry journalism on the one hand and surrealist hysteria on the other. But isn't the Amichai piece a political poem, put in the locality of love? Isn't restraint part of the effect? Isn't the intimacy of the metaphor, the singleness, the localized detail, the essential *modesty* of the self and its language here, emotionally more resonant than grand pronouncements about the politics of technology? I confess that I think so.

Here is another poem of modesty and political or philosophical wisdom at times seemingly foreign to America, C. P. Cavafy's "Hidden Things," taken from *Passions and Ancient Days,* translated by Edmund Keeley and George Savidis (The Dial Press, 1971):

> From all the things I did and all the things I said
> let no one try to find out who I was.
> An obstacle was there transforming
> the actions and the manner of my life.
> An obstacle was often there
> to silence me when I began to speak.
> From my most unnoticed actions
> and my most veiled writing—
> from these alone will I be understood.
> But maybe it isn't worth so much concern
> and so much effort to discover who I really am.
> Later, in a more perfect society,
> someone else made just like me
> is certain to appear and act freely.

In *Another Republic,* you will find a poem by Nicanor Parra, "I Take Back Everything I've Said," which speaks to the same issue.

In the same collection, there appears a poem by Fernando Pessoa, "Tobacco Shop," which begins, "I'm nothing. / I'll always be nothing." Try to imagine certain American poets writing, in their own voices or through personae, "I'm nothing. I do not contain multitudes, only myself—which is unimportant.

My opinions do not matter. My famous versatility with language—in particular, with comparison-making—is a flawed system of devices, a ruse and a self-deception." Etc. Can you imagine most American poets not wanting to be God, or at least king? Book blurbs which rank poets are born of this royal vanity, as is the contempt of some reviewers.

Carrying my rhetorical and fanciful questions even further and generalizing, dare we imagine American poets ending their love-affair with idiosyncrasy and the self?

I do. In fact, I think that that is what is happening right now, and that our interest in the poetry of the poets in *Another Republic* and others is an indicator. We are tired, finally, of poets who say, "Look at me!"—sometimes at great length. We are sick to death of those who publish their sorrows and ask mercy only for themselves. And we have come to the end of our belief in those who claim to speak for all men but who offer little more than political wisecracks. American influence is shrinking, and so are our egos. In the end, our materialism inescapably diminished and our individualism revealed for its selfishness, we may be freer than before.

From *Another Republic*, here is a poem by Carlos Drummond de Andrade, translated by Mark Strand, "Souvenir of the Ancient World":

Clara strolled in the garden with the children.
The sky was green over the grass,
the water was golden under the bridges,
other elements were blue and rose and orange,
a policeman smiled, bicycles passed,
a girl stepped onto the lawn to catch a bird,
the whole world—Germany, China—all was quiet around Clara.

The children looked at the sky: it was not forbidden.
Mouth, nose, eyes were open. There was no danger.
What Clara feared were the flu, the heat, the insects.
Clara feared missing the eleven o'clock trolley,
waiting for letters slow to arrive,
not always being able to wear a new dress. But she
    strolled in the garden, in the morning!
They had gardens, they had mornings in those days!

How wondrously simple! A portrait of a lost way of life. It is, surely, a poem of imagination, yet it does not strain. Nor does it leap about. It is balanced, even circular, and at ease with its circumstances. If the translation is not misleading, it is at ease with its own language. We are shown Clara's world and, in the final line, we are let in on the speaker's (poet's?) attitude and opinion, if briefly—all in the tone.

Yet there is artifice to this "plain speaking." Perhaps it is worthwhile to interrupt the flow of language in this poem so that it can be held up for inspection. As for the title, we need only note how much it increases the poem's dimensions. Imagine, in its place, a title such as "The Garden"—a mere label. The real title extends the circumstances of the poem in both space and time and, in its hyperbole, supplies emotional coloration.

The poem neither leaps nor strays. Rather, it takes us back and forth between the unquestionable and the imaginative, then between the unquestionable and the revealing. It wins us over with single-minded patience.

After what must seem the easiest and most direct of first lines come two lines which seem quite as matter-of-fact but which are not: the sky is *green* over the grass, and the water *golden* under the bridges. The green sky leads to the less remarkable golden water and on to the fourth line which can raise no question either of veracity or meaning. Moving from description to event, the poem continues to play upon the reassurance of the specific and the familiar even as it heightens, selects, transforms. Nothing unusual occurs in line five, something much less usual occurs in line six, and line seven is wholly imaginative: the *whole world* is quiet around Clara (and if we doubt this, there is the charming evidence—*Germany, China!*).

In this respect, consider the balance of the four halves of lines one and two of stanza two. There is nothing strange in what the first and fourth parts of those two lines report: that the children looked at the sky and that there was no danger. But there is something revealing about parts two and three. To say that "it was not forbidden" suggests, suddenly, that it might have been or perhaps that it might have come to be. To note that the children's mouths, noses and eyes are open is to dwell curiously, with almost medical detachment, on that sensory freedom we should not take for granted.

There follows a list of some minor troubles of Clara's—not one of them unknown to all of us, not one of them raised to a stage of cultural prominence. The list is so clearly illustrative over and over of the relative safety of that former life that all there remains to do is to remind us of what *they* had, and when. Finally, it is a pretty little poem, mixing nostalgia and, yes, politics, and all without striding, without showmanship, without self-congratulation, superiority, threats or self-pity. More important, perhaps, by its very method it reveals its author's respect for common people and ordinary readers. It is decidedly humane.

In another poem by Drummond de Andrade collected in the same anthology, the speaker makes an elephant of scraps— a "poor elephant" who stands for the self and for a belief in natural forms. At night, tired of searching for friends "in a tired world," the elephant collapses: "The paste gives way / and all his contents, / forgiveness, sweetness, / feathers, cotton, / burst out on the rug, / like a myth torn apart."

Wouldn't many American poet-critics downgrade an American poem which explained itself with a line such as "like a myth torn apart?" And wouldn't they collapse into their reserve in the presence of "forgiveness, sweetness"? But here is the clincher: the poem contains one more line. What do you think it is? Is it an allusion to an illustrative myth? An echo of Rilke? A line of contempt for half the world? The strangest image ever made? No. The line is, "Tomorrow I begin again."

It is in accepting lines like "Tomorrow I begin again" that we see that we need to reclaim from bad popular verse the whole range of common expression we turned from in justifying the "difficulty" of modern poetry.

There is reason enough for trying to. In "Tobacco Shop," Pessoa writes, "Today I'm bowled over, as if the truth had seized me. / Today I'm clearheaded, as if I were going to die. . . ." And in Milosz's "Dedication," there appear these lines: "You whom I could not save / Listen to me. / Try to understand this simple speech as I would be ashamed of another. / I swear, there is in me no wizardry of words. / I speak to you with silence like a cloud or a tree."

Do not be misled into thinking that "silence like a cloud or a tree" is surreal or mysterious. He is speaking to the dead of his nation.

*Another Republic* contains the work of Yehuda Amichai, Johannes Bobrowski, Italo Calvino, Paul Celan, Julio Cortazar, Carlos Drummond de Andrade, Jean Follain, Zbigniew Herbert, Miroslav Holub, Henri Michaux, Czeslaw Milosz, Nicanor Parra, Octavio Paz, Fernando Pessoa, Francis Ponge, Vasko Popa and Yanis Ritsos. The editors have excluded from the collection poems by many who have already received much publication and attention in English—including Neruda, Borges, Char and the best-known Russian poets. There are no poets from the Scandinavian countries.

Nor is there any representation of Rafael Alberti, whom Strand translated so superbly in *The Owl's Insomnia* (Atheneum, 1973). The editors point out that Alberti was a precursor to the less self-conscious international style of the anthology. Yet I cannot resist offering here one example of Alberti's "surrealism" for its coherence. With an imaginative propulsion via the image second to none, this poem still shows what a "surreal" imagination can create when it is not in love with itself. This is Alberti's "They Have Gone":

They are the leaves,
leaves destroyed because they wanted to live forever,
because they didn't want to think for six moons about what
    makes a wasteland,
because they didn't want to know why a drop of water insists
    on hitting a naked skull already nailed to bad weather.
Other disgraces could occur to us.
What's the date today?

The leaves sweep themselves into piles with the bones that in
    life never acquired rights to a tomb.
I know that I hurt you,

that there is no place to escape to,
that the blood in my veins has suffered a seizure of smoke.
You had yellow eyes and now you obviously can't understand
    that they're ashes.

We *are* not.
We *were* this or that.

Of course, I deliberately selected a short one for this article. Nor need I dissect the images. How strong they are, yet how developed is the whole poem. It does not leap or loiter or carouse. Nor was the poet afraid to conclude with a wholly abstract, metaphysical and explanatory couplet. I admire that ease of will in general and the range which derives from such ease. I have included the Cavafy and Alberti poems here to indicate that, while the work of the poets in *Another Republic* by its very "international style" invites us to notice an ease of language and an avoidance of flashy techniques, we might have noticed it earlier and elsewhere. I might have mentioned Seferis, Radnoti, Akhmatova. . . .

A student tells me that he wishes he had a nickel for each line he has taken out of his poems because it did not seem sufficiently "cool" to be part of an American poem. A colleague tells me that she often notices in foreign poets the influence of Whitman. Whitman! (*Another Republic* contains a "Salutation to Walt Whitman" by Pessoa, as well as a poem "To Robinson Jeffers" by Milosz.) I think that these are two sides of the same coin: we find much poetry from other countries seductive, yet we fail to see just why and so deny its essential qualities to our own poems.

It is true, as I said, that we sometimes also overlook posing, confusion or sentimentality in foreign poems because they seem so "Spanish" or so "French" or whatever. It is also true that the quality of translation makes all the difference. For example, in choosing the Keeley translation of Cavafy's "Hidden Things," I rejected certain versions which seem to me inferior as poems, however literal.

Hence, I am not suggesting that foreign poetry is superior to American poetry, nor that we should be instructed by any and all foreign poetry. Rather, I am suggesting only that, in our stereotyping and self-denial, we have too often eliminated from our work the good with the not-so-good. Toward our own work, we sometimes exhibit an astonishing meanness of spirit. We have been technocrats of intensity. Even those poets who made careers of revolution against what they perceived to be the technique-oriented poetry of the fifties in many cases ended up replacing it with a poetry of artificial intensity: merely another kind of technical gee-whiz.

In the article previous to this, I said that poetry is language that makes a difference, and I tried to show with an example that this is so even in the seemingly most artless of poems. I do not now take back that loose definition. Yet I think any such definition, which begins in craft and moves outward in application, requires a companion definition—one which begins in content and narrows in application to look at language. Many might serve, including Pound's for literature: news that STAYS news.

For the editors of *Another Republic* rightly point out that the poets in their anthology exhibit characteristics "not indigenous to any country or literary movement. They are international. . . . And because of the great amount of translating that has been done in recent years more literature has been available to them than to any previous generation of writers. It is largely through translation that they know each other's work, and even manage to be influenced by it. Such a situation would seem to render false Frost's dictum that poetry is what is lost in translation, for in fact it is poetry that is retained in translation."

I am aware that *Another Republic* is a selection of poets who exhibit this "international style," and that it may be this common style which permits translation in which the "poetry" is retained. Nonetheless, this collection serves excellently to remind us that our notions of individual style (and even of a distinctly American literature) may limit the range and power of our poetic expression. In any case, such notions are beside the point. .

Nor is there any need to distinguish between outward-turning and inward-turning poetry: the distinction is false. I would hope that the Alberti poem illustrates the falsity of such a distinction. To the extent that American poets, like these poets, are becoming aware again that the self and the subconscious cannot be separated from that which is not the self and all conscious existence, then something is happening, without benefit of poetry gurus. *Another Republic* contains a poem by Zbigniew Herbert in which the poet witnesses the execution of five men, confesses to himself that he has always known of such events, and asks, "so why have I been writing / unimportant poems on flowers". Then he lists what the five men had spoken of the night before: dreams, a brothel, poker, booze, "of girls / of fruit / of life." The poem goes one stanza further:

> thus one can use in poetry
> names of Greek shepherds
> one can attempt to catch the color of morning sky
> write of love
> and also
> once again
> in dead earnest
> offer to the betrayed world
> a rose

This simultaneous grasp of realism and art seems very attractive to me. It is not a matter of form, minimal here, but of content. The content is a matter, primarily, of structure. And structure is form, raising again the question of just what it is that is retained in translation. But we begin with content.

# From Tangier

Trying to write poems in another country—particularly in a culture as different from one's own as the Moroccan is from the American—throws one back on how little we know about the writing of poetry. That is because personal need is the heart of it.

I expected no difficulty writing poems here, nor any new insights into the writing process. I had been to Morocco before, with my family—to Tetuan, Meknes, Casablanca, Marrakech, Kenitra and Tangier. We had been told not to go: it was seedy and dangerous. But we had gone anyway and been glad to get to a culture not trying to be European or American. The physical ways of the people, threatening to some, appeal to me—probably because I grew up in a town of fishermen, farmers and small shopkeepers. Hence, the plan this time was to stay mainly in Tangier and Marrakech, and to write every day.

Previously, I had always had trouble writing while travelling or displaced. Others have done better. Galway Kinnell wrote and revised sections of *The Book of Nightmares* in motels and while teaching for one semester in Iowa City. John Logan has been able to write while on the move. Once he finished a gorgeous lyric of affection and desire titled "Suzannah" (later changed to "Suzanne," to accord with the fact) while visiting me but briefly.

My experience had been different. Given my first nonholiday vacation ever in the summer of 1967, I did what I thought all poets did when they were given time off. I went to another country: Mexico. Dorothy, Nathan (who was seven), Jason (who was one) and I drove until forced to decide, then chose Guanajuato—at that time relatively free of foreigners. We lived in Marfil, three miles up the mountain. Grateful to have time free from work, I felt I should write every day. The poems piled up for three months, the final two and a half weeks in Ajijic. In the end, however, I had no more poems worth saving than I would have had at home writing less often—when I both had to and could have. The obvious lessons of that trip were that the need to write takes precedence over the will to write, and that the need comes and goes on its own erratic and sensitive schedule.

Given an entire semester free from teaching in 1970, I added the summer. I thought, then, it would be good simply to change the landscape, and we went to live in California—at first in Santa Cruz, later in San Francisco. Yet, even having stayed in the States, I found that I wrote no more than usual—not because I felt foreign and culturally uprooted as in rural central Mexico, but because moving and setting-up, particularly with a family, always takes time, and because problems which arise under such circumstances inevitably seem (to my displaced center) more difficult, more constant, more time- and thought-consuming, than they do at home. The writing lesson that time was that even a small move makes one a tourist in the new place.

Five years later, having again been given a term off, I took our family to Spain where we lived first in Nerja, a small Andalusian fishing village in the south (from where we took our first trip to Morocco), and later in Sitges, a slightly larger, more international town just below Barcelona. After that we travelled in France and England. Although I spent most of my writing time at a long poem since abandoned, I was not discouraged. By then I had realized that whenever my emotional center was in suspension because uprooted it would be best to save the new circumstances, the new views, for the writing back home. A simple obedience to Wordsworth's methodology: emotion recollected in tranquillity.

Similarly, I had to live in Iowa for ten years before I began to comprehend the people and the land. I try to read with sympathy the inevitable "Iowa" poems written by those who come to live there for a short time as students or teachers, but it is nonetheless clear to me that these poems are rarely about Iowa but often about the aggravated loneliness, isolation and neuroses of the sensitive transient. Given the mobility of American writers, I wonder how many poems are predestined by the special weakness of the sadly displaced transient or ga-ga tourist.

Thus, when I received a fellowship for 1976 (but postponed by me for a year), I knew where I should be to write poems: right at home. To write of what one sees elsewhere—not merely to take note of it, but to write at some length and with some depth about it—would be, for me, I now knew, to write a kind of tourist poetry. It is not natural to me to understand a place I have not lived long in, and it is equally unnatural to me to circumvent that difficulty by writing about the past culture and history of a place: I am neither very cultured nor very learned.

Nonetheless, I returned to Tangier intending to write while here. In turn, the effort has thrown me back on who I am and what expression is authentic to me. William Stafford once referred to his "portion" in writing. I feel that my portion, and yours too, is not to be analyzed, but derives more mysteriously than we sometimes admit from need. That is why Rilke suggested that only love, not criticism, could hope to grasp works of art—which are, he wrote, "of an infinite loneliness."

We must accept our individual portions—those of us who have the need, neurotic or healthy, to understand the world and the self through writing. I must accept, for example, the fact that the first finished poem to emerge during this stay in Tangier is not about the Cave of Hercules, nor about the fishing town of Azila, nor about the Moroccans in their djellabas, nor about the expatriate lives on the "Old Mountain," nor about the call to prayer of the muezzin. No, the first of the poems I accept as authentic and which clearly fills a personal need is, revealingly, a poem about what I go through here to write a letter home. Reading it, I know more about myself. When I was writing it, and it began to take a shape I knew would be completed, I felt for the first time that I could stay here and write.

Later, the cave and the muezzin may find their way into a poem, but only as counters for a life centered elsewhere—as, for instance, Williams remembered the hills and caves of Granada, not to write of Spain, but to write the local truth of a lifetime in "Asphodel, That Greeny Flower." For the moment, the lesson is clear. And I feel the broadening possibilities of travel for literary expression, given a coherence of self, for the first time.

Nor is Tangier a poor place for an American poet to think about aesthetics. Two others, Carol Muske and Daniel Halpern, and I go into the kasbah day and night. The maze of narrow passageways holds a sea of shoppers. Everyone is open in the intermittent rains: spice-sellers, perfume chemists, rug-merchants, the keepers of hundreds of tiny stalls of brass and djellabas. Cafés and kif-houses are packed. The smells and the music are strong, and the crowds move *en masse.* How many people there are in these alleys, in the squares and cafés! And how many readers do you think you have here? Well, we did see a literary sight the first night: a young shopkeeper reading a novel in English. *War and Peace? Herzog?* Not in your lifetime. It was Erich Segal's *Love Story!*

To be fair, I should note that there *are* literary lives here. Paul Bowles is still here and Edouard Roditi comes and goes. And there are others. The writer Mohamed Choukri stopped us the other day in the *Medina* to show us a book he had just received: M. L. Rosenthal's *The Modern Poets*—all in Arabic!

We know little of our own needs and motives, less about others'. The academic life is dangerous to talent, not because it is tame (even academics travel, dare and fail—privately all the time and sometimes in public), but because it offers too many definitions. The Academy often trusts language almost without reservation. Writers who matter to us do not.

When I began to write these informal essays in 1975, I was not at all sure what the effect would be—on you or on me. I knew only that I wanted to direct attention toward poems rather than away from them, to offer the positive testimony of a reader, and to avoid self-promotion. I wavered once, in using the unnamed author of a first book of poems as a straw man and, when I saw it in print, I regretted it, and said so to the author. Now, two years and nine articles from the beginning, starting the essays of 1977, it seems right to risk these few remarks (confessions?) about writing and teaching in the service of reminding myself and you too of how little we know about them. Into this stew, begun from this base in Tangier, I plan to toss in words by Saul Bellow, my father, Robert Frost, James Wright, Samuel Johnson and John Ciardi.

Incidentally, I brought Whitman's poetry with me—the only book I brought—but Whitman doesn't read all that well here. His spirit abides. But his universality of address and his preachiness seem essentially immodest and ethereal in this country of modesty, secrecy, strong scents and hard bargaining. It must seem heretical to some of you to say this, and I report it with reluctance, and unsurely. No one will be more sorry than I. Nor does it mean I am ready to break my pact with his spirit. In portion 24 of "Song of Myself," he describes "Walt Whitman, a kosmos, of Manhattan the son, / Turbulent, fleshy, sensual, eating, drinking and breeding, / No sentimentalist, no stander above men and women or apart from them, / No more modest than immodest." And I still would believe in him, though the democratic optimism which informs his work seems at this remove still a tentative experiment.

Oh, but how I welcome his common spirit. A central position—intellectually, linguistically, psychologically and emotionally—has come to seem to me the best place for the poet when possible: best because healthiest, best because that is where the truths outside oneself are, best because language can go that far safely but little farther.

"In his Nobel lecture at the Swedish Academy," the Associated Press reported (I tore this from a newspaper *en route*), "Bellow said that writers do not adequately represent mankind, in particular America, and the notions that have become respectable among intellectuals about society, sex, politics and human nature are insufficiently challenged.

"Speaking of books that confirm the thought of Marx,

Baudelaire and D. H. Lawrence, Bellow said: 'How weary we are of them. How poorly they represent us. The pictures they offer no more resemble us than we resemble the reconstructed reptiles and other monsters in a museum of paleontology. We are much more limber, versatile, better articulated; there is much more to us, we all feel it.' "

"'With increasing frequency,'" Bellow continued, "'I dismiss as merely respectable opinions I have long held—or thought I held—and try to discern what I have really lived by and what others live by.'"

"'One can't tell writers what to do. The imagination must find its own path. But one can fervently wish that they—that we—would come back from the periphery. We do not, we writers, represent mankind adequately.'"

Bellow is an educated man. I am not. Yet I tried to accept some of those opinions too—those he rejects now with increasing frequency. I never could put them on adequately, however. In fact, I recognize now that I came to poetry partly because it seemed, at its best, *defiantly* true. Of course, I too am only a product of my background.

My father, Saul Botsian (changed to Saul Bell), was an immigrant from the Ukraine and, like so many of our fathers, a man of great common sense. He knew from experience that the Tsar's men and the Bolsheviks were two sides of the same coin. He had seen great evil, and did not confuse it with personal vice, minor flaw and human failing. He would refuse our easy complaints against others with the remark, "Well, he has to make a living too." In an impure world, we would do the best we could. He was a man of character, courage, good humor and charity. Although he had taught himself English and would read the daily tabloid, it would not have been easy or natural for him to read fiction or poetry.

Nor for me. Nor is it now.

The act of reading is not easy for me. My older son, Nathan, reads thousands of words a minute, and remembers all of it. My younger son, Jason, can read mythology by the afternoon-full. My wife, Dorothy, can't find enough decent fiction to satisfy her. Yet I feel as if I read thirty words a minute when I care about what it is I am reading. And heaven help me if a sentence continues from the right-hand page to the next: I may have to recheck the syntax three times. The rest of the time, I tend to dawdle over a phrase or even a word—lost in what it reveals about the author, intended or unintended suggestions, the logic or illogic of it—and often responding to what I take to be the writer's ignorance or evil with a thundering mental "No!"

Moreover, I much prefer reading philosophy to reading fiction, though there are of course specific fiction texts I admire and friends' books that engage me at first on the level of friendship. And I confess to having read much fiction and drama in the past—especially when a graduate student. But I found it interesting most of the time only as an occasion for conversation, because I don't really *like* literature.

"Poetry," says Marianne Moore, "I too dislike it." And do I know what she meant! John Berryman (whose distant cousin, Ellen Berryman, ironically, has shown up here in Tangier this week!), through the Henry of his *Dream Songs,* says, "literature bores me, especially great literature," and I know what *he* means! When David Ignatow writes, "No theory will stand up to a chicken's guts / being cleaned out. . . ." I nod in agreement and there goes literary criticism.

Still, I read a great amount of poetry, which does not seem to me to contradict my essential distaste for what Pound called *kulchur* and (out of personal bearing) for the fancy language of overdistinction.

The right speed for reading a good poem has always seemed to me to be the speed at which a two- or three-finger typist might type it. That seems the pace at which the nuances of words, the grace of rhythm and the mental shapeliness of organization will reveal themselves for sure. It is good preparation for the teacher to type the student's poem slowly, just as it is commonplace to hear a student expressing new understanding of a poem he or she has had to type slowly—perhaps for a class.

We are not a nation of readers in any significant sense. Nor do we trust literature, or any art. We trust literature less than others because literature (mis)uses the very materials with which we tell specific truths. We associate literature with the Academy, and we do not trust the Academy—which (mis)uses language to make opinion seem fact. We do not trust politicians or journalists, with good reason—more misusers of language.

I represent this national philistinism (or common sense) as well as anyone. Like most people, I am by instinct and upbringing more interested in what is "out there" than in inventions from "within." I do not stay long interested in the dead-end aesthetics of idiosyncracy, however interesting they are when they start out. The question of poetic form is broader than that, as Frost notes in the essay with which he introduced his *Complete Poems* (Holt, Rinehart and Winston, 1949), "The Figure a Poem Makes."

There he notes an old desire of philosophers and a new desire of artists to play with the "toy" of abstraction—in the sense of separating out a part or aspect of art. Because "sound is the gold in the ore" of a poem, says Frost, "we will have the sound out alone and dispense with the inessential. We do till we make the discovery that the object in writing poetry is to make all poems sound as different as possible from each other, and the resources for that of vowels, consonants, punctuation, syntax, words, sentences, meter are not enough. We need the help of context—meaning—subject matter. That is the greatest help towards variety. All that can be done with words is soon told. So also with meter. . . . And we are back in poetry as merely one more art of having something to say."

So meaning will vary tune in—Frost would prefer it this way—meter. Similarly, it is theme, he says, that permits a poem to have "wildness and at the same time a subject that shall be fulfilled."

"The figure a poem makes. It begins in delight and ends in wisdom. . . . It has an outcome that though unforeseen was predestined from the very first image of the original mood—and indeed from the very mood. It is but a trick poem and no poem at all if the best of it was thought of first and saved for the last."

And, finally: "I tell how there may be a better wildness of logic than of inconsequence. But the logic is backward, in retrospect, after the act. It must be more felt than seen ahead like prophecy."

All of this from an American poet who wrote as accessibly as anyone, and so much from the local. Hardy was another. Work like theirs lasts because of it, because their voices and views (or visions, if you like) are personal without being idiosyncratic.

James Wright, asked to write about his poems for the first edition of *The Distinctive Voice* (ed. William J. Martz, Scott, Foresman and Co., 1966), put it this way: "In the work of the best poets that I know, the voice of poetry is an articulation of true feeling and thought, at once personal and general, shaped in such a way as to evoke from many readers an equally personal response. Any poet begins with the effort to be true to himself. But the poets who matter most are those who discover and demonstrate that the effort to be true to themselves inevitably results in being true to others." And here Wright quotes Samuel Johnson's *Preface to Shakespeare:*

> Nothing can please many or please long but just representations of general nature. Particular manners can be known to few, and few only can judge how nearly they are copied. The irregular combinations of fanciful invention may delight awhile, by that novelty of which the common satiety of life sends us all in quest. But the pleasures of sudden wonder are soon exhausted, and the mind can only repose on the stability of truth.

In the same book, John Ciardi distinguishes between "style" and "a style," as between "voice" and "a voice." It is a matter of emphasis to make the distinction, he rightly notes, but useful nonetheless in distinguishing between "the way the medium is used to forward 'the subject' or 'the aesthetic experience' (*style*) and the way the medium is used to forward the author's individuality (*a style*). 'Style' is, at root, representational . . . whereas 'a style' is signatory."

Ciardi wonders (in 1966!) if we do not err in favoring "a

voice" over "voice." "For when the impulse is first to achieve a unique way of speaking and then to find the world, the danger is that not enough world will be found."

Some of the implications of these reports, confessions and quotations are obvious, some perhaps not. They serve to remind me that a fine congruency of form and content is always mysterious—a fact that should limit our confidence in what we say about how to write. There is so much we do not know. For example, responding to the poetry of students should be difficult because we do not know the sources of the work. How much is neurosis and how much art? How much is talent and how much will? There are two kinds of teaching which I think must inevitably be destructive: the teaching of tricks (in which the student is left to make a life of surface invention) and master classes (in which the insufferable or hypnotic example of the teacher creates the limiting dogmatism and idolatory of the second-best).

One might go further into implications having a personal twist. For example, my personal rules for teaching, if I had any rules, might include: Know what to encourage; Do not injure the personality; Stay in the world; and so forth.

Another implication might be that proper reviewing would seek to describe the work carefully in *its* terms, and to excerpt what one likes most.

But the really important implication, I think, is that one's aesthetic must fit one's self and one's life. If art is ruining a life, it is not art; it is self-destruction.

The reasons I like particularly the late work of Williams, Whitman even so, much of Stevens, Jarrell's later work, and much of the poetry coming to us in translation from Eastern Europe and Latin America is because now their aesthetic fits me. I don't say that it is superior to any other. But I know that, however crucial a period of inventing language has been to me (and I still think it can benefit anyone), it has been necessary finally to consider how important it is to me to write so that anyone can read it (*very* important) and what the aesthetic implications are. I feel that I have come to a beginning (a mature aesthetic)—in my case, a beginning that would not be reached, I always knew, until about the age of forty. I am thirty-nine, and feel lucky to have come this little way already.

I also feel that, whatever I can do, anyone can. It is not that much. But it is my life, and the greatest pleasure and power of all is still, in Iowa or Tangier, that of self-recognition.

# The Technique of the Right Attitude

I propose to describe (in the sense of "talk 'round") a poetry of consciousness, economy and profound ease. In so doing, I will be talking about mental disciplines which require time and effort and on which everything else in the writing of poetry may depend.

I take for epigraph two short texts. The first is by Charlie Mingus, the jazz bassist, speaking about creativity in the July, 1977 issue of *Mainliner:*

"Love of something sparks creativity. . . . You get hooked on something early and that's your outlet. When I was a baby, I heard some tune on my mother's crystal set—da-da-da-da-da—I was paralyzed. After that, always when I was unhappy, when I got a whipping, I went to the piano. And it all came out. First the piano. Later the bass.

"That's once I got hooked. The other time was when I first heard Charlie Parker. I was a studio musician then, but hearing Bird changed my life. Charlie Parker was the essence of creativity. Bird wasn't just playing, he was composing as he played. And where did it come from? Where in Kansas City did he learn to quote Stravinsky while he was playing?

"Creativity is more than just being different. Being different isn't necessarily being original. Anybody can play weird; that's easy. What's hard is to be as simple as Bach. What you have to do is know where you're coming from, be able to do what's gone before, but go on from there in your own way. . . .

"My son's a painter. All through school his teachers tell him he's a genius. I tell him to paint me an apple that looks like an apple before he paints me one that doesn't. Go where you go, but start from somewhere recognizable. Making the simple complicated is commonplace; making the complicated simple, awesomely simple, that's creativity."

.   .   .   .

The second of the texts I propose for its epigraphic value is by Samuel Johnson, from his *Preface to Shakespeare.* James Wright, in speaking about his own poetic values, incorporated this statement into his remarks in the 1966 anthology, *The Distinctive Voice,* edited by William J. Martz. This is Johnson: "Nothing can please many or please long but just representations of general nature. Particular manners can be known to few, and few only can judge how nearly they are copied. The irregular combinations of fanciful invention may delight awhile, by that novelty of which the common satiety of life sends us all in quest. But the pleasures of sudden wonder are soon exhausted, and the mind can only repose on the stability of truth."

Johnson equates truth in art with "just representations of general nature." Behind such an equation rests the concept of recognition. "Particular manners can be known to few, and few only can judge how nearly they are copied."

In keeping with the Johnson text, therefore, my intention is to tell you only things that you already know. For example, we know what most people think of poetry. Most people do not recognize "just representations of their general natures" in poetry at all. Most people think poetry is lies and decoration, mystification and good manners. It seems too strenuous, too strident, at other times too frivolous, to be read without a feeling afterwards of diminishment. Or it poses: the poet as the melancholic sensitive, the poet as the wounded, the poet as the self-righteous, writing as Literature. Most people know what poetry is. Poetry is a waste of time.

Therefore, when poets show up in popular art, they show up as clowns or dopes. Perhaps you remember the poet of the old television series called "Meet Millie." His name, alas, was Marvin, and his odes to bathtubs and the like destroyed any interest I might have had in serious poetry at the time. In the reruns of Ernie Kovacs, you can see his poet, Percy Dovetonsils, endlessly cooing "Flower in the Crannied Wall." And there's Henry Gibson, with his oversized daisy and his not-quite-funny verses. Even "Happy Days," the current hit television series, once offered us a young bohemian lady marvelling over that wonderful book of poems, *Warts on My Soul*.

Of course, it isn't poetry that is so widely jeered and dismissed. It's poeticizing. "Poeticizing" is what I would call it. A good copy desk editor would probably call it, simply, "over-writing." Unfortunately, the word "poetry" is common, while the word "poeticizing" is rare. In the common vernacular, "poetry" and "poeticizing" mean the same thing. "Oh, that's only poetry," is what people say. Therefore, I must agree not only with those who say about poetry, "I, too, dislike it," but also with those who actually do. What I dislike in poems, and what I think defeats them, is the *"poitry"* in them, the thoughtless stylization that becomes the style of the art of one's time, what my friend Stanley Plumly calls "creative writing." (The other thing I think defeats poems is the prose in them, but that's another matter.)

Now obviously, I couldn't be offering these remarks if I didn't, like you, carry a sense, if not a definition, of good poetry, and if I didn't love it and learn from it. Nonetheless, I think it may be helpful to remind ourselves occasionally that language is rarely the vehicle for truth and beauty. One need only read the newspapers and magazines, listen to television or radio, or—alas—read most poems to know that language is, most of the time, the vehicle for lies, distortions, hyperbole and just plain busywork.

It is my hypothesis that, in poetry, such errors can derive from the strain of aesthetic ambition: from thinking of poetry as universal art rather than as personal expression, and from thinking of poetry as righteous vision rather than as obsessive viewpoints.

We know that poetry begins in self-expression and/or in

verbal game-playing. Verbal game-playing is what Auden was endorsing when he said that he saw no promise in the student who wished to write poems because he or she had things to say, but did see promise in the student who wanted to hang around words to see what *they* had to say. If self-expression by itself leads to what we might call "popular poetry," distinguished by its sentimentality, verbal gamesmanship by itself leads to what we might call "literary poetry," distinguished by its on-high presumptions and its reductiveness, whether in the Academy or in the streets. It is my opinion now that neither self-expression nor gamesmanship are sufficient apprenticeships or happy pursuits unless they are combined with mental attitudes which have little to do with verse forms or syntax, or with what is on our minds.

William Stafford is a good example of a poet who plays the game of poetry, though not at all as Auden would have it played. He writes all the time and, like all of our best poets, he is willing to fail. In a short essay about his method, called "A Way of Writing," he takes the position that words are cheap. "A writer," says Stafford, "is not so much someone who has something to say as he is someone who has found a process that will bring about new things he would not have thought of if he had not started to say them."

.    .    .    .

Stafford is easy about the materials of poetry. He trusts them. He is able to use anything that occurs to him because he unburdens himself of the weight of significance. He doesn't have to play for keeps. It is sometimes, he says, like practice. In this respect, I have noticed, as I'm certain that many of you have, how often the poem written as an exercise, perhaps on assignment, turns out better than the poem which was written out of great ambition for our perceptions.

Yet perception is, in the end, the better part of poetry: that stability of truth on which the mind can find, according to Samuel Johnson, its only repose. Perception has two meanings: sight and insight. I believe that both sight and insight derive from fierce consciousness, whether it begins in looking at a small object or in paying attention to all of the implications and resonances of an idea or image. "Paint me an apple that looks like an apple before you paint me one that doesn't." I believe, also, that conscious perception is our only path to both the conscious world and the unconscious. Everyone knows that Frost's poem, "Stopping by Woods on a Snowy Evening," is about taking a breather between towns. And everyone knows what it's *really* about.

I mean to emphasize here a sense of consciousness as awareness. P. D. Ouspensky's first five lectures, available in *The Psychology of Man's Possible Evolution*, will serve to elaborate on this.

There, he refuses the usual distinction between the conscious and the unconscious. Instead, he defines four states of consciousness: sleep, waking state (in which we are influenced by the dreams and slight sensory impressions of sleep, and which differs little from sleep), self-consciousness (not the nervousness of the adolescent but adult consciousness of the self) and objective consciousness.

It is Ouspensky's view that, although man has the possibility of these four states of consciousness, he actually lives in only two states. One part passes in sleep, and the other part in what is called "waking state," though in reality his waking state differs very little from sleep.

"In ordinary life," he says, "man knows nothing of 'objective consciousness'" (the fourth state). The third state, "self-consciousness," occurs but rarely and sometimes goes unrecognized. According to Ouspensky, "these glimpses of consciousness come in exceptional moments, in highly emotional states, in moments of danger, in very new and unexpected circumstances and situations; or sometimes in quite ordinary moments when nothing in particular happens." Ouspensky further claims that what we remember long after—say, from childhood—we remember because those were our conscious (that is, self-conscious) moments: our moments of heightened awareness, if you like.

Now suppose we were able to banish from the final versions of our poems all lies disguised as the truth, including distortions and exaggerations, all hypotheses about which we know better, and all the arty overwriting. What would be left, in fact, would be perception . . . in both senses of the word. Sight would occur as telling detail, and insight as wholly inevitable suggestion and idea.

.  .  .  .

Now I would like to show you a poem by a beginner. For all practical purposes, this is her first poem. Because she had signed up for a writing class, she had tried one poem before this, but it was both short and little, obscure, impersonal, concerning nothing of interest to her or to anyone else—in short, unexpressive. It was a mite arty, that's all, and she disowned it. Eventually, she came to see me, beside herself with her inability even to begin a poem.

I offered nothing complicated. We talked about simply looking at things. We talked about looking at things but not saying the first thing that enters one's mind. We talked about *using* whatever is put into a poem rather than just mentioning it—that is, developing rather than accumulating. We talked about trusting one's instinct toward speech. But most of all we talked about writing about little things, starting small, and not worrying about significance or "art." Here, then, is her "first" poem. As Stafford has said elsewhere about any of our efforts, it's not *Paradise Lost* but it's not quite unforgivable either.

### On The Bank

In this hot noon, the trees
would gather their shade back
into themselves.
But I find room under the willow,
and in the split-maple's split shadow,
eight or more ducks spread their brown fat,
and sleep, bellies flattened in the dust,
their legs, I guess, tucked up
somewhere.

The river slips South,
its loose skin, more brown than green, wrinkling,
and folding on itself, and floating slicks
of sunlight; running,
more green than brown,
where it folds and falls in shadows.
Below the ripple, in its black bed,
the river is a more solid thing.
It sleeps and spreads. It slides
toward the Gulf.
And in the great willow's green heart, beneath the bark,
grey, wrinkled, cracked,
the river seeps.
The leaves turn, and turn over
their grey undersides.

—Anne Welch

What is going on in this poem is this: a girl is paying such close attention that she, and what she attends to, form personal combinations. She isn't creating new forms for content we can't yet imagine: that is a matter for genius and the Age and is beyond premature discussion. But she is finding, already in this first poem, something of her world and herself. For one thing, she has located death and life and seen them run together right there on the bank of the Iowa River. And, because she is looking and responding, rather than explaining what she might have thought beforehand, she is not preempting the essential mystery of life.

Art ought to make the mysteries of life deeper. It should neither render them shallow by partial explanation, nor replace them with artificial mysteries—that is, mystifications. And there is enough apprehensible mystery to go around. You can see it in the woods in the snow if you happen to stop long enough between towns. That is, if you keep trying. If you *keep* on trying, you can see it on the bank of the river in your home town as easily as in, say, Rome or Athens.

As I said, Anne Welch's first poem is not perfect, even in its own terms. When she reaches the stage at which she can hear it, we might hold up a standard high enough to suggest more criticism than would be helpful at first. You may not agree, but I think the phrase "hot noon" insufficient to the heat of the day. I think that the last two sentences in the poem end the poem but do not quite finish it. And the phrase "the river seeps" does not seem to me sufficient to the perception behind it. Also, there is an ordinariness to most of the verbs which allows some of the lines to seem merely informational.

But there are also lines in this poem in which the sensibility of the poet mixes nicely with information: for example, the way in which she says that she sits in the shade: "But I find room under the willow." Sensibility gets into that line because of the imaginative maneuver in the preceding sentence, where she hypothesizes that, on a day like today, the trees themselves would take back their shade.

There are other indications of the poet's sensibility in this poem, sometimes in a turn of phrase, sometimes in what is noticed. Paralleling the maple and its shadow, with the phrase "split-maple's split shadow," even as she parallels herself and the ducks, is one such. Numbering the ducks "eight or more" is, I think, charming. Hypothesizing that the ducks' legs are tucked up "somewhere" (because she cannot see them) is a bit coy but this is, after all, her first poem. And the detail is not without significance in revealing her concerns. Saying "the river is a more solid thing" is expressive, I think. And there is something worthy in letting the heart of the great willow be "green," though because she is at pains to make sure that we know everything to be true she injures the line somewhat by telling us that the heart is "beneath the bark."

The point is that we can work with this poem. We can be particular in our arguments and criticisms, and even in our *un*critical responses as simple readers, because the poem itself is particular—and because it is *responsible*. That perception in it which is sight derives from what is real; that perception in it which is insight, likewise. There is, thereby, the further possibility of recognition—for her, then for us—and of the stability of truth. The path to sight and insight is, in this poem, conscious attention. The poet and the act of writing are not an issue in the poem. After all, the poet will be in the poem regardless.

. . . .

Much of the arty writing in poetry, yours and mine, derives from anxiety and egomania. Most student poems have a secret subject: the worth of the poem. When the poet values too highly the speaker in his or her poem, then the personality of the speaker is likely to be an issue in the poem. Therefore, it is necessary to clear the ego from the path of perception. The weak ego and the strong ego are the same thing: they are the ego.

. . . .

I have been describing an attitude here. I mean to suggest that one's writing benefits from a certain mental position and emotion toward the world and the poem: a heightened awareness at the least and a fierce consciousness at best, along with an easy feeling about what a poem is. About that *easy* feeling—you know, were you to keep always in mind model poems, you could never write a poem unlike your models. Self-expression, acceptance, paying attention, sticking to the subject (that is, using and developing rather than mentioning and accumulating), getting the facts straight: these don't sound like very high falutin' aesthetic principles. That's why I like 'em.

Moreover, such simple principles can help us, I think, to approach what Ouspensky calls "objective consciousness," and an emphasis upon unselfconscious awareness leads us to the mystery and richness of life. In this regard, I am going to incorporate here a lovely, inspiring essay by the late Soetsu Yanagi. Dr. Yanagi, who was Director of the Museum of Folk-Crafts in Tokyo, delivered this essay during his visit in 1952 to the Archie Bray Foundation in Helena, Montana. It concerns a kind of pilgrimage Dr. Yanagi made from Japan to Korea, and I must ask you to remember that the rural Korea he describes may no longer exist. The essay first appeared in *Craft Horizons*, and is titled, "Mystery of Beauty":

"In South Korea stands the village Ampo, a lonely hamlet, remote from towns. To visit this village was a hope I had long cherished, for I had seen many examples of beautiful turnery (wood turning) made by the villagers. Nearly all Korean woodwork, especially turnery, suffers some deformity in its shape. But this slight crookedness always gives us a certain peculiar asymmetrical beauty, an indescribable charm that entices us into a sense of beauty that is free and unrestricted. From what source and by what means Korean craftsmen obtain such natural asymmetrical beauty had long been a question for me.

"In Japan we find also a great deal of turned works. Some are extremely good, made so precisely that they are almost perfect in shape. But their symmetrical perfection lacks the quality of unrestricted beauty. In turning there is an accepted rule that the wood used should be thoroughly dried; otherwise cracks will almost certainly appear. In Japan the wood is air dried for at least two or three years. This is common sense. In modern factories, of course, the drying is done quickly in kilns. In any case, all turnery should be produced from well dried wood.

"Fortunately, I was favored with a rare visit to that Korean village where those beautiful turned goods are made. I was excited by the opportunity of seeing these Korean craftsmen at work because I thought that I might grasp the mysterious beauty of their products.

"When I arrived after a long, hard trip, I noticed at once beside their workshops many big blocks of pine ready to be lathed. To my great astonishment all of them were sap green and by no means ready for use. Imagine my surprise when a workman set one of these blocks in a lathe and began to turn it. The pine was so green that turning it produced a spray redolent of the scent of resin. This use of green wood perplexed me greatly, for it defies a basic rule of turnery. I asked the artisan, 'Why do you use such green wood? Cracks will appear pretty soon.' 'What does it matter?' was the calm answer. I was amazed by this Zen-monk-like response. I felt sweat on my forehead. Yet I dared to ask him, 'How can we use something that leaks?' 'Just mend it' was his simple answer.

"I was amazed to discover that these artisans mend their turnery so artistically and ingeniously that a cracked piece seems better than a perfect one. Consequently they do not care whether it is cracked or not. Our common sense is of no use to Koreans at all. They live in a world of 'thusness,' not of 'must or must not.' Their way of making things is so natural that man-made rules are meaningless to them. They are attached neither to the perfect piece nor to the imperfect. So it was that at this moment when I received the artisan's unexpected answer I came to understand for the first time the mystery of the asymmetrical nature of Korean turnery. Because Korean artisans use green wood, their wares inevitably deform while drying. Therefore, the asymmetry is but a natural outcome of their state of mind, not the result of conscious choice. In short, their minds are free from any attachment to symmetry or asymmetry. The deformity of their work is the result of nonchalance, freedom from restriction. This explains why Japanese turnery looks hard and cold in comparison with Korean. We are attached to perfection; we want to make the perfect piece. But what is human perfection after all?

"In modern art, as everyone knows, the beauty of deformity is very often emphasized, insisted upon. But how different is Korean deformity. The former is produced deliberately, the latter naturally. Korean work is merely the natural result of the artisan's state of mind, which is free from dualistic man-made rules. He makes his asymmetrical turnery not because he regards the asymmetrical form beautiful or the symmetrical ugly but because, as he works, he is perfectly unaware of such polarities. He is quite free from conflict between the beautiful and the ugly. Here lies buried the mystery of the endless beauty of the Korean artisan's work. He simply makes what he makes without pretension.

. . . .

"One who has had the chance to visit a Korean potter's shed may notice that the wheel used for throwing pots is never exactly true. Sometimes it is so crudely mounted that it is not

even horizontal. The asymmetrical nature of Korean pots re-
sults in part, therefore, from the uneven movement of the
wheel. But we must understand that Koreans do not make
such wheels because they like unevenness and dislike evenness.
Rather they simply construct their wheels in a happy-go-lucky
way. This unevenness, then, is but a natural outcome of the
untrammeled state of their minds. They live just as circum-
stances permit, without any conception of artificiality. Of
course, if the wheel is canted too much, they may correct it to
some extent, but even then it will not be precise. They are
scarcely troubled by accuracy or inaccuracy, for in their world
these qualities are not yet differentiated. This state of mind is
the source from which flows the beauty of Korean pots.

"Why did our tea-masters, men of keen eyes, prefer Korean
pots to all others? The asymmetrical beauty, free from all pre-
tension, was immensely attractive to their aesthetic eyes. They
so ardently loved to gaze upon those Korean pots that they
finally tried to analyze the beauty expressed in them. They
enumerated ten virtues as the elements of which their beauty
consisted. It is quite remarkable that the eyes of our tea-mas-
ters penetrated so deeply into the beauty of these pots.

"Paradoxically, however, their very analysis initiated the
history of an erroneous attitude which has poisoned nearly all
the later tea-potters in Japan. They imagined that they could
make good pots by isolating the indispensable elements of
beauty which characterized Korean tea utensils. But what was
the result? In spite of their careful craftsmanship and passion-
ate love of beauty, their analytical self-consciousness has never
been able to produce pots as beautiful as the original Korean
ware. Why? The reason is obvious: they did not understand
that the Korean pots were not the result of intellectual analysis
but of a natural and spontaneous condition of the mind. If our
tea-masters had told the Korean potters about the ten virtues,
the Koreans would not have known what to say.

"The Koreans simply made pots, while the Japanese pro-
ceeded from thought to action. We have made nice things, but
they are different. We proceed upon a conscious differentia-
tion of the beautiful and the ugly, while the Koreans' work is

done before such differentiation takes place. Which is better? I do not say that the analytical approach is useless, but if we are confined by analysis, we cannot be assured of producing pots of indescribable beauty. Why is it that self-conscious potters cannot make beautiful pots with ease? Because it is extremely hard for them to make things in that state of mind described by Buddhists as 'thusness.'

"Once there was a Buddhist devotee named Genza. Though an illiterate peasant, he was actually an enlightened man. He had a friend named Naoji. Attaining together the age of nearly ninety years, both fell ill and took to bed. Naoji, realizing that the end was at hand, began to be anxious about his death, for he wanted to die peacefully. So he sent his niece to his friend Genza to inquire how one may die with a peaceful mind. Genza replied simply, 'Just die.' A week later, it is said, both of them died peacefully.

"His answer is magnificent. If anyone can just die, what problem remains? Death is powerless to trouble a man if he can just die. But it is difficult for most men to die in peace, for they do not want to die or they think they should not die yet or they fear the unknown or pity themselves. Some even commit suicide. All troubles, anxieties, agonies come from attachment to life and from ignorance of the meaning of death. If we can escape the dualistic conception of life and death, we can just live and we can just die at any moment and in any place without anxiety. This state of mind is called 'Buddahood attained' or 'Enlightenment.'

"All beautiful crafts are nothing more than the expression of attained Buddahood. Enlightenment means liberation from all duality. If we want to make a truly beautiful object, we must before all else reach this state of mind which is free. In comparison to this radical condition, degree of skill, depth of knowledge, even the quality of materials are secondary considerations. This is the utter simple truth implicit in every Santo or Retablo painted by those Mexican devotees of the humble mind.

"Of course it is far better to have good training, knowledge, and well chosen materials, but the one absolutely indispensable thing is the attainment of that state of mind which is free from all dualistic fetters. If this one condition is lacking, all skill, knowledge and materials will be wasted."

Should we not include in the category of "dualistic fetters" that of form and content? And should we not also include influence and originality or, if you prefer, "tradition and the individual talent"? For poetry remains personal expression. In one's own language. Not trying to sound like others. Not trying not to.

And style takes care of itself. Eventually, we all come to say things in our own way. Elegant diction, rhyme and meter are not more expressive or precise than other ways, but are merely signs of a style. Nor do colloquial diction, continually varying rhythms and an absence of rhyme signify a greater sincerity, but again merely a style.

. . . .

Finally, since I don't want to waste your time, I'll tell you right now the secrets of writing poetry. Since all gall is divided into three parts, there are three of them. First, one learns to write by reading (of course one has to be writing too). That is, the quality of what one reads makes a difference, and the quality of one's reading attention makes a difference. That's number one.

Number two (and not everyone may agree with this), I believe that language, compared to the materials of other art forms, has only one thing going for it: the ability to be precise. All suggestion in a poem, and the quality of the emotion in a poem, derive from precision. All other so-called "aspects" of poetry—even to rhythm and sound—are in its service. Actually, words cannot be precise about *things*. No matter how particular the description of a *thing* in a poem, when the poem moves on the description of the thing remains limited and the thing described remains one of a class, not one of a kind. What words *can* be precise about is ideas, ideas that come from the relationships of the modestly particular things in a poem. The things, in turn, derive from the workings of sensibility, which derives from personal obsessions. Therefore, serious poetry is profoundly adult. It is an adult art, deriving its finest moments from a fully developed heart and mind. Trusting oneself to the language as Stafford does—"adventuring in the language," as he phrases it—implies the richness of the mature self behind that trust. Therefore, the second "secret" is to look into the distance—not only to see how small one is, but also to see how far one can go.

And the third and most important secret is that, if you do anything seriously for a long time, you get better at it.

# The Question Remains

I haven't seen it but I like it already. In *The Encyclopaedia of Ignorance*, edited by Ronald Duncan and Miranda Weston-Smith, fifty-eight scientists write of what remains unknown.

Naturally, what remain unanswered are the fundamental questions: How was the universe formed? What is consciousness? Where and how does the brain store memories? A book like this is surprising to some and fun for all because it's always a treat and a relief to hear the scientists admit that they are working on the outskirts, just fooling with the dials without the slightest idea of where the message has come from, how it originated or what it means.

Most artists would be happy to admit the same. *More* happy to admit it. Painters get away with it the most easily. In Michael Crichton's book, *Jasper Johns*, the author asks Johns why he has just made a change in the handle of a spoon in a lithograph on which he is working. Johns answers, "Because I did." The author asks, "But what did you *see?*" Johns: "I saw that it should be changed." Author: "Well, if you changed it, what was wrong with it before?" Johns: "Nothing. I tend to think one thing is as good as another." Author: "Then why change it?" Johns, after a sigh and a pause: "Well, I may change it again." Author: "Why?" Johns: "Well, I won't know until I do it." One imagines the author continuing to ask "Why" and "Why not," while the painter goes on with what, where, when and how.

Later, the author asks, "How do you work on a painting?"

And Johns replies, "Well, I begin at the beginning, and go on from there."

Was Johns simply enjoying the frustration of the investigator, or trying to make good copy? I don't think so. Rather, he was trying to avoid oversimplification of behavior, motive and response, as well as the distortion that accompanies the transliteration of one form of expression into another.

No less than the painter, the poet doesn't want to spell out what he or she cannot know either. Pound, in the *ABC of Reading*, cautions against trying to make art by measuring art. "Give your draughtsman sixty-four stencils of 'Botticelli's most usual curves'?" he writes. "And he will make you a masterpiece?" And everyone has heard many times the Imagist dictum that the poet compose "in the sequence of the musical phrase, not in the sequence of a metronome."

There is mystery (the title of Soetsu Yanagi's wise and delightful essay, reprinted in part in my previous column, is "*Mystery* of Beauty") and there is ignorance. We write from ignorance to discovery, but we do not "solve." The mystery remains.

It's good to know, from *The Encyclopaedia of Ignorance* and elsewhere, that the mysteries are safe. When we resist the behaviorists and gene-fiddlers, we protect whatever is infinite and infinitely various from mutilation and reduction. On a lower level, let's be honest: who still thinks the education departments in our universities, with their emphasis on simpleminded methodology and their disdain for content, have done anything but harm to our school system? Who still believes that the sociologists, with their love of statistics, know what counts?

Knowledge is a form of purity and needs language, even numbers. We cannot escape the essential quality of the word, which is that it limits. Nor should we wish to. Yet we write from ignorance and the impure.

Ignorance and mystery are acknowledged by the importance in poems of space and silence. Poetry that uses up every bit of space and/or makes a continuous sound seems shallow, the busy plane of a crossword, the flat numerology of the Scrabble board—though this is unfair to the spacings in crosswords and Scrabble and the psychological resonance of the players (more on this later).

There are fine poets who have made space and silence in part their subject matter and sometimes imitated it in form: John Haines, Gregory Orr, once Robert Bly, and others. But I do not limit it to apprehensible acknowledgments. James Wright has become one of our best poets by reducing his language and expanding his heart, and the reduced language of his more recent poems is no less expressive for being of fewer words. Jon Anderson seems to me an example of a younger poet whose poems resonate with silence and space. Well, there are many.

It is tempting to come up with a new definition of poetry: say, poetry is the conscious use of interval in language. John Cage credits his aesthetic to Thoreau, who said, "Music is continuous; only listening is intermittent." Without interval, however, music is noise, so Cage composed our listening, and both silence and noise became part of the musical expression.

And we write from ignorance of motive and effect. We know that poetry is a kind of naming in the service of understanding and taking control. But what does it take control of? Certainly not the thing named! The plague continues, the lover still goes away. The poem enables us to take control, if at all, only of what we feel.

Put another way, with obvious reference to other theoretical questions, If a tree falls in a poem, does it make a sound? The answer might be Yes, it does, but not the sound of a tree falling. One might say, with some strain, that the sound made in a poem by a falling tree is the sound of the notion of a tree falling.

We write to take control of what we feel. That sounds about right. Let's go further and say, right out, that we write to avoid death, then to confront it, then to accept it, maybe later to toy with it and redefine it or just to prepare for it. One of the great examples of a poem written squarely before death is Williams' "The Descent."

It has been said often: it is easier to be a poet at twenty than at forty. I am forty and I am here to tell you that this is true, though you hardly need my word on this.

Take the simple things first. The young or beginning poet can set down anything. Everything is a discovery—of form, of content, of self, of the world. Things can follow. Things can imply and mean. Things can surprise. We are not just what we thought, etc. But for one who has been doing and thinking about it for a very long time, that first line or phrase or sentence signals much of its possibility, including what has already been done, what is not worth doing, and what is merely convention.

Writing these essays is fun for me because I approach them out of ignorance. I might still be twenty. When it comes time to make up a new article for *The American Poetry Review*, I look forward to it as a little exploration. No Perry, I just go into the back woods and play a little. It's like childhood, it is not solemn.

In these, I look forward to an exploration that arrives. Like Johns, like the poet at twenty, I can start anywhere. My motto is the motto of the mongoose family in Kipling's "Rikki-tikki-tavi": "Run and Find Out." (The motto of most critics, on the other hand, is "Divide and Conquer.") Moreover, I have a weakness for starting out from the lowly, the simple and the common, and letting them lead, if they will, to what is elevated, complex and, I believe, also common (naturally). So I (or you) could easily begin an essay about poetry from a children's book or cartoon but for the desire to impress. You see, I know that, by this time, in this essay, I have already lost those readers who would have stayed, had *The Encyclopaedia of Ignorance* been followed by Croce, Black Humor, Projective Verse, Pliny or Structuralism.

I don't write for those people, and neither do you. They look upon written expression as if it were a keen executive awareness of the audience, an act of theatre, even vaudeville—no small accomplishment. But you and I write differently, I think—a step at a time, some rhythm to our walk, the compass not to be used until we are lost somewhere new.

The young or beginning poet can do this more easily than

the poet at forty: can walk off into the woods without a thought. And *should*, again and again. Never mind the critics, especially those older poets who will tell you that you're only playing. They have forgotten their youth and its importance. Death is all over them and now their art will become, more and more, a matter of character.

But for you, it is still a matter of exploration. And yet. . . .

And yet, the poet cannot wait for the critic, but has the need and duty to see and decide among his or her discoveries. Without becoming so self-conscious that new work becomes increasingly impossible. Consciousness is the main benefit of the academy. Self-consciousness is the tuition. Can you afford it? Then, can you make back what you must spend? Every example another answer.

In accepting death, do I give up too much? I have written a poem for this column, a risky gesture with which to discuss the territory one can explore and the sense one must make of it. I have written it quickly and in a way intended to defeat planning and earnestness.

If you have played Scrabble, you know that it seems that words already formed on the board create unconscious associations leading to other words. Lay down the letters for one flower, and you can be sure two others will follow, if not "thorn," "dirt" and "berry." Put down "sex," and parts of the body show up soon after. One item of food leads to a menu.

I had taken down the words from two Scrabble games, thinking I might create an assignment for some students, but I neglected to. Instead, late last night, it occurred to me to do the assignment myself, just to create an example of discovery and judgment—an example immediate to my memory of its origins, an example that would endanger no one but myself. This is the poem that resulted, written in perhaps ten minutes, if that.

> A puff of woe has blown
> the teal from the garden,
> the rouged tissue from *Madame*
> and the parasol from the picture,

while elsewhere bees chime
in the white air above the rye.
Nine who espy will savor, adore,
while the tenth spots in the icy lake
a navy of quail, lax fauna,
data of the deft ruse, the moot,
the veil, the fib, the virtual.

Putting aside articles, conjunctions and prepositions, both from the poem and the Scrabble boards, this poem contains twenty-eight words which appeared in the two games. The words which did not appear are "blown," *Madame*, "picture," "elsewhere" and "spots."

One doesn't write by word, but by phrase. Poetry is not an art of words so much as it is an art of phrases. (And if this omits for the moment such "poems" as concrete poems, typographic poems, architectural poems—not unlike those fold-out calendars of The Twelve Days of Christmas—we must say what most of us think: Who cares?)

It is the phrase which is the unit of breath and perception both. In this case, it was the words "puff" and "woe," the former vertical before me and the latter horizontal, which signalled me in combination. For a "puff of woe" sounds and says that outdated prettiness which was all the world of the Impressionists and is now a seduction practiced by poets who pose us their wounds.

So the scene is set: a complex of what is missing and remains, that person (*Madame*) who belongs there and can have us, and the gradual announcement that this is also art in which the painter (or photographer, say, but let's say painter) of course both shares and does not share the attitude of *Madame*.

What Romantic, having succumbed to the combination of "teal" and "garden," could resist pairing "rouge" and "tissue" and creating someone to mourn them?

Yet I have feelings about *Madame*, her scene and the art that announces it and, no matter how rapidly I worked at using up words, I could not avoid them. It was only a matter of time and the right word. The word was "nine."

"Nine" suggested to me a group to view the picture. No doubt they would love it and be wholly seduced. They would not simply "view" such tenderness; they would "espy" it. But always there is another way. It is in my nature to believe this. I believe in the primacy of fact and have not abandoned the wish to maintain it in the "lie" that is art.

Hence, the tenth viewer will spot another scene, the actual, the artifice, the virtual. No doubt I identify with the tenth as much as with the first nine. And, if I must choose, I choose The Tenth Viewer. The poem *could* have been written thusly:

> Nine will spot in the icy lake
> a navy of quail, lax fauna,
> data of the deft ruse, the moot,
> the veil, the fib, the virtual.
> The tenth will see that bees chime
> in the white air above the rye,
> that a puff of woe has blown
> the teal from the garden,
> the parasol from the picture
> and the rouged tissue from *Madame.*

Having changed the poem as little as possible except for the order of the lines (one might say sections) and, ignoring the unhappy alterations in rhythm, sound and syntax, it is possible to see that this other version not only changes sides in the argument between appearance and reality but redefines the meaning of perception. In the first version, the tenth viewer perceives that all is not as it seems and that the picture of life in the painting is a ruse, nothing we who are alive should expect to encounter. In the second version, the tenth viewer's seeing-through serves to discover implication and plot and to treat them as if they *are* the facts of importance.

Which is the better and truer version? If I must answer, I will choose the first because its argument seems to me more important, rarer and more timely, and because it is reasonable to me to suppose that most viewers of such a scene would be, like me, utterly seduced, thoughtful only later. I confess that I also like beginning with that combination of the natural and the poignant which first arrested me in "a puff of woe," and ending on the word "virtual."

These were the words then which, made into phrases, put me into a poetic circumstance, if tiny, and led me on with the promise of honest feeling. The discoveries made thereby do not excuse me from viewing the whole at a psychological distance afterwards, judging it for sense and truth.

Surely any of us could go on from this circumstance to our own. I could easily enough follow "a puff of woe," "teal," "lake," "quail," etc. to eastern Long Island, my boyhood home. Frank Holzman, a writer of poems and my friend from childhood, reminds me that the town in which we fished, stole boats and explored, which shone clean and clearly for us, now seems "like a dump." It is, he tells me, as if the whole town were just waiting to be pushed out to sea. He wonders which has changed the most, the town or our viewpoint. I could go there from here.

But I set out to stay near the exercise. Someone else might have begun with other words from among those available. It would have led elsewhere to join "axe," "adze," "size," "hub," "weld," "jug" and "gin," not least because they sound as well as make a different circumstance. Someone could have used "wok," "broth" and "dine." I have to admit to the appearance of both "id" and "zoo." How about "lab," "arid," "quit" and "gene"? "Toke" is there and so is "howl."

More could be said. It is not my way to write in this manner or by this method. Nonetheless, I assert this example to affirm for the self-conscious and inhibited the worth of play and the truth of process. It is the love of process and play which causes Picasso, asked which of his paintings is his favorite, to reply, "The *next* one."

"The next one" has to begin. Let it begin anywhere, from nowhere, from ignorance. God knows, one does not always begin with a first line, the first line does not always remain first or even survive, yet it is interesting to see how much is contained in many first lines. Then it is interesting to see whether or not the poet follows up.

For the poet can say anything at the start. That is why almost anyone can write a good line. Writing a good poem is a matter of being sensitive to the implications, formal and sensible, of a (first) line. ("Line" is a rough border, sometimes a sentence, sometimes just a phrase: a first unit of perception.) The first line of a poem, so many times, wins or loses us, and is in any case symptomatic.

When John Berryman begins a "Dream Song," "Golden his mail came at his journey's end," I'm hooked. When John Logan begins his "Lines on His Birthday," "I was born on a street named Joy," I go with him. And when Elizabeth Bishop begins her poem "In the Waiting Room" with the lines, "In Worcester, Massachusetts, / I went with Aunt Consuelo. . . ," we know we have been engaged by a poem of another stance and circumstance entirely than, say, that of James Merrill's poem, "The Mad Scene," which begins, "Again last night I dreamed the dream called Laundry."

Sometimes, plot is the hook, as in Richard Wilbur's often-anthologized poem, "Love Calls Us to the Things of This World," which begins, "The eyes open to a cry of pulleys. . . ." When we read further, we find ourselves wound up in a combination of body, spirit and laundry, and only one who had none of these could stop reading.

The good first line is used by the poem. The bad first line uses up the poem, just as summary epigraphs do. After the bad first line, there need be no other. Opening lines which go unused are just lines, not first lines. The young poet, rather than struggling with theme and idea, should thank heaven for his or her ignorance, and get into action, settling for subject matter rather than theme, circumstance rather than idea, and that sensitivity to the implications and resonances of a phrase which, joining subject matter, make for the poetic circumstance.

Then it might happen quickly. Here is a story from *Zen Flesh, Zen Bones,* compiled by Paul Reps:

### The First Principle

When one goes to Obaku temple in Kyoto he sees carved over the gate the words "The First Principle." The letters are unusually large, and those who appreciate calligraphy always admire them as being a masterpiece. They were drawn by Kosen two hundred years ago.

When the master drew them he did so on paper, from which workmen made the larger carving in wood. As Kosen sketched the letters a bold pupil was with him who had made several gallons of ink for the calligraphy and who never failed to criticize his master's work.

"That is not good," he told Kosen after the first effort.

"How is that one?"

"Poor. Worse than before," pronounced the pupil.

Kosen patiently wrote one sheet after another until eighty-four First Principles had accumulated, still without the approval of the pupil.

Then, when the young man stepped outside for a few moments, Kosen thought: "Now is my chance to escape his keen eye," and he wrote hurriedly, with a mind free from distraction: "The First Principle."

"A masterpiece," pronounced the pupil.

The question remains, How did he do it?

# The Last Column

There appeared in the *Iowa City Press–Citizen* for Wednesday, April 19, 1978 the following report:

*Father, son*
*shot to death*

NEW SHARON, Iowa (AP)— Authorities today were investigating an incident in which a rural New Sharon man and son were found shot to death in an apparent murder-suicide.

Roy Victor, 83, and son Bob, 59, were found Tuesday with .22 caliber bullet wounds in the head, said Mahaska County Sheriff Harold Van de Pol.

He said the elder man apparently shot his severely retarded son, then himself.

The bodies were found by neighbors at Victor's farm house 12 miles northeast of Oskaloosa.

A third of a year later, the story still breaks my heart. Not that I'm less crusty than anyone about newspapers, crime and tragedy. How else live to act? It is not the reporting or the picture it makes in the mind that continues to shake me, but the story behind it. Perhaps I should better say "within it." For at the center of this straightforward record is fifty-nine years of two men's lives. How much tough thought and brave living prefaced that moment when the father must have known for certain that he could no longer care for his son? And how much love? And what frustrations and angers? And what steps, even, to keep oneself fit for the sake of the other?

Oh, almost anyone can conceive the story, and perhaps write it. There must be many poets who could type out three or four easy, related poems in a night. I myself can value the mention of it within a poem about something else. But to try to think about it at length! To do so is a wide variation on such disciplines as sometimes ask of the initiate that he or she attempt to concentrate on the most horrible thing imaginable.

I have tried before to distinguish between mystery and mystification. Craft is a surface operation. Superficially applied, it can mystify beautifully. It is like lovely clothing on a mannequin.

We can prettify, poeticize and mystify by means of style. Of course, style is an aspect of craft and, without that minimum of craft we call "care," all is lost. But I should prefer to think not about style, which is a mode of expression, but about expression itself. I mean this to be a sign of our primary regard for mystery . . . or the wordless. At the center of the news story quoted earlier is a lifetime of selfless love and courage that will not survive your words. If you must approach it, the simpler words will do better. (Unless, of course, it is your own mastery for which you beg recognition.)

There is some question of form which subsumes such aspects of craft and style as rhythm (including meter), sound (including rhyme), line and stanza. It nags at me to be found out and set before you. Our interest has been freed to pursue it—perhaps forced to take out after it—precisely because a kind of free verse bearing the memory of accentual or accentual-syllabic verse has become the loose convention of our time. Some have sought refuge from the confusion and the problem in forms they still wear well. Some have sought refuge in force of imagery, some in plain or fancy diction, some in an appropriation of aspects of prose and fiction, some in epic concern and some in translation. Of all these methods, translation, at first glance, seems to be the head-in-the-sand approach, yet only translation, it seems to me, has, by indirection, seen into the problem.

The other methods, except for that of staying put, set out for direct change. Translation, however, has discovered something as if by accident. It has discovered that, as Charles Simic and Mark Strand say in introducing *Another Republic*, "in fact it would seem that poetry is what is retained in translation." (You recall that Frost said that poetry is "what is lost in translation.")

I believe that good poems—poems worth rereading—are always formal in some important way. I believe this simply because I have never seen an exception. Furthermore, from reading I must conclude that good free verse has quite as formal an effect as good verse in received forms. And, moreover—and this may seem heretical to some—it seems to me that neither the looseness nor tautness of the line nor the level of diction in a poem is decisive. Simic and Strand speak of an "international style"—further evidence that "forms" as we usually discuss them (this meter, that stanza, parallelism, circles of organization, etc.) are symptoms of something larger.

For lack of a better word, I would say "structure." The poetic imagination is structural and enables us to "see through" (as opposed to fancy, which rhapsodizes with endless inventiveness so that all of our attention is occupied.) For lack of a better word, I would say "wordless." The center of the poem is the inexpressible. To apprehend it, one must maintain the entire structure of its enclosure.

(I do not believe this is only true of the would-be-hermetic lyric, though it is easier to see in the lyric than in the epic or the dramatic.)

I have another clipping to insert at this point. It reports on a local conference about behavior and reads: "Novak was skeptical of tendencies to over-analyze human behavior, and criticized the use of highly involved verbal approaches to deal with child-rearing and marital problems. Once a theory is developed about a human response, he said, the original meaning will sometimes be lost in the words defining and categorizing it. 'We are cursed by education,' he charged. We reach levels at which spontaneous reactions are 'submerged in wave after wave of articulation.'

"'In an attempt to be rational, we are most irrational of all; we falsify,' Novak said. 'Truth-telling is exceedingly difficult.

People who encourage us to talk things out are encouraging us to be false.'"

I lean to agreement. If the quality of emotion is what counts most in a poem, it is still not *any* emotion nor, I think, emotion wholly said (and baldly) in a line or two *about* emotion. No, if language is the method, the mind has plenty to do. Sometimes the mind is the only metaphor large enough and various enough to the task. It was true of Williams in *Journey to Love* and *Pictures from Brueghel*, of Eliot in *Four Quartets*, of Stevens all of his writing life. It was true of Dickinson and of Whitman. It is so patently true of Ashbery that he has caught the eye of critics who regularly miss the same thing elsewhere.

The mind provides a complicated metaphor unless one opts for speech and circumstance. Uncomplicated, the metaphor straightens out the poem, makes the surface taut enough to be penetrated. Again, we may signal here the difference between poetry which performs without flagging and poetry which envelops almost anonymously. The metaphor—that is, the whole dramatic circumstance or the center of attention in the poem—makes the line straight.

I have to stop and start again, this time by way of photography. For I noticed this past summer several excellent photos in the campus newspaper, *The Daily Iowan*. Somebody knew how to print and present them, and the effect was magical. One photographer, in particular, stood out for a clear perspective and clean execution worthy of Walker Evans.

I should probably have been less surprised, therefore, when she solved, by simplicity itself, a problem that has defeated the mixers of media over and over: that of combining words and still photos.

I have to say that I do not think it has been done well to any extent. Even the text of Robert Frank's *The Americans*, a famous example, seems to me quite detachable from the photos.

Here is what Mary Locke did. She used three photos of one (changing) scene with a simple declarative text of sixty words. You will have to take my word that the three photos, arranged vertically, have that head-on particularity, zonal range and love of gray that sit in Evans' photos. The text at the bottom reads:

> In an alley in downtown Muscatine a deserted
> doll lay on the fire escape to an upstairs
> apartment. A boy came out with a coathanger in
> one hand, slapping it against his other hand.
> Half a minute passed in the stifling heat; he
> took the doll by the hair and flung it into the
> doorway. Then he disappeared inside.

I confess to being charmed by the quality of attention in the text—its small, disarming graces. Though never intended to be more than a newspaper caption, it seems to me more interesting than many of the prose poems around now. They, for the most part, are consciously, willfully, "poetic"; this is not. They often say such literary buzz-words as "dream." This caption contains, but does not say the word for, the dream. They lack the coathanger and Muscatine. They do not value the scene as much as they value the writer. They do not call a doll "deserted" unless they mean to make a literary point about loneliness. They do not use a semicolon nearly so interestingly, nor note the heat and the passage of half a minute. They are "poems"; this is just words.

I prefer the words—here, in the company of the images. Note that they do not plot out a further story for us, even though from the photos one might deduce, for example, poverty and politics.

Speaking of the poetry of John Ashbery, Richard Kalstone writes, "He is not simply reminding us that poetry has access to the inner life; he is emphasizing the unique power of language to reveal how much of external life the inner life displaces."

Richard Poirier, writing of the poems of Frost, says, "Frost denies or negates the reality not of local and obvious but of remote possibilities, as if to reassure his readers that he is not a visionary poet. But it is in doing this that he allows himself to be visionary. He is like an attorney who knows that evidence stricken from the record is apt to remain more strongly in the mind."

And, in a recent issue of *Stand*, Desmond Graham writes about Robert Lowell: "Throughout his career, Lowell possessed and knew he possessed a seemingly incurable gift for words: a capacity to transform anything to rhetoric, to elevate and give resonance to whatever came under his hand; a capacity which he increasingly saw as the dangerous ability of art's order and resolution to triumph over the mess of life. And in his later writing (though the process started as early as *Life Studies*) he sought to hold at least partly true to this mess by checking art's triumph."

Now here is another caption to a photo by Mary Locke: "A flock of pigeons circled a field near Tiffin on Sunday and passed up an empty farm cart as roost before flying off to find greener pastures." The phrase "greener pastures" is, in part, a sop to clichéd journalism (and, in part, a sop to Midwestern reality!), but the sentence is still notable for its length, for the detail of the empty farm cart, for the twist of lingo in "as roost," and for its addition of motion and narrative to the single, fixed image.

The *most* interesting aspect of this caption and of the other, however, is their use of the past tense. Appearing in a newspaper, with its conventional (and false) ever-Present tense, the use of the past tense in these captions sticks out like a beautiful thumb.

The inner life is, indeed, the source and the recipient of our best expression—in poetry and elsewhere. But the inner life will not be apprehended by a frontal assault. Poetry is a method. When the method succeeds, it can produce that representation of the external which somehow contains or holds the internal. But we must not be fooled into thinking we can cut the process short.

The past tense has about it the denial of the present in the *presence* of the present. Nostalgia and memory have about them the ability to be *unable* to fully hold or articulate. These are tiny symptoms of the perfection of the roundabout. But of course I am not suggesting poems should be written in this tense or that, or should look backwards rather than forwards. When they are, however, they indicate the nature of poetry in that they exemplify the way in which poetry avoids to include, the way in which it tells us what is not to be seen or thought so that we may realize something else.

All I'm saying is that the subject matter of a poem is, in the best poem, metaphor, and that much of a poem's work is to articulate and then dismiss what is expressibly *next to* the inexpressible. Want another clipping?

In the Iowa City police report for March 15, 1977, there appears this item: "—At 1020 Fifth Street. A woman reported at 11:07 a.m. that 'a big, hairy, mean, long-nosed, big-teeth furry animal' was hanging in a tree there. An officer found a ground hog and shot it down from the tree."

I think the fact that it turned out to be a ground hog gives dimension to the story and character to the woman, but I am happy to have it left in the form of straightforward information. It would be a big comedown, I think, to be told, for example, that the lady then apologized. Just as I would have thought it a comedown in the first of the photo captions had I been told, say, that the shorts-clad boy who faces us from the doorway in the middle photo, and is seen climbing back up into the doorway in photo three, had retrieved the doll for his sister at the request of his mother.

Nor would it be, for me, of the essence of the story to be told, say, that the farmer who at eighty-three killed his fifty-nine-year-old severely retarded son and himself did it following an argument between them. Even if true, I resist the truth of easy cause-and-effect in favor of the possibility of that which is no less real but less easily said.

To be fair to you, I must now get down to matters of craft. (But not the craft that dresses the mannequin.) For the poet, craft is the trick on the self. One can list the ways by example: James Wright's many introductory remarks and apparent asides preceding the small story that is the destination of "The Old WPA Swimming Pool in Martins Ferry, Ohio"; Randall Jarrell's "The Truth," in which a boy of ten gets things wrong until the end; Norman Dubie's lists of that which "has nothing to do with . . .";  Stevens' open exclusions; Pound's gaps between fragments of history, languages, music even—in which, somehow, the content of *The Cantos* almost takes shape; Dickinson's personal symbols, including such words as "circumference," "noon," "grace" and "seal"; Whitman's trick of the "I" whereby he employs the pronoun and syntax of confession but tells you, of himself, nothing particular; Berryman's deflective insistence on the separate identity of Henry in the *Dream Songs.* One could list techniques almost endlessly: the "Kubla Khan" high, Black Mountain breathing, dramatic monologues (see Browning, see Richard Howard), dialectics in two voices (see Elder Olson), personification of almost anything (see William Stafford, Russell Edson), etc., etc., etc. All are ways of surrounding the inexpressible, which shrinks from too much self and disappears entirely where thought to be directly approachable.

No one can quite say what form is. Anyone can describe convention deriving from forms already found. Still, no one can quite say what form is in any way that takes part in the future. And the finding of future forms is what often occupies, delights and instructs those of us who write poems.

So no one can say what form is. But many can say what craft is. Still, craft without an exploratory formal sense is little more than polite convention. Hence, American literary life is always threatened by shallow teaching—the teaching of free verse conventions of creativity. Students who learn these tricks without a sense of the deeper levels of the process are condemned to write cardboard.

At times, we are all condemned to write cardboard. We wake up somedays with half a brain or a broken heart. We wake up every day incomplete. I have carried in my head for precisely ten years a few lines which hint for me a form and content I have never been able to apprehend. The first two of them are:

> The rain
> is too heavy a whistle for the certainty of charity.

I will never get "rain," "heavy" and "whistle" to cohere, perhaps. I refuse simply to explain them as I go because I sense—perhaps only wish for—a formal context within which they already cohere. Something astral, perhaps, but not surreal.

Once I attempted to go forward simply by saying what was nearby:

> The rain
> is too heavy a whistle for the certainty of charity.
> The moon
> throws us off the sense.
> The wind
> happens at night before you drop off.
> The mountains
> on them sufferance blisters its skin of paint.
> The oceans
> in which this happens.
> The ash
> of which we are made.

You can see in sentence two the poet already relaxing his hold on the metaphysical. He grabs on again in sentence four. Ten years later, he is still trying to find that combination of the external and the internal, as well as that mix of reaching and reticence, which will bring the poem home.

The poet has to look from an angle, even to look aside. Much Eastern European political poetry is successful because it looks from an angle. The poets of Eastern Europe have not thought irony to be little more than wit and attitude and tone, to be renounced when something else comes along. For them, it has been a necessary strategy. So much American political poetry is lousy because it launches a frontal assault—brave but fatal.

The poet needs to affect innocence before his or her subject, lest the art become craft only. My hunch is that it is better to affect too much innocence than not enough. For any poet, young or not, but particularly for the former, this may take the form of fixed forms, exercises or personae. Anything to see at least part way out of the self.

Hence, I offer up an "exercise" by Tess Gallagher, "The Horse in the Drugstore." It was written because a poetry writing class she wished to take in Seattle was oversubscribed, leading the teacher to require of applicants that they each write a poem using six assigned words in ten lines. Five of the words appear in Tess Gallagher's poem, and she squeezes an extra line into the title:

### The Horse in the Drugstore

wants to be admired.
He no longer thinks of what he has given up
to stand here, the milk-white reason
of chickens over his head in the night, the grass
spilling on through the day. No, it is enough
to stand so with his polished chest among the nipples
and bibs, the cotton and multiple sprays, with his black lips
parted just slightly and the forehooves doubled back
in the lavender air. He has learned here when maligned to
    snort
dimes and to carry the inscrutable bruise like a bride.

The words are "bruise," "horse," "milk," "reason" and "bride." "Drugstore," interestingly, is the poet's own contribution, and it is crucial. It creates the circumstance within which the horse can be "real" yet surrounded by such manufactured goods as bibs and multiple sprays. It affords his polished chest and his ever-doubled-back forehooves.

The main thing is that the poet had to use certain words (four of them standing for things), yet required of herself that reality have its say. So motivation can be attributed to the horse: he "wants to be admired." But the horse in the drugstore turns out not to be Secretariat, or even Angelfoot (Tess Gallagher's horse), but the very sort of "horse" one finds in a drugstore: a dime ride for kids.

Finally, it's easy enough to see that the requirement that the poem use both "bruise" and "bride," evaded as long as possible, results in the last line in a discovery of (one might say, "extra") content. Held, those words seat themselves on the back of the horse with that richness that often seems peculiar to metaphor. Will the horse ever be free to run off with his admiring bride? Or is he—lips parted just slightly, chest polished, forehooves bent back—the very image of resignation, and of making-the-best-of-it, amidst the tokens of use, of survival, of pleasure?

What I *can* say is that it is a better poem for having been made to go somewhere—without knowing, at the outset, where. One might venture that the best affliction for the young poet is a clear nearsightedness that nonetheless goes easily beyond the self. Seeing things close can lead to knowing more, but can a willful farsightedness ever fill in the gaps?

Still, the clipping with which I began this piece remains for me a place that keeps the largest problems of what we call "form." Art *is* form; we have no other way of recognizing it. When what is expressive seems to lack or contradict form, we have some difficulty changing our definitions, but we always manage. Writing about Picasso, Gertrude Stein tells us that what is truly new in art always strikes us first as ugly. She argues that those who follow will refine the new and make it beautiful. I would be happy sometimes to do without those craftsmen of the pretty and just let the audience wake up.

1956

## UNDER DISCUSSION
### Donald Hall, General Editor

Volumes in the Under Discussion series collect reviews and essays about individual poets. The series is concerned with contemporary American and English poets about whom the consensus has not yet been formed and the final vote has not been taken. Among those to be considered are:

**Elizabeth Bishop and Her Art**
*by Lloyd Schwartz and Sybil P. Estess*

Adrienne Rich *by Jane Roberta Cooper*
Richard Wilbur *by Wendy Salinger*
Robert Bly *by Joyce Peseroff*
Allen Ginsberg *by Lewis Hyde*

*Please write for further information on available editions and current prices.*

*Ann Arbor*          **The University of Michigan Press**